Praise for
FIGHT FOR THE FORGOTTEN

"Justin is the truest tough guy and in one of the most grueling sports in the world. In this book he is standing up for those who are less fortunate. It's a great book and it will inspire all who read it."
—Bill Glass, founder of Behind the Walls, NFL Super Bowl Champion, and author of *Champions for Life*

"Justin Wren is a true inspiration, not only to the MMA community but to people all over the world. His story inspires me to be a better human being."
—Adrian Ramirez, elite strength and conditioning coach of UFC fighters/champions, and trainer for Team Takedown

"Justin Wren loves God and loves people and his passion is truly inspiring. He's committed to do everything he can to help people in any way he can. His story will move you to become more of the person God created you to be and show you how you can push back darkness in the world!"
—Jud Wilhite, author of *Pursued* and senior pastor of Central Christian Church

"Justin's story is an example of what any man or woman can do when they discover and embrace who they are and what they are made for. This is not a story of a special person who has superhuman will, this is a story of a man set free to become himself. How can you change the world? Listen to God's voice, and then act. Justin did and that is what makes the difference. His story points us all to the power of our own stories. Read. Listen. Act."
—Bob Hamp, author of *Think Differently Live Differently*

"A fascinating read about transformation. Justin Wren is a big man and blessed by Christ with a new heart. The Mbuti Pygmies of the Democratic Republic of the Congo have been on the receiving end of Justin's transformation from UFC fighter to freedom fighter. God has used Justin in a remarkable way to minister His word to these forest people."
—Malcolm S. Morris, chairman of the Millennium Water Alliance

FIGHT FOR THE
FORGOTTEN

HOW A MIXED MARTIAL ARTIST STOPPED FIGHTING FOR HIMSELF AND STARTED FIGHTING FOR OTHERS

JUSTIN WREN

with Loretta Hunt

HOWARD BOOKS
AN IMPRINT OF SIMON & SCHUSTER, INC.

New York Nashville London Toronto Sydney New Delhi

Howard Books
An Imprint of Simon & Schuster, Inc.
1230 Avenue of the Americas
New York, NY 10020

Some names, locations, and identifying characteristics have been changed.

Scripture quotations marked (NLT) are taken from the Holy Bible, New Living Translation, copyright © 1996, 2004, 2007. Used by permission of Tyndale House Publishers Inc., Carol Stream, Illinois 60188. All rights reserved.

First Howard Books hardcover edition September 2015

HOWARD and colophon are trademarks of Simon & Schuster, Inc.

For information about special discounts for bulk purchases, please contact Simon & Schuster Special Sales at 1-866-506-1949 or business@simonandschuster.com.

The Simon & Schuster Speakers Bureau can bring authors to your live event. For more information or to book an event, contact the Simon & Schuster Speakers Bureau at 1-866-248-3049 or visit our website at www.simonspeakers.com.

Interior design by Renato Stanisic

Manufactured in the United States of America

10 9 8 7 6 5 4 3 2

Library of Congress Cataloging-in-Publication Data is available.

ISBN 978-1-4767-6558-7
ISBN 978-1-4767-6561-7 (ebook)

For my beautiful bride, the love of my life, EmmyBear.
And, Mom, thank you for teaching me to dream.
In memory of Andibo, lil Mo, Babo,
and my dear friend Kaptula.

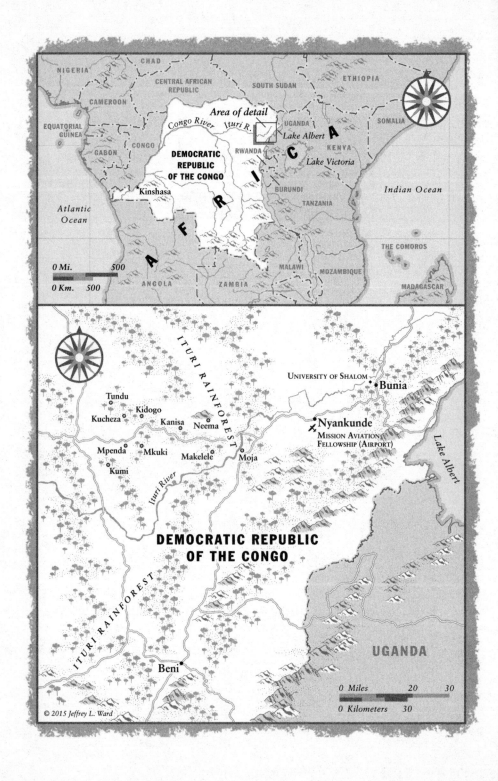

Contents

PART I

CHAPTER 1

Andibo

His name was Andibo. Blood was still trickling from his ears as I took his small body in my hands. Eighteen months old, he had died moments before we crawled into the simple, twig-and-leaf hut he and his mother called home. I held his tiny, lifeless hand, and as I cupped his head, which fit in my palm, blood dripped onto the tips of my fingers. Andibo's mother sat off to the side, listless, watching me cradle the remainder of her family. Her ribs protruded on both sides of her gaunt frame and the roots of her jet-black hair had turned pure white. She was suffering from such drastic starvation and malnutrition that she didn't have tears or the energy to cry. I hadn't known that was possible.

I had only two more days before I left the Democratic Republic of the Congo following a monthlong stay. It was my second trip in a year to the war-torn country to see the Mbuti Pygmies, a peaceful, but heavily persecuted indigenous people buried eighty miles deep in the Ituri rainforest, a twenty-four-thousand-square-mile region of dense jungle in northeastern Africa.

Only two years earlier, I had been a professional cage fighter in the sport of mixed martial arts. I'd been on a hit reality TV series. I'd made it to the Ultimate Fighting Championship, the pinnacle organization that every hopeful dreams of fighting for. But I'd given all that up to become a missionary in a rainforest halfway around the world during its rainy season, tending to the most hated and unloved people on the planet. I'd gone from fighting people to fighting for them.

My goal for this second trip had been a simple one: to live among the suffering Pygmies, to listen to them, to learn from them, and then figure out a practical way to love them. I was on a quest for the knowledge that could help end their anguish, or at least ease it. I had no clue the lengths or depths it would take to acquire this "head knowledge" and transform it into "heart knowledge."

With only forty-eight hours left, my missionary buddy, Shane, and I had hoped we'd already seen the worst. The things we'd seen on that trip no human should have to see, much less live: children with tuberculosis, rape victims abandoned by their husbands, orphans with HIV. We'd heard the most gut-wrenching, heartbreaking tales any human being could tell, stories of indignities, persecution, and even cannibalism.

We'd watched the Mbuti Pygmy tribes struggle to survive under the oppressive control of their Mokpala slave masters, who exploited the hunting-and-gathering peoples' dependency on them after deforestation had taken away the only way of life they'd ever known. The Mokpala claimed the land underneath the Pygmies' feet and forced them to either work it for pitiful "wages" or move off it. The government didn't recognize Pygmies as citizens, so, devoid of the most basic human rights and with nowhere else to go, they quietly complied with the Mokpalas' cruel degradation.

During my trip, I'd witnessed a sixty-year-old Mbuti slave woman get paid twenty cents' worth of bananas for a twelve-hour workday in the fields. I'd watched another Pygmy woman carry 120-pound sacks of jagged coal on her back for three miles through the treacherous terrain and receive a patch of goat fur, not as clothing but as food. I'd observed Pygmy children, no older than four or five, wield machetes as big as themselves, clearing the fields for their slave masters. With my own eyes, I'd seen an elderly Mbuti slave gladly accept two tiny minnows, normally only used as bait, for his daily toil to take home and share with his sickly wife.

Just two more days and I would have missed Andibo altogether. In another village, I'd been shown the graves of eight other infants, but I hadn't truly believed the stories of Pygmy children dying after being denied medical care at hospitals. *Nurses and doctors get into medicine to help people, don't they?* I just couldn't imagine it.

Holding Andibo's lifeless body in my arms made it all sink in. *How did this happen? Why, God?* These questions raced through my mind over and over as Shane and I tried to assess the situation at hand. We'd delicately gather the details of Andibo's story over the next two days as we tried to help his village mourn and begin the healing process.

Our first priority was Andibo's mother, who was nothing more than skin on a skeleton. I handed some money to our two Congolese translators, who hiked back out of the jungle to a dirt road where they caught a ride on a boda-boda, or motorcycle taxi, for the three-hour ride to the town center where the Mokpala lived. Sending them ensured the Mokpala wouldn't jack up the prices the way they would have if they were selling goods to a *mzungu*, or white man.

They returned hours later with fresh mango, passion fruit juice, tilapia, and rice, which we fed to Andibo's mother slowly, reminding me of my wrestling days when a teammate would carefully rehydrate his body after a hellish weight cut. Gradually, her hollowed-out eyes began to flicker with life again. She was able to stand, and then a single tear fell down her cheek, chased by another and another as she began to weep.

Earlier, I'd quietly asked our translators to also purchase a shovel and a casket. In another village, the Pygmies had given me the name Eféosa, which means "The Man Who Loves Us," and if I was really going to be this man, I wouldn't let these starving slaves dig a grave. I was here. I was able. I wanted to ease their burden in any way I could.

The next day, myself, Shane, and our two translators took turns digging until our hands blistered and bled. The tribe wailed in unison for hours as we worked silently. I never knew the shedding of tears could be accompanied by such a horrific sound of pain. When we laid down Andibo's thin, wooden casket—covered by an ill-suited bright blue fabric dotted with vibrant red roses—the mourning villagers covered their faces. Though they'd attended funerals countless times before—as many as one in two Pygmy children die before the age of five—they still couldn't bear to watch. I wanted to cover my eyes, my ears, and my heart all at the same time.

I wish we'd been able to bury just a little bit of this village's heartache in that grave, but the Pygmies' grief was a continuous, never-ending circle. During our dig, the chief had asked if we'd make a second grave for Andibo's mother. Like her son, tapeworms had burrowed into her stomach from what little contaminated food she'd been able to get. Through the polluted water supply, parasites had found their way into her blood. The Pygmy adults had stopped going to the hospital altogether; it wasn't worth the half day's journey only to be turned away. So it was a foregone conclusion that she'd die as well, said the chief, and there would be some solace in that. She'd lost her husband and a second son to disease and was now alone. She had given up, he said.

As we spoke with the chief through our translators, we gathered that Andibo's mother had previously taken him to a local hospital run by the Mokpala for aid. The first time, the staff had turned them away because they were too dirty to even enter and didn't have the money to pay. In desperation, the village had culled their sparse resources together and had returned to lay out firewood, salt, a chicken, eggs, and the equivalent of three dollars on the hospital steps—more than enough to cover the cost of Andibo's medicine. This time, the staff made it clear that no amount of money would be enough. They wouldn't waste the medicine on a "Pygmy animal."

Andibo's ailments had not only been preventable, his cure of just one pill had been affordable. It would have cost only a few dollars to save him. Instead, I spent $48 on his coffin.

As I'd quickly learn with the arrival of the tribe's Mokpala slave master, Andibo was a name we were never supposed to know. Andibo was a child we were never supposed to have heard of, and his was most definitely a story that was never supposed to be told. Why? Because there were countless others with stories just like this one and the Mokpala were determined to make sure they never left the confines of this jungle. The slave master argued with the chief as I stood on the fresh grave I'd just filled with my own hands and described what I'd witnessed into the camera phone that Shane had fixed on me. When the slave master approached to make me stop, trying to intimidate me with harsh words and threatening gestures, it took all I had not to beat him senseless. Fighting, at least the kind where I used my hands, was not the answer on this day. I'd have to fight for the Pygmies in a different way.

Before we said good-bye, I made arrangements and left payment to make sure Andibo's mother would be given the right medicine and not an overpriced handful of useless Tylenol, like a greedy staffer had doled out on a previous occasion. Two days after we'd gone, the translators delivered her to the hospital, where she recovered for a week before she returned to her village.

As we packed up to leave for the airport and said our final good-byes, the Mbuti chief made one final request of me. It was something I'd been asked before, but never agreed to for fear of not being able to come through for these poor, disenfranchised people.

"Can you help us have a voice?" asked the chief. "We have none."

With Andibo occupying my thoughts, for the first time ever I mouthed what my heart had been screaming all along: *Yes.*

On the plane ride home to Dallas, visions of the last month danced around my mind. How had God placed me in this position, in this dilemma, in this exact location, in this brutal place? I'd had such a drastically different plan for my life. A life immersed in the everyday comforts of the American dream—that had always been my plan. Was it a sense of adventure that had brought me to this uncomfortable, war-torn jungle filled with creepy crawlies? Had this all begun with some misguided and uneducated desire to go on a human safari of sorts that brought me to this sickness-ridden, slave-driven region? Did I need some false sense of purpose that I was really making a difference with my life?

Maybe I was secretly carrying a death wish to want to travel to such a rebel-infested jungle in a chaotic country with an unnatural taste for blood. Or maybe I was really there for just one reason—to love the most unloved people, as God did. Living among them, I'd fallen in love with the Mbuti Pygmies of the eastern Congo rainforest. Though they looked and lived so differently from me, I'd found my second family. Whatever I'd hoped to learn, I hadn't learned with just my head, but deep within my heart. Whatever motivation I'd gone there with, God had now turned it into something that would fuel future goals that most people would either laugh at or never dare to achieve.

How did I find myself as a voice for an entire people? It's a responsibility I never knew I'd have to carry. It's one I almost wished I could hand off to someone more fit, but it's one I knew I had to uphold. *If not me, who?* This question haunted me for days and months to come as I settled back into my comfortable, familiar life of grocery stores, running water, and goose-down beds in heated houses that kept the rain out at night.

It would have been easier to forget what I'd seen, what I'd heard, what I'd felt, to tell myself I'd done all that I could and resume some semblance of a normal life. And then I'd think of Andibo, the most innocent of this destitute group of undeserving victims, and the questions would come flooding back. *If I didn't care for them, who would? If I didn't give them a voice, how would they be heard? If I didn't love them, who would?*

I knew what it was like to not have a voice. I'd been bullied in my childhood, alone in my suffering. I had lived in my own private prison of depression and drug abuse and it had nearly killed me, until God pulled me out of that dark dungeon. God had breathed purpose into a life I didn't think was worth living, and I had been set free. I knew the same God who loved the Hell out of me deeply desired to love the Hell away from my new family, the Mbuti Pygmies. Using me, somehow, He'd make sure they weren't forgotten.

CHAPTER 2

First Contact

It all started with a vision I had four years earlier. Clear as day, I saw myself in a jungle—surrounded on all sides by thick, green vegetation—like a film playing on a screen in a movie theater. I gazed up at massive, ancient-looking trees that shot up into the sky far past what the eye could follow; their leaves created a thick canopy roof that darkened my surroundings as if it were dusk. Small thin rays of light fought their way through the thicket. The rainforest ignored my presence; insects chirped, birds squawked, and monkeys scattered among trees above me. The air felt sticky and hot, much worse than one of those humid August days we'd get in Dallas. Perspiration dripped from every pore.

Among the forest's white noise, I heard a faint sound of lively music being played, but not like anything I'd heard before. I started walking toward the music.

My size-13 boots spilled over a small, practically invisible path, so narrow it was as if a child had made it. My arms swam into the thick tangle of branches, leaves and vines brushing against me from head to toe, until that barely discernible path opened into a clearing where I could finally see in front of me.

My eyes took in the scene. There were a hundred to a hundred and fifty people in my vision, living in a cluster of twenty or so huts that formed a circle. Some were interacting with one another. To the right, a group sat around cooking in a beat-up pot on an open fire. Another woman was using a homemade wooden mortar and pestle to smash leaves together. To the left, a mother held her baby, while a group of men stood a few feet away, talking. Their conversation was fluid, as if they were singing or yodeling to one another.

As I took a step forward, the vision in my head stopped and I was bombarded by flash-fast images that emanated emotions and stirred deep-seated feelings in me. I saw the drastically sunken-in cheeks of a malnourished child's face. I saw the caved-in collar-bones on a starving old man. I saw ribs poking out of his skin that created crevices in the rib cage. I saw a man suffering in agony inside of his hut, dying from a disease that was eating him alive from the inside out. I saw a woman bent down next to stagnant, disease-infested water, cupping her hands to her mouth. I saw a man having to work for another man and I knew that the first man was hated and abused by the second. I saw that they were treated like outcasts, less than human, and they felt like they didn't belong among others. They felt forgotten. More than anything, that was the biggest thing I got from the vision, from the elders, the parents, the kids—they all felt forgotten as people and, more important, forgotten by God. My vision only lasted about a minute, but it unhinged me emotionally.

If there's ever been a time in my life when I felt flooded and overwhelmed with emotion, it was that moment. I felt their suffering piling up, layer after layer, onto them, pushing them down. I began to cry so uncontrollably that I had to catch my breath. My body began to shake.

I felt all these feelings for these people I'd never seen before in my life, and a thousand questions popped into my mind at once. *What just happened? Who were they? What did I just see? How do*

I find them? What am I supposed to do about it? Is this too much for me? How will I make an impact?

I had never shed more than a couple of tears in my life, but this time, I left a silver dollar–sized puddle on the back cover of my Bible. Still puzzled by what had just happened, I pulled a scrap piece of paper and a pen from my Bible. I wrote down key words to describe what I'd seen.

In big bold letters, I wrote down *Forgotten* and then underlined it. Underneath it, I wrote down *Hungry. Starving. Thirsty. Dirty Water. No Access to Clean Water. Dying of Sickness. Extreme Poverty. Enslaved. Hated. Oppressed.* I folded the paper to put back in my Bible and, by chance, opened the book to Isaiah 58:6–7 (NLT):

> *No, this is the kind of fasting I want: Free those who are wrongly imprisoned; lighten the burden of those who work for you. Let the oppressed go free, and remove the chains that bind people. Share your food with the hungry, and give shelter to the homeless. Give clothes to those who need them, and do not hide from relatives who need your help.*

That scripture seemed to match up with what I'd written down from my vision. My heart had felt every word that my eyes had read. The vision and those words were the closest thing I'd ever experienced to a conversation with God. I instantly knew that He was trying to tell me something or point me in a new direction.

Later, I told my missionary friend Caleb—who was, coincidently, about to leave for a trip to Africa with another missionary named Colin—about my vision. I described the huge rainforest and these people, who were hurting, sick, starving, enslaved, and hated. And these people were always reminded that they were despised.

A knowing look came over Caleb's face.

"Justin, those are the Pygmies," he said.

If you asked me today how to describe the Pygmies, I'd say they're some of the most amazing and sweet people on the planet earth. But four years ago, I thought a Pygmy might be a miniature-sized goat, hippo, or marmoset. I didn't know the Pygmies are the oldest people group in Africa. I didn't know that 250,000 to 600,000 Pygmies inhabit the rainforests in the Democratic Republic of the Congo,[1] a war-torn country that is anything but a democracy. I didn't know that *Pygmy*, translated from Latin, means "the height between the elbow and knuckles," in reference to a Pygmy's average height of four-foot-seven. I didn't know the Pygmies were one of the most disenfranchised people groups on the planet. And I couldn't believe slavery still existed in the world. But I got to see this all with my own eyes when I met my first Pygmy tribe just over three weeks later.

Meeting the Pygmies, or what we like to call "First Contact," went down just like my vision. The rainforest was dense and treacherous. We heard this unique-sounding music and drifted toward it. We pulled the forest's green curtain away to reveal a village of about one hundred Pygmies gathered around their stick-and-leaf huts.

I literally had to squat down, I was so overwhelmed by the moment. I stayed like that for the first few minutes, taking it all in. This was my vision. These were the sick, the poor, the hungry, the thirsty, the oppressed and imprisoned people I'd seen in my vision.

I'd found these people who were broken and hurting, who were being enslaved. I just knew instantly that this was all God. I couldn't have planned all this in three weeks. I had this vision in my mind and it happened so quickly and then all was provided for me, right down to a last-minute passport. I had no idea that God could really speak to me in this way.

------

[1] *http://www.theguardian.com/environment/2007/oct/04/congo.forests*

The Pygmies began to dance and share their culture with us—I'd learn later that it was because they had no food or drink to offer us. I could tell right away that they were starving. You could see all of the bones in their hands. Their elbows jutted out. The elderly women were topless and you could see their AC joints protruding from between their clavicle and shoulders. The ones that couldn't work were the worst off.

We hadn't brought any food with us, as we didn't know how many Pygmies we'd encounter and we wanted to make sure everyone got something. Caleb, Colin, and I were also concerned that bringing food or clothes might also put locals out of work—a day or two of lost wages could do lasting damage. We didn't want to hurt the places we were going to. We thought the best way to avoid that was to watch and learn. The first trip was a scouting trip. See, learn, and pray. We didn't go there with a bunch of answers. And there was plenty to painstakingly see.

One Pygmy man led the dance and others followed him in a circle. The women yodeled as they danced. Many of the men played bamboo flutes of different sizes that made various tones when they blew into them. The flute players were all playing together as if they had sheet music in front of them that they'd practiced before. A younger man sat on a log and played a complicated beat on an overturned yellow five-gallon jerry can with a stick. There were a few other men hitting various objects to make up the rest of the percussion session.

As in my vision, the collaborative sound was like nothing I'd ever heard before. It blew my mind that they could come up with songs on the fly and that each person made their own sound at a certain time to create this polyphonic masterpiece.

From this clearing, we could see the sun was still out. Caleb and I noticed some of the women and children were off to the side, too scared and skittish to join in. We jumped in with the others dancing and that seemed to ease them right away and make them laugh.

The kids had never seen light blond hair like mine, let alone a white man, and they weren't used to arm hair. I squatted down to where I was eye to eye with them and put my open hand out. I rubbed my own arm to motion that it was all right for them to do it. Every time they touched my arm hair, their eyes would get very big or they'd smile or laugh. Or they'd say, "Aye! Aye! Aye!" and shake their heads, the Pygmies' way of showing disbelief. I didn't know it was going to be that big of a hit, but they were mesmerized.

One of the two translators we'd hired motioned for us to stop mingling in order to meet the chief, who wore a leopard headdress that was gold with black spots and had a tail like the raccoon-looking thing that Daniel Boone wore. I instructed our translator to tell the chief we'd come to visit, that we wanted to understand their life and wanted to learn the culture. We wanted to spend time to get to know them as friends and love on them. Was that okay?

The chief said yes. We were told that we weren't the very first visitors the tribe had accommodated, but it was the first time they'd been approached in this way. In the past, they'd only had "bad" visits. At the time, I hadn't known what the chief meant, and I didn't press the issue. This would come to light later.

We danced with the Pygmies for an hour and a half (give or take, with a few breaks on our part). I tried to mingle with those watching and used my translator to ask some questions. *What does this dance mean? What are your daily lives like? We heard you have great suffering. Is that true?* I walked by their huts and I peeked in. There wasn't a stitch inside of them—no mattresses, no blankets, no pillows. Just dirt. They had nothing but one another and their music and dancing.

I was invited to sit down among the chief and his elders in a chair made of sturdy sticks that were twisted, tied with vine, and splayed in such a way that it could support you. It was a pretty comfortable chair, but with my six-foot-three, 265-pound frame, I felt like I was sitting in a kid's chair in a kindergarten class. I began to ask the chief my questions and he conferred with his elder group before answering. He spoke in a hushed tone.

"We work from sunup to sundown for little food or sometimes nothing at all," he started. "We used to be able to support ourselves, live free, and move around the forest as we wished."

The chief looked around him for some reason before he continued, like he had a secret to tell. He said that animal conservationists and rainforest preservationists around that area had bought up their land and pushed them off of it. They'd been threatened at gunpoint and treated as poachers.

The ones who could work wore modern-day clothes as payment, but there were holes upon holes in them. Their clothes were falling right off their frail bodies. A Pygmy teenager we'd come to call Freddy wore pink Minnie Mouse shorts made for a little girl. You could just tell that this was all they had.

The ones who couldn't work—the elderly and the little ones under four or five years old—wore leaves, natural materials from the forest, or nothing at all.

I knew we were only hearing and seeing the tip of the iceberg, but after three hours—with a lot of that time going to translation through the two sides—we were told to leave. The translators were worried about the sun going down and the rebels traveling through the forest, looking for villages in which to wreak havoc. The translators said the rebels also came out at night to put up illegal roadblocks or they'd appear out of the forest and shoot out your tires or windows. We had to get back to the hotel by nightfall, they said.

"A hotel?" I asked. "Why can't we stay here tonight? I've brought a tent with me."

The translator shook his head.

"Ask them if we can stay," I told the translator.

"Oh, I don't think they'd like that," he answered without even asking.

"Why not?"

"They don't let visitors stay," he said, trying to end the conversation. But I was persistent. I accompanied the translator over to the chief to watch him ask. The answer we got back was that they'd love us to stay, but they'd already suffered so much. They were enslaved, abused, and murdered, and they didn't want to attract any more attention to themselves. Having a *mzungu* staying in their village would attract attention from rebel groups that might want to steal from them. I took the translator at his word and sadly prepared to leave with the others.

I didn't know it, but Mokpala slave masters had been hovering in the background, watching over our exchanges with the Pygmies that day. There'd been two taller guys talking to our translators, though our translators hadn't pointed them out as such.

It had only taken us three flights (totaling seventeen hours); a six-hour bus ride from Kigali, Rwanda, to walk over the Congo border into Goma; a two-hour flight within the Congo; a five-hour ride in a 4×4 on crazy, bumpy, dirt roads; and a half-hour hike through the jungle to reach the Pygmies. On top of it all, our flight within the Congo had been delayed from Monday until Thursday, and we lost four days of our trip. I wanted to hike back to the truck, get our bags, and go back and get permission to stay the night, but our translators again reiterated that the area was far too dangerous and the Pygmies didn't want us there.

We drove back an hour and a half to Komanda, the closest town. We checked into an eight-room hotel riddled with bullet holes from previous years of rebel warfare. We were sleeping where the rebels had shacked up when they overran the town the previous year. My room had a locally made chair from the wood of the forest and a mattress with a mosquito net above it. All the guests shared one toilet and shower, both being a hole in the ground. There was limited electricity that ran on a generator, when it worked, but I couldn't complain. It was a palace compared to the conditions I saw the Pygmies living in.

I sat in bed that night, too excited for the next day to sleep. I couldn't wait to get back to the Pygmies. I just couldn't wait.

The next morning, the translators told us the area we'd visited had been too dangerous and they wanted us to meet other tribes. So we took a different road in a different direction. It was noon when we arrived to meet our second Pygmy tribe. Like the day before, we left our vehicles on the road and walked into the forest for another thirty-minute hike. When we arrived at camp, there was no singing and dancing at first. Some of the Pygmies were hanging out, but most were coming back in from their day's work.

One of those men was Yoda, a name we gave him out of endearment when we failed to pronounce his real name correctly after countless attempts (which really made him laugh). Yoda, maybe in his fifties, had a spunky personality and was the best dancer of the older crowd. Most of the older Pygmy men sat out the dancing, but not Yoda. He was very personable and happy, so I made a friend in him off the bat. Yoda was jovial until we asked about his personal struggles, and his face stiffened.

Yoda's village had been found out by rebels and his family was massacred in such a heinous, inhumane way that I didn't believe it when I was first told the story. At gunpoint, Yoda watched his nephew, who was a master hunter, get shot, cooked, and eaten. Yoda watched his nephew's wife get kicked to her knees and, with a machine gun to her head, she was force-fed her own husband. It was one of the most evil things I've heard of on this planet earth, but it happened just a few years before I got there. Hearing this story gave me such a mix of emotions because I was falling in love with these people, but at the same time I hated what was happening to them.

We stayed with this tribe for about four hours. The chief asked why we had come. I told him we wanted to meet some of the world's most amazing people and to learn why they were suffering. But then I sensed it was an opportunity to share some of my life story and hopefully encourage them. I shared my difficulties and struggles, though I knew they were nowhere near what the Pygmies were going through. I told them that God, and a relationship with Him, is what ultimately fulfilled me and became my joy whenever I let Him come into my life. It wasn't a man-made religion, but each man's personal relationship with God, the One who made us, that fulfills us. It wasn't about the stuff I did or didn't have. It was God being in my life that finally made me happy and saved me from being a suicidal drug addict.

The Pygmies couldn't believe that I ever wanted to kill myself. They'd never heard of suicide or been that depressed that they wanted to kill themselves, they said. Maybe it was a cultural thing, but suicide was never really an option for them. Among the Pygmies, family is the most important. Families are always together. They suffer as one. They suffer together out in the open with their tribesmen. Slavery, starvation, death—all were suffered together openly.

I felt I'd really made a connection with this Pygmy tribe, and again, as night approached, I asked the translators to inquire about spending the night in the Pygmies' camp with them.

"Let's ask the Pygmies," he said. I noticed his question to them seemed very short, like he hadn't translated what I'd asked, word for word.

"Yeah, they said they want you to stay," explained the translator, "but they don't want the rebel groups coming here because they have a white person in their village. They're already disliked by everybody. You being here will just bring more harm upon them."

I certainly didn't want to do that. We wanted them to know we loved and cared about them. We didn't want to bring them harm in any way. On the third and final night we asked if we could stay with the Pygmies, if they wanted us to, and it was the same answer. We only wanted to stay, hang out, and experience their life with them. I was accustomed to "learning by doing." That's the way it was in fighting—you had to get in the cage to fully grasp it.

"I was hoping something was going to happen here," Caleb said as we drove away from the last Pygmy village to continue our trip into Tanzania and Kenya. I privately asked God if this was really the people He wanted me to help. I had had that moment of first contact when we'd gotten there, but then all of these obstacles had been thrown at us.

"These are the people I'm supposed to love, bro," I told Caleb, but inside I was praying, *God, why did you bring us here? We got nothing done. Did You bring me here just to show me how small I am? God, if there's one place I never want to come back to, it's here.*

But when I said "I want," I opened my Bible again right to Isaiah 58:6–7 and "I want" was staring up from the page at me.

> *No, this is the kind of fasting I **want**: Free those who are wrongly imprisoned; lighten the burden of those who work for you. Let the oppressed go free, and remove the chains that bind people. Share your food with the hungry, and give shelter to the homeless. Give clothes to those who need them, and do not hide from relatives who need your help.*

On the plane ride home, I told myself I was done with this, that I didn't know why He had asked me to come to the Congo. Everything had gone wrong. I felt like these people weren't treated like they were human, and when they had visitors, they were observed like animals in a zoo. If we'd been able to stay longer with the Pygmies, learn more about their way of life, and begin to cultivate friendships, I would have felt like it was a success. However, our corrupt translators cheated both us and the Pygmies; they assumed we wanted to go on a "human safari," and I feel like that was the vibe some of the Pygmies got. I told God that I'd go anywhere He wanted me to and would do anything He asked, but please don't send me back to the Congo. Literally, I felt a question pop instantaneously into my mind: *What if I ask you to?* That really made me think. What if this wasn't about what *I* wanted but about what *He* wanted?

CHAPTER 3

Religion and Sports

ompletely surrounded, they poked, prodded, grabbed, shoved, and shook me while trying to cast the demons out of me. I'm twelve years old and have just been physically and emotionally bruised by my counselors at a Christian summer camp.

I was so desperate to fit in I agreed to go to church camp with a kid I hoped to befriend. Unbeknownst to me, the camp was organized by one of those extremist, over-the-top, charismatic denominations that lured kids in with the promise of Jet-Skiing, swimming, and a summer-load of fun. They really sold me on "The Blob," a forty-foot-long crash pad of air that sat in the campground's lake. In one of my favorite childhood movies, *Heavyweights* with Ben Stiller, I'd seen the heavyset kids propel the average kiddos twenty, thirty, even fifty feet into the air. I thought with this human catapult, and my weight, it was finally my chance to make a huge splash with some of the other kids my age.

When the bus pulled up to camp, we all shuffled off and were handed a King James Version of the Bible and a tambourine. I was told these were my "sword of the Spirit" and my "shield of praise" for the week. The days consisted of some of the fun stuff I mentioned and a lot of weird religious stuff. When the churchy music began, the worshippers would run up and down the aisles with ribbons or sometimes march with flags. When the preacher spoke, people would randomly pass out. It was shocking to watch my peers act like God had given them spur-of-the-moment epilepsy and convulsive seizures.

During one of the evening services in the week, our group leaders told us we were going to "speak in tongues," as an exercise I guess.

"Just let it go, Justin, speak in another language," said one of the counselors. "Just like a baby does. Come on, try saying 'Goo goo gaga' and ramble until the words begin to flow."

Under pressure, I thought about faking it, but I couldn't find it in me to do so. When I didn't pick it up quick enough, a few of the male leaders took it upon themselves to teach my peers how to lay their hands on my head and pray for the demons to leave me. Needless to say, that didn't help me make friends at church camp.

On the last night, we were told we would take part in one of God's many miracles. We all crowded into the dimly lit tabernacle and were informed that God was going to make us "drunk in the Spirit." I watched as the other kids began to stumble around and lean on one another's shoulders, pretending they were drunk, like they were walking home from a bar. Others squirmed on the floor, their eyes rolled into the back of their heads, laughing hysterically. I was beyond startled, and honestly, I was shaken, so I withdrew to the back of the room. When I didn't join in, the camp speaker stepped down from the stage and had the other leaders circle me in a corner. I was "possessed," they said, and needed to be "delivered." While I was being shoved and shaken by a huddle of adult men, I remembered having one distinctive thought. *Look around, guys, please! How in the world do you think that I am the one possessed and not the others flopping around on the ground like fish out of water?*

I asked them to stop because they were hurting me, but they didn't know if it was me or the demons talking. When they felt satisfied, they stepped back to take in their handiwork. This happened in front of the rest of the kids, who then ostracized me. I hopped on the bus back home a total outcast.

You can say that "religion" not only gave me the heebie-jeebies; it had prominence in my life early on. Some of my family were deeply religious and believed that it was all about living up to an impossible set of rules. No tattoos, drinking alcohol, swimming coed, or wearing shorts—any of these trespasses could or would send you straight to Hell. It was both fear-based and fear-inducing, as well as being absent of a whole lot of love.

Not surprisingly, I had some extremely confusing, jacked-up experiences when it came to religion. My parents sent me to Catholic high school—absolutely one of the best moves they could have ever made for my self-esteem and future athletic career, but at times I was bewildered by what I saw. The priest could drink, and the parents could throw us "keggers" on homecoming and prom so we wouldn't drink and drive. But if you used contraceptives, whether you were married or not, you were living in sin.

From my past experiences with religion, I think you can see the kind of web my mind became entangled in and understand why I was so eager to escape and remain free.

One church taught if you drank—ever—you were headed straight for the pits of Hell, that if you couldn't let God make you drunk, then you were obviously possessed by demons. While the other church said we could all get drunk together, but if we used a condom (or any contraceptive), there would be Hell to pay. I thought, *How can any of this make sense?*

The strict focus on the rules and my personal experience with religious people pushed me far away from any kind of organized religion, especially churches and Christians. In high school, my favorite quote came from Mahatma Gandhi. "I like your Christ, but I don't like your Christians," he said. "Your Christians are so unlike your Christ."

I'd seen so much fake stuff, I was exhausted from it. During my formative years, every religious activity I took part in either bored me to tears or repelled me further away. The differing "men of the cloth" constantly contradicted one another in their teachings. They all claimed to worship the same God, but it was hard to believe He was the same guy. I went to a church with relatives that preached that if you didn't attend their specific church, Heaven could never be an option. Even as people attempted to convert me, I used these instances as ammo to show why religion was phony and definitely not for me.

On top of the ever-puzzling theology, my personal wounds kept stacking up. A tormenting bully at one of my childhood schools raised hell with me all through the week, but then turned into Mr. Goody Two-shoes on Sunday and led the youth in prayer. Oftentimes, it was the people promising Heaven who burned me the most. The religious people I knew felt like some of the most judgmental people alive. They spoke about a God of love, but their actions showed hate. Anything that had to do with God began to look not only unbeneficial, but parasitic, something that would suck the blood and life out of me. Despite what they said, I just didn't see a loving God in any of it.

I ran from religion, but I sprinted toward sports. Since my early childhood living in Dallas, Texas, I always knew I wanted to be a professional athlete. Both my parents encouraged me to try every sport I could. I played Little League baseball, basketball, football, soccer, then later competed in shot put, tennis, and even calf-roping at rodeos. Sports were my family's common bond. My father was a successful sports photographer who worked with professional sports teams in the NFL, NBA, MLB, MLS, and NHL, among others. My mother had been a two-time high school state tennis champion and two-time national barrel-racing champion.

My parents were my biggest supporters, and my mom was my rock growing up. She and my father attended my games and carted me around to what must have been more than a thousand practices.

My mother clearly cared about my sports future, and because of her athletic success, she was always able to guide me down the right path. I also think I inherited most of my competitive traits from her, but because she is so sweet-natured, you might not know it from just a glance. My father was just as supportive of my athletics, but in a different way. He was both passionate and serious, and expected a lot of me from the sidelines. Outside of school, my schedule was completely filled with sports. I'd miss practices to go to games, trying to please my dad by keeping up that pace. It's no wonder that sports were where I gauged my value as a person. Yet, even with sports in my life, my insecurities would take root at an early age.

CHAPTER 4

Bullies

The first thing I hear is her laugh, that apathetic cackle signaling the oncoming humiliation. I'm a thirteen-year-old eighth-grader in my crush's backyard, at her birthday party, and cameras are flashing in my eyes. Jennifer is the most beautiful girl in school. Curly brown hair. Captivating eyes. You'd think she'd want nothing to do with me: the short, pimply, chubby kid with the chili-bowl haircut— the one who often sits alone in the lunchroom, getting pelted in the back of the head with chocolate milk spit wads.

But I have the invitation she hand-delivered, which clearly states that this is a costume party. It slips from my hand as I realize she and the rest of my school's cool kids are pointing and snickering at me. I'm the only kid wearing a costume.

Jennifer was in on it. She must have been told how much I liked her. It must have sounded like a fun thing to go along with when the boys devised their plan with her.

"What costume are you wearing?" a classmate asked me the day before Jennifer's party. Jennifer had given me the invitation herself that Friday morning. I have to admit that I was excited, nervous, and a bit puzzled as to why I'd been invited, but I knew Saturday night was my chance to finally catch her eye.

"I've got something up my sleeve," I said, looking down at the card. It read: *Best costume gets a prize.*

Desperate to gain Jennifer's affections through my all-important costume selection, I quickly asked around for some insight into her life. Her family loved Dr Pepper and there was paraphernalia all over her house, including one of the mauve soda machines with the big white lettering. An idea sprang into my head.

I took about ten different Dr Pepper cardboard cases, and duct-taped my armor together. The twelve-pack was great for covering my arms and the twenty-four-pack made a great helmet. I even made "boots" to wear over my sneakers. Transformers had been fairly popular at my school at the time and I banked on Jennifer liking them, too, so I became Dr. Optimus Pepper. I would be her knight in cardboard armor.

I got to Jennifer's house at six P.M. sharp, her present in one hand and the Dr. Pepper sword I'd fashioned in the other. Her grandmother answered the door.

"Oh, what a nice . . . costume," she said. She was so sweet that I didn't notice the hesitancy in her voice. She walked me down the hallway plastered with Dr Pepper advertising signs and into the backyard. I made a grand entrance with my chest popped out and sword drawn.

The next thing I felt was the blood rushing to my face. I was flush all over, extremely embarrassed, hurt, and confused. I found out later that everyone had been invited at 5:30, as not to miss the loser's big entrance. "You're so worthless you should just kill yourself" I heard someone yell out as I exited shamefully.

Hours later, my mom picked me up down the street at the local Dairy Queen. Some of the staff had spotted me distraught and crouched down in between the dumpsters. I still had the sticky remnants from the duct tape in lines all across my clothes. My mom was heartbroken for me.

I can honestly point to that moment at the party as the beginning of my battles with suicidal thoughts. It can be a brutal experience in a kid's life when they believe what others say about him. Kids can be mean, and because I was still in my earlier years, I took a lot of those words to heart.

I didn't leave my room that weekend except to go to the bathroom or to get something to eat. I was too "sick" on Monday, Tuesday, and Wednesday to go to school, and when my parents made me return, pictures of Dr. Optimus Pepper were circulating, ensuring no one would forget this incident anytime soon.

By then, alienation wasn't too uncommon for me. When I was transferred to public school in third grade, I got into my very first fight on the first day. I tried to walk away from a kid who'd jumped my back and started hitting and choking me. I pulled him off me, but the teachers carted me off to the principal's office as well. When word got out that I hadn't fought back, the kid and his friends used that to bully me at every turn. I got called fat, received barrages of "titty twisters," and got picked last for kickball games. I was generally timid and quiet and, people might say, a bit of a loner. When I opened up, or tried to laugh things off, I was usually giving the bullies more ammo to use against me. I learned at a young age how it felt to be oppressed.

I so wanted others to like me but failed many attempts to earn acceptance in any social group that would take me.

I tried to become a skater kid, but I wasn't great on a board and I didn't fit their mold. I was unceremoniously kicked out of that group. The outcast kids wore big baggy jeans, dark clothes, and lived by the doctrine of metal rock groups like Korn and Insane Clown Posse. I had a sort-of friend in this group, so that was my "in," but these kids went to a pretty dark place. I watched them blow up frogs, screaming and jamming out to the lyrics to Papa Roach's suicidal song "Last Resort," and felt I'd be better off depressed on my own.

The more I became an outcast, the more I withdrew from the world. In seventh grade, I quit sports altogether, which upset my dad, especially with football, where I'd been one of the best linemen for both offense and defense. I quit basketball and left baseball not even halfway through the season—the teasing had become that inescapable in the dugout.

I don't know why I was bullied in school. Maybe it was because I was chubbier, or maybe because I was too nice and let the other kids walk all over me. I don't feel like I showed too much weakness, but my classmates sensed it and took advantage.

A popular girl asked me to one of the homecoming dances. In Texas, homecoming football and dances are a very big deal and grounded in tradition. It's customary for a guy to present his date with a "mum," Texas's version of a corsage. Mums are more like gaudy prize ribbons, worn on the chest and decorated with everything from cascading sparkles to stuffed animals to flowing ribbons down to the ground. They literally have all the bells and whistles. (The most extravagant can have all of these. Google it if you don't believe me.) The mum I ordered had both my date's and my names on it. When I picked it up from the flower shop, I woohooed all the way home.

During halftime at the homecoming game, with the whole school watching, it finally dawned on me that I'd been duped. Another kid, also named Justin, approached me. He looked at Jessica's mum and grabbed the ribbon that spelled out *Justin and Jessica Homecoming '99* in puffy, white carnations.

"Thanks," pseudo-Justin said. "This is the perfect mum for my date." He wrapped his arm around Jessica, who, to my mortification, had a front-row seat. They walked off together, much to the amusement of the crowd that had turned to watch us.

Some people ask these days why middle school kids—and even elementary-level kids—are committing suicide because of bullying.

"They should just suck it up," people say. Even I've thought that before, but looking back now, I absolutely understand.

I struggled deeply with suicidal thoughts. I was blessed to have a loving home, for without that, I would have been a goner. Depression compiles and compiles and has you rolling down the side of a mountain in an unstoppable snowball of overwhelming loneliness, sadness, and hurt. Some days you feel like you've dropped off a cliff and gone splat. Taking the option to get out can be an eerily appealing way to escape. And when the other kids told me I'd be better off killing myself, I started to believe them. If my parents had had a gun in the house, I probably would have used it. That's how bad I felt about myself.

My parents weren't oblivious to my struggles. They knew something was up in middle school, but what kid wants to admit to his parents that he isn't cool and nobody likes him? Around age thirteen, my parents took me to our family doctor, who diagnosed me with attention deficit disorder and depression. I started taking medication for the ADD, but I wouldn't accept that I had depression and I refused the medication. I wanted to prove the doctor and my parents wrong.

My parents put together a plan to help me begin high school on a different note. They transferred me out of the school district where I'd been bullied. I began my freshman year at Southwest Christian School, a K–12 private school, in Fort Worth, Texas.

Luckily, Southwest Christian had a strong athletics program. I was excited to find out that a father of two of the younger kids coached a club wrestling team in the school's basement.

Wrestling and I clicked from the start. I wasn't very good right away; I was actually horrible, but I loved it. Alan Rodger, my club team coach for the Eagles, was incredibly dedicated, caring, and inspiring. With wrestling, I was molded into a different person. Competitive, goal-oriented, and more self-assured. For the first time in my life, I'd found something to be passionate about. It gave me something to focus on, someone to aspire to be, and was an incredible outlet for my self-esteem struggles.

When it came to wrestling, my parents didn't have to encourage me to go to practice or to eat right. They didn't have to give me any extra motivation. Noticing a radical change in me, my parents got behind me and helped me pursue my newfound passion. I began working extensively with Coach Rodger outside of school, and traveling around the country with his select group of seasoned wrestlers. I normally lost every single match. It wasn't even close.

I was just a warm-up match and tossed around like a rag doll for any of the Okie boys or corn-fed huskers who I'd face. I was years behind the curve. Many wrestlers (and even teammates) discouraged me and told me I should just cut my losses. Behind closed doors, fellow coaches would advise Coach Rodger that I was a good kid who'd never be a good wrestler. The best thing was to let me down easy, the other coaches told him.

Still, Coach Rodger saw something in me that other coaches didn't, nor did I see in myself. He told me work ethic, experience, and lots of meticulous mat time, both practicing and competing, were what was important. He took me under his wing, he mentored me, and I looked to him for advice in wrestling and in life. Coach Rodger would become a second dad to me.

I was still having back-and-forth problems with my peers in school, though, and the teasing continued. I'd thought a fresh start, at a new school, with new classmates meant a chance to reinvent myself. I'd thought if I'd try and become the funny guy that maybe everyone would laugh *with* me for a change. I became the goofy Chris Farley character with my orange *Beverly Hills Ninja* T-shirt. It didn't go over very well.

I was the only high school wrestler from Southwest Christian. The popular kids had decided to boycott wrestling because it was for "sissies who wore spandex and got sweaty with other boys." Wrestling was social suicide, I'd soon find out.

I tried to get a wrestling team started, and actually got twenty-three guys to sign up. It was more than enough to start a bona fide team, so my enthusiasm was through the roof when I showed our athletic director the full list of names. Coach Rodger even hopped on board and offered to get Coach Jack Spates from the University of Oklahoma, a powerhouse among wrestling colleges, to come to the first practice. That first day of practice came and only one kid showed up. The big joke was on me. The rest of the guys who'd signed up had no intentions of coming at all. Hilarious.

Without a team, I couldn't compete in team meets, so I could only enter independently at individual tournaments and keep practicing with my club team. Finally, during my sophomore year, some momentum built in my direction. Coach Rodger, who also happened to be the director of Texas High School Wrestling, told me a spot had opened up in the state championship. I was the youngest and smallest heavyweight wrestler in the tournament and I Cinderella'd myself right into the finals.

Nobody had given me a chance to get that far, and the finals were no different. I was up against the big, nineteen-year-old senior who had won the state championship the year before. Honestly, I was intimidated because he was from Bishop Lynch High School's powerhouse wrestling team and had been coached by not just one, but two Olympic gold medalists. Early in the match, he made a mistake trying to go for a big throw. It was basically a fluke when I fell on top of him, but I hung on tight and squeezed with all my might. I pinned him to the mat in the first period and became the first state champion from my school at only fifteen years old. My mom, dad, and coach were all there to see the big upset.

Due to more extracurricular fights with the bullies, I was asked to leave Southwest Christian shortly after that, though the timing couldn't have been better. Someone had been watching from the other side of the mat at the state championships and had seen a glimmer of talent in me. With the full support of my parents and with Coach Rodger's encouragement, I was heading to Bishop Lynch, which had the second-best wrestling team in the country.

CHAPTER 5

The Mbuti Pygmies of the Congo

The Pygmies have a saying that there are three things you can't take away from them:

1. The forest
2. Their fire
3. Their singing and dancing

There was a time when the Pygmies lived alone and unfettered in the Ituri rainforest, darting freely among the trees for the ample wildlife that fed their families. The forest gifted the Pygmies with everything they needed to survive, from food to water to shelter. The bond between the two was strengthened by the spiritual significance the forest and some of its inhabitants had to the petite-people group. Some believed the trees were holy hosts to the spirits of their ancestors. Others believed the python, a variety of which slithered around the forest, was a holy creature never to be touched. And still others worshipped Gingi, a spirit god who ran through the forest looking for mischief. The forest served nearly all of the Pygmies' needs, so they lived peacefully away from the rest of the world.

Exploration brought the Arab nations to central Africa in the early 1800s, and the booming ivory trade made them stay. It is said that the Arabs were the first among the non-African tribes to make contact with the Pygmies of the Congo, and the invading group spurred on intertribal wars to divide and conquer many of the tribes into slavery.

The Europeans chased the Arabs out of Africa in the late 1800s and took up their own trade with rubber, which could be peeled from the endless supply of trees like corn husks. Keen on acquiring the well-placed territory, King Leopold II of Belgium laid official claim to it in 1885 and renamed the country the Congo Free State.[2]

Under the decades-long "Rubber Terror," millions upon millions of the Congolese people were either enslaved or killed in Belgium's race to export rubber worldwide. King Leopold, a greedy, aging royal known for his bushy white beard, ruled the Congo Free State with an iron fist, stationing Belgium officers in posts up and down the waterways (where the rubber was often transported) and hiring locals willing to pledge allegiance to his crown as enforcers. During Leopold's reign, slavery trickled down into every village. Chiefs were paid to capture others or give up their own people as slaves, which some did gladly. Soldiers regularly raided tribes of their able-bodied, then took livestock and burned huts, leaving the remaining villagers destitute. Soldiers shot and killed whole villages that wouldn't submit to the slave trade—it became customary for a soldier to cut off a hand of the ones he'd shot, to show his superiors that the bullets hadn't been wasted. Severing hands also became an acceptable punishment for those living natives who resisted Belgium's sovereignty over them. As many as 10 million people, half of the Congo's 20 million in population at the time, were massacred in the slave trade.

---

[2] *Hochschild, Adam.* King Leopold's Ghost: A Story of Greed, Terror, and Heroism in Colonial Africa *(New York: Mariner Books, 1999).*

If the Mokpala weren't enslaving the Mbuti Pygmies by this time, slavery was on full display all around them. The Pygmies, smaller in stature and thus able to maneuver the forest better, could get something valuable that the non-hunting Mokpala could not—wildlife from the forest.

When people stateside ask me how in the world the people around the Pygmies can ever believe them to be literal animals, I tell them that a hundred years ago in America, we stole a Pygmy from the forest and put him in the monkey cage at the zoo.

In the early 1900s, some Pygmies were transported to Europe and the U.S. as exhibits for zoos and world fairs. Most famous among that group was Ota Benga, who was bought out of slavery in 1902 for a pound of salt and a bolt of cloth. Benga, a Mbuti Pygmy, was "displayed" at the St. Louis World's Fair, then at the Bronx Zoo, where he was, at times, housed in the monkey exhibit.[3] Benga, whose teeth were sharpened to points back in Africa as a part of his people's tradition, stayed in the zoo until 1906, when he was released into a reverend's custody. In 1916, realizing he would never return to the Congo, he shot and killed himself in his early thirties.[4]

In a 1960 *National Geographic* article, the Mokpala-Pygmy relationship was described as a symbiotic one.[5] In exchange for protein, the Mokpala paid the Pygmies in items they couldn't get in the forest, including scraps of metal, corn, beans, cassava leaves (similar to spinach), and rice. The Pygmies would use the scrap metal for the tips of their wooden arrows and spears and to make knives. The Mokpala would use gathered herbs from the forest for traditional medicines that the Pygmies had perfected over

[3] *Bradford, Phillips Verner, Harvey Blume.* Ota Benga: The Pygmy in the Zoo *(New York: St. Martins Press, 1992).*

[4] *http://www.encyclopediavirginia.org/Benga_Ota_ca_1883-1916*

[5] *Putnam, Anne Eisner. "My Life with Africa's Little People."* National Geographic *(February 1960): 15 pages. Print.*

thousands of years of trial and error. The article described the relationship as one of serfdom, but that the Mokpala slave masters admirably oversaw the Pygmies with a gentle hand.

Since the 1920s, the Congo Free State had gone through many leaders and a few name changes. It was renamed the Belgian Congo in 1908, when the Belgian government wrestled it out of Leopold's hands. It was christened the Democratic Republic of the Congo in 1965 when a coup d'état propelled Colonel Joseph Mobutu Sese Seko into presidency. Mobutu changed the country's name to Zaire in 1971 and proceeded to embezzle millions from the country's infrastructure into his European bank accounts over the next thirty years.[6] In 1997, when Mobutu's dictatorship was overthrown during a series of civil wars, the country went back to its first name, the Democratic Republic of the Congo. (For the purposes of this book, I refer to the DRC simply as the Congo.)

In that time, industrialization came to the forest. Deforestation sent the animals scattering, as trees as wide as two side-by-side Mack trucks were ripped out of the earth. This tipped the Pygmies' delicate relationship with the forest out of balance. Without protein, the Pygmies had nothing to offer their slave masters, so they were put to work in the Mokpala's fields farming and transporting various food crops, charcoal and firewood, and bright red-orange cooking oil made from palm nuts. As the shortage of wildlife grew, the Pygmies became more dependent on their slave masters, who, in turn, started paying less for more work. Fourteen- to sixteen-hour "workdays" became the norm, and without the privilege of daily food, the Pygmies began to starve.

In 1994, neighboring Rwanda experienced one of the world's worst recorded genocides, with as many as one million deaths in a

---

[6] *http://news.bbc.co.uk/2/hi/africa/1120825.stm*

hundred days, according to the United Nations.[7] Millions of Rwandans took refuge in the Congo, but the migration also brought warring rebel groups to the forest, like the still-ruthless Hutu militia group known as the FDLR (or the Democratic Forces for the Liberation of Rwanda). The name sticks even though their fight hasn't been in Rwanda for more than twenty years. Still, they've stuck around to exploit the Congo's wide array of natural elements. The Democratic Republic of the Congo is, by far, the most mineral-rich country on the planet.

Today, the Congo has more than thirty invading rebel groups controlling different parts of the east for their mineral supply. Homegrown rebel groups include the Cobra Matata ("the Cobra Problem") and the Mai-Mai, who've specifically hunted down Pygmies for mass rape, torture, murder, and cannibalism. There is a standing superstition that eating a Pygmy will give a warrior impenetrability and bullets will fly right through him.

The discovery of vast reserves of gold, diamonds, and, later, coltan—which is used in every smartphone, laptop, flat-screen TV, among other electronics—have drastically affected the Pygmy way of life. Rebel groups have even chained and shackled some Pygmies into slavery (including children), taking advantage of their smaller frames to dig through the narrow mines faster. Some have claimed that the Congo's civil war ended in 2003, but those who live there, including the Pygmies, know the war for natural resources still rages on, and its battlefield is almost always the mineral-rich jungle.

According to a 2011 CNN.com article, "Eastern Congo has been called the 'rape capital of the world' by U.N. Special Representative Margot Wallstrom. Reports record that 48 women are raped every hour."[8]

Today, the Pygmies are still one of the most primitive hunter-

---

[7] http://www.un.org/en/preventgenocide/rwanda/education/rwandagenocide.shtml

[8] http://www.cnn.com/2011/11/24/world/africa/democratic-congo-rape

gatherer societies left on the planet, but they are still denied proper representation and aren't recognized by the Congo's corrupt government. They are denied medical care and opportunities to make actual money for their labor, and can't afford to go to school, which is one of the reasons why the Mokpala are able to enslave them and keep them that way. Frequently, the Mokpala claim they've bought the land that the Pygmies live on, using falsified documents the Pygmies can't contest because they can't read or write.

In the Congo, you're not going to find a Pygmy in a good living condition. I don't think there's a Pygmy on the planet that has that. The Pygmies are denied clean water from existing wells and forced to drink stagnant water that animals have defecated in. Waterborne diseases, malaria, and dysentery are three of the top killers among the Mbuti, and every Pygmy suffers from these throughout their entire lives. Some also suffer from tuberculosis, HIV/AIDS, and even leprosy.

The Pygmies of the Congo might have the world's worst child mortality rate. On my trips to Pygmy villages, I'd see mothers who had lost five out of seven children, all due to illness. Nearly all the mothers I met had lost at least one out of two children before their child reached the age of five. Some had lost all of their children. It's rare to see Pygmies in their fifties and sixties.

Pygmy children become slaves as soon as they can be of some help in the Mokpala's fields, which is a lot younger than you would think. I've seen Pygmy boys who are already aces with the machete but can't string together sentences. I've seen children as young as five years old chopping down massive trees.

A 2014 report penned by the United Nations Development Programme stated that the Congo had the second-lowest level of human development in the world.[9]

---

[9] http://hdr.undp.org/sites/default/files/hdr14-summary-en.pdf

It's a poor country all around, stunted by government corruption. There are far too many officials who really don't care about the people in their country. Disputes and disagreements are decided on a local level and the ones who have the biggest guns or the most money are the ones who have control. It's the Wild Wild West. Every people group of the Congo suffers, except for a select few that have government and military jobs. The corruption that these officials wield cripples the country.

Caleb, Colin, and I experienced that prevailing corruption on our first trip—we just didn't know how much until I traveled back to the Congo a second time. I'd suspected something wasn't right the first time around, and learned on the second trip that our previous translators, whom we'd blindly hired, had been lying and trying to scam us the entire time.

On my second trip, I calculated all the ways we'd been duped the first time. We'd rented a 4×4 for nearly $200 a day on account of there being a high risk in an active conflict zone. On the second trip, I saw the same vehicles renting for $30 to $50 a day. Our "translators" had pocketed the difference. When I went to buy machetes, they only cost $2 to $3 each, not $10, as they'd said. I was also upset to hear from our new, local missionary friends that the Pygmies had really wanted us to stay overnight all along, but our translators wouldn't stoop themselves that low, and they thought we wouldn't, either. We started to put two and two together on our third and last day with the Pygmies.

"We'll take you somewhere really off the grid," said one translator. "Somewhere no one has ever been. You'll see when we get there. They won't be wearing any clothes. Just leaves."

I thought we had to be going very deep into the jungle to see that. It took us a few hours to drive and hike there from our already remote location. When we got there, the Pygmies were as the translators said they would be, naked except for leaves and other materials from the forest. Right before we left, I decided to dive into some of the huts to check out their stick-frame structure from the inside. This was the first time I got to enter their huts, and the construction was so delicate and intricate. I went inside three huts, and in one, I noticed clothing, like shorts and a T-shirt. In our final minutes with our translators, we had a pretty incredulous conversation in which they tried to get five figures out of us. All along, we'd told our Congolese translators that we really wanted to help, and now they had a way for us to do so.

"Listen, if you really want to help, you need to give us thirty-eight thousand dollars," said the second translator. "We'll buy machetes for the Pygmies, so they can get through the forest. They really need that." They said the machetes alone could total $20,000 (two thousand–plus machetes at $8 to $10 each), and they had a list for the rest, which included perishable food and bottles of water for another $18,000. How in the world did they think we'd just dish out thirty-eight grand to them? Looking back on it, I wish I could have added up the con men's math much, much quicker.

But the hardest realization I had from that first trip was that I'd been tricked into becoming a spectator at a human safari. Like Ota Benga's admirers, I'd taken pictures with the Pygmies. I'd depended too much on the honesty of our shady translators, who had a system down pat when "tourists" like us stepped right up to see the human oddity.

Over the next few years, I'd see the real definition of corruption. And at the very bottom of this miserable heap were the Pygmies, the most bullied people on the planet. I'd been heavily bullied throughout my childhood, so the Pygmies' plight resonated with me on a very deep level. I knew what it felt like to be stepped on, pushed around, and called names.

CHAPTER 6

Karelin

W hat's this?" my father asks. He points to the stack of video-tapes in front of him, the ones I've been stashing under my bed. I'm thirteen years old and I've just been busted.

My father acted like he'd stumbled upon my secret porn collection. But no, it was something far worse. I was watching . . . cage fights! I'd found the tapes at a local flea market and smuggled them into my room for late-night viewing, one eye always fixed on the shadows underneath the door crack.

When my dad told my mom, she shook her head and said that I'd grow out of it. What my mother didn't realize was that my real motive for watching the fights was to become a mixed martial artist, and more specifically, fight in the Ultimate Fighting Championship.

To me, a UFC fighter was a modern-day gladiator. A warrior. The UFC fighters were the absolute opposite from me. I thought if I could ever be like them, I'd have the significance and purpose that I was searching for. I'd have something to be passionate about and my life would be fulfilled. I'd have money, success, fame—I'd have notoriety for being good at something and thus worthwhile. Heck, I'd have real, actual friends. *I'll never be this dude who I am right now ever again,* I thought. I'd stop being the victim, because who'd bully an Ultimate Fighter?

Ultimate fighting, cage fighting, MMA: they're all names for mixed martial arts, a hybrid combat sport that was introduced to America in 1993. MMA is just what it sounds like. It basically combines four major combat sports: two striking components—boxing and kickboxing, or muay Thai, where you combine punches, elbows, knees, and kicks—and two grappling disciplines—Olympic-style wrestling and Brazilian jiu-jitsu, where you use chokes and holds, armbars, and other joint manipulations to submit someone—kind of like the little brother saying "Uncle" to his big brother.

There are other disciplines involved—judo, karate, and other, more obscure martial arts—but no fighter can ignore the four corners of MMA's foundation. The quicker a fighter can master all four disciplines and blend them together seamlessly, the more successful he'll be.

Though MMA gets a bad rap at times—Senator John McCain dubbed it "human cockfighting" in its earlier days—I believe it to be one of the purest sports out there. It's one fighter's heart against another's, both digging down deep to find out what they are capable of.

MMA can be just as dramatic as other sports. Good MMA fights tell stories: the two legends who met for the trilogy fight that decided an ultimate winner, the surefire fighter who crumbled under pressure, or the underdog who should've been put to sleep in the first round but made it all the way through round five and won.

Wrestlers have a very good track record in MMA. It's always a solid base discipline to build upon. If you're getting in trouble on your feet, you can always take the guy down. And because wrestlers are so disciplined, they transition well into MMA's complicated regimen.

At Bishop Lynch High School in Dallas, wrestling was king.

Coached by two Olympic wrestling gold medalists, the Lynch squad was a powerhouse. As many people came to Bishop Lynch wrestling meets as its basketball games, and both teams were state champions. At the time, Lynch prided itself on being the number-one program for high school wrestling in Texas and the second best in the country. For my amateur wrestling career, it didn't get any better than this.

Still, I was terrified to go to Bishop Lynch. The kids drove Hummers, Porsches, and Mercedeses, and I worried the entire school would find out about the "real me" and shun me. I decided to fly in under the radar. For the first week, I didn't really speak to anyone. Being a big kid at this point, six-three and 285 pounds, the other kids were intrigued, and maybe even a little intimidated. I was the mysterious new heavyweight scouted by the wrestling team. By that weekend, I'd been invited to a couple of senior parties at my new classmates' swanky houses.

You ever see one of those comedies where the dork gets in with the "in-crowd" and is suddenly cool? At Bishop Lynch, I became a different person socially. Things completely turned around for me because I was a good wrestler. I was accepted and actually popular. I went from being the laughingstock at Homecoming to getting nominated for Homecoming king. Now anytime I saw someone getting bullied, I'd stick up for them, and the bullies would listen and back off without a second thought.

Lynch was sixty-one miles from my home, and my parents drove me back and forth every day, in Fort Worth and Dallas traffic jams, until I got my driver's license. They made it happen. They sacrificed the time and money, which I know was a struggle for them, to make sure I had every opportunity available. In return, I tried to be the best wrestler I could be. I got up each morning to run or lift weights before school, and devoted more time to wrestling than I did to my schoolwork. I taped a reminder to the ceiling over my bed so it would be the first thing I saw every morning. It read *National Champion*, and I'd placed pictures of my two favorite wrestling moves on either side.

Olympic gold medalists Kenny Monday and Kendall Cross coached the Lynch team. I wrestled with Coach Monday a lot because he was the only wrestler big enough to work out with me. My specialty was high-amplitude throws, like back suplexes (where one wrestler throws another fighter, feet up, in an arc, over his shoulder). These were dynamic moves for the heavyweight division. Of the three wrestling styles—folkstyle (only practiced in the U.S.), freestyle, and Greco-Roman—the latter was my favorite because it offered the most opportunity for throws.

Wrestling was a perfect outlet for all the anger that had built up in me over the years. On the mat, I became a tenacious aggressor with a bit of an attitude. My coaches kept telling me I could be a national champion, but I'd have to get meaner. I was a Texan (Texas isn't known for its wrestling) who'd only started wrestling at age fifteen when others had begun as early as six or seven. I didn't get much, if any, respect from my opponents, so I pushed them out-of-bounds to get a rise out of them and to let them know they were in a real match. I had to earn respect by being the aggressor, constantly pushing my opponents onto their heels. My opponents were way more experienced than me, and I needed to create some sort of edge.

In the off-season, I got the opportunity to wrestle outside of high school on the national and international circuit. Most of the matches were on U.S. soil, but I got to wrestle guys from Cuba, New Zealand, Uzbekistan, Kazakhstan, Bulgaria, Russia, Canada, Poland, Puerto Rico, and more.

During the summer between my junior and senior years, I took a twenty-day trip with a team through Russia, the Caucasus, and Dagestan. I was a seventeen-year-old kid wrestling opponents who had beards, and hair on their chests and backs like sweaters spilling out of their singlets.

In my most memorable match, I suplexed my opponent for five points. Heavyweights usually didn't land moves like that and the fickle crowd started cheering for me and not the hometown guy. I won that match with a "tech fall" by getting ten points ahead—wrestling's version of Little League baseball's "ten-run rule." None of the other wrestlers or their coaches believed I was seventeen until we showed them my passport.

Wrestling is revered in Eastern Europe and we were mini-celebrities when we traveled there. The locals held parades for us as we made our way to the arena. Kenny Monday was given standing ovations when he walked into the arenas because of his Olympic gold medal. We had guards to keep the fans from mauling us, as many wanted to take pictures. The crowds were so taken with us that a lady put her baby in my arms like I was the pope. But the biggest accolade I received was when the fans pointed at me and said, "Karelin." Alexander Karelin was Russia's most famous heavyweight wrestler and my hero. This trip helped me see for the first time that I could actually be the best at something. Wrestling gave me purpose, worth, and a feeling of belonging.

Most important, wrestling steered me down a positive path. Before wrestling, I'd been battling depression big-time and had haunting visits from suicidal thoughts. It had gotten so bad that I *really* don't know what might have happened if I hadn't found wrestling.

I blossomed as an athlete during my senior year, when I won two national titles—one for my high school and another in the 2005 Junior Greco-Roman National Championship.

The Greco-Roman tournament at the Fargodome in North Dakota was one of my career high points. I had a picture-perfect performance—not a single person scored a point on me in my seven matches leading up to the finals. There, I was set to face Erik Nye, who currently has the number-three national ranking with Team USA.

Nye was the returning favorite. He'd won a championship the three previous years, and everyone was expecting to watch him take his fourth. Nobody gave me a chance except for my coaches. Nye had just bumped up to heavyweight that year and Greco-Roman was his strongest style.

As far as matches go, this was probably the most important of my wrestling career. I'd had some interest from the big wrestling colleges, including Oklahoma State University, where the legendary John Smith coached, but I'd told them all that I wanted to go to the U.S. Olympic Education Center instead. To get a spot at the USOEC, I'd have to win the Greco-Roman Nationals. Essentially, my future was riding on this match.

My mother knew how important this day was to me. Before the tournament, she gave me a handwritten note that I put inside the blood rag I carried in my singlet. I took it into battle with me.

It was a close match. It was 0–0 after the first round, so we were started in "the clinch"—each wrestler having both an underhook and an overhook—a fifty-fifty position, where the wrestlers start on even ground. The clinch is where most of the throws happen, too. The clinch was my sweet spot. If I had you there, I was going to throw you.

As the referee put Nye and me into place, I could see from the corner of my eye that my mom, the coaches, and the Texas fans were getting excited. They all anticipated what was coming.

The whistle blew and I picked Nye up, sucked him real tight into my hips, whipped around to the side of him, clinched my knees around his thigh to pin one of his legs with mine, and popped my hips. It's called a step-around body lock, a five-point throw rarely executed in the heavyweight division. The only heavyweight that could accomplish the move at the Olympic level was Alexander Karelin.

I beat Nye, 6–0, and was the only opponent to score a point on him the entire tournament. I had one of those slo-mo moments out of a heart-tugging sports film when a teammate threw a cowboy hat down from the stands. Being the first Texan to win Nationals in this style of wrestling, I grabbed the hat, put it on, and took my victory lap, tipping the hat to the crowd. Then I ran up into the stands and kissed and hugged my mother. "Dream big, win big," I whispered, reciting the note she'd written to me.

I graduated high school on an upswing. I'd received the grant I'd needed to continue my wrestling career at the U.S. Olympic Education Center on the campus of Northern Michigan University. It was a lot like regular college life, with dorms and cafeteria food cards. But our "academics" included training two times a day, five days a week, and could bring us a few steps closer to an Olympic bid.

At the Olympic Education Center, we continued to wrestle on the international circuit. At the New York Athletic Club Wrestling Invitational that first winter with the team, my momentum came to a grinding halt. I ended up in a bad position when I wrestled against a thirty-two-year-old Olympic bronze medalist and world champion. Rather than give up the point to him, I let him gut-wrench me against the mat, twisting my arm behind my back the wrong way with my palm facing up. My arm snapped like a twig. One of the other wrestlers, a future Olympian no less, puked when he saw it happen.

It happened so fast that the referee hadn't had time to step in and stop it. I was in terrible pain from my neck down to my hand. My elbow was broken and dislocated, and I'd torn the ulnar collateral ligament. There was nerve damage. It was the whole package. The doctors told me there was a thirty percent chance I'd never wrestle again.

I was only midway through my first year at the Olympic Education Center and I already had to undergo major surgery. It took six months of waiting, battling an insurance company all the way, to get the surgery done. Doctors replaced the ligament with one of the three tendons from my hamstring and performed a nerve transposition. (Because of the surgery, I no longer have a funny bone. Literally. If I talk on the phone too long, my three exterior fingers fall asleep.) The doctors said it would take a year of rehab before I could wrestle again.

While I'd waited those six months for surgery, I was given painkillers to get through the grind of shuttling myself back and forth from home to the Olympic Education Center. The first doctor gave me twenty hydrocodone, then bumped me up to Oxycontin when I finished them too quickly. I went through a month's supply of Oxycontin in a week. It was too early to ask for a refill, so I went across town to another oblivious doctor and got a prescription for more. At one point, I had three different doctors in three states, some of them prescribing one hundred pills at a time. When I couldn't readily get my pills, I started smoking marijuana, which I scored from a wrestling buddy who helped me get my pills. He told me pot was better for me anyway.

The blissful combination of narcotics and weed handled my elbow pain and kept me high while I watched from the sidelines as my team trained without me. I pretended to be optimistic; I was the youngest guy there and had shown a lot of promise and potential. I put on a good show. Inside, though, it was becoming a nightmare.

Unable to practice or compete, I left the U.S. Olympic Education Center after fourteen months. After addiction set in and my physical therapy began, I started at Des Moines Area Community College on the recommendation of undefeated, four-time NCAA champion and 2004 Olympic gold medalist Cael Sanderson, who was introduced to me by another friend. I was ecstatic that someone as experienced and decorated as Cael would take any interest in my wrestling career. He had a plan for me to attend DMACC, a smaller sister school to Iowa State University, for one year. Then I'd transfer to ISU to wrestle on a full scholarship. That arrangement worked well at first. I'd go to Iowa State and train with the team when my elbow felt okay, but Cael wasn't keen on my idea to fight professionally while I waited to get cleared to wrestle again. Cael would have no sway in that matter.

CHAPTER 7

MMA

My opponent curls up into a ball underneath me as I repeatedly punch the will to continue out of him. He moans with each fist that tenderizes his ribs. I'm nineteen years old and making my debut as an MMA fighter.

I wasn't actively seeking my first MMA fight, but one kind of fell into my lap. I went to Oklahoma City to corner one of my best friends, Justin McCorkle, in an MMA fight. As soon as I landed, I got word that Justin was hospitalized from a severe staph infection in his leg. Needless to say, McCorkle wasn't going to fight, and I was the one elected to go tell the promoter at the pre-fight weigh-ins. When the promoter told Justin's opponent, he started to mouth off.

"McCorkle only ended up in the hospital a day earlier," he said to anyone within earshot.

"He would've ended up there tomorrow night anyway," added his classless cornerman. I stood a few feet away, trying to hide my simmering anger. The promoter, who'd recognized me when we'd spoken, walked up to me.

"This guy's a striker," he said, laying out a game plan. "He's a kickboxer. He coaches at a kickboxing gym. If you stand up with him—"

"What do you mean if I stand up with him?" I interrupted, trying to slow down his building enthusiasm.

"Justin, I've seen you wrestle, and I can see the steam coming out of your ears. Don't you want the chance to shut this guy up?" the promoter asked with the subtle persuasiveness of a snake oil salesman.

"I don't know," I said, really thinking about it. "I've never fought before."

"I'll give you the opportunity tomorrow night. I need someone to fill your friend's slot."

A million thoughts raced through my mind. I had no MMA training. My elbow felt good, but it'd only been seven months since the surgery and I'd been strictly told to wait a year. But this was my childhood dream: to become a professional fighter. Was I ready? I hadn't even fought as an amateur yet. How would I go pro?

"Don't I need some kind of paperwork or approval?" I asked.

"Well, that's the good thing about Oklahoma," the promoter said with a grin. "We aren't very regulated yet. Look, you stand up with him and you're going to get knocked out. But if you take him down, just pound on him until the ref pulls you off."

And with that, I had my first professional MMA fight the next night—a co–main event no less. My opponent was thirty-five years old and looked like a country bumpkin straight off the farm, but I wasn't intimidated. I watched him warming up on the pads, and I saw wide-open opportunities for me to take him down. I knew he might get to throw one punch, and if I could avoid that, he'd be on his back.

McCorkle was in my corner, shouting instructions and encouragement from cage-side. The rest of the crowd cheered on the hometown favorite. I took him down easy enough, got top position, and started punching, nobody noticing that I could only use my left arm in my attack. And, just as the promoter said he would, the referee jumped in to stop the fight. From bell to bell, it'd only taken one minute and forty-five seconds, and when they put my opponent back on his stool, he slid right off of it. McCorkle hobbled on his crutches into the cage to give me a big hug.

I'd finally done something I'd wanted to do since I was thirteen years old. Dan Henderson, an Olympic wrestler turned very successful MMA world champion and legend, was sitting cage-side and he came up to shake my hand. "Nice throw," he said, and my friend and I nearly lost it in all our excitement.

Backstage, the promoter handed me $600 in cash. "When can I fight again?" I asked him with haste. "I'm available next weekend."

My third professional fight took place in Ames, Iowa, at the county fairgrounds. My friend and I were deep into our third round of beers when the promoter entered the cage. He announced that the heavyweight fight of the night would be canceled. One of the fighters hadn't shown up.

The jilted fighter took the microphone and apologized to the fans for not giving them their money's worth, when an idea struck him. "I came to fight tonight," he said. "If there's anyone over two hundred six pounds who wants to fight, let's do it."

I looked at my buddy and he looked back at me. "What are you thinking?" he asked.

I chugged down the rest of my beer, glanced at my friend, and said, "I'm gonna fight."

I had a pair of wrestling shorts and shoes in my truck. I used another fighter's gloves. To protect my teeth, someone gave me a new mouthpiece that didn't fit at all. I hadn't felt comfortable with hand wraps for my first two fights, so I didn't tape my hands under my gloves, but made it look like I had on my wrists. And to top it all off, I had to borrow a cup and jockstrap from the sweaty light-heavyweight fighter who'd just had a barn-burning three-round fight. Good thing I'd had some beers, right?

Since my first two fights had been a breeze, I thought I might try some stand-up in this one. We touched gloves and I could tell that this Iowan wrestler was about to change levels and attempt to take me down. I stepped back and threw an uppercut that caught him pretty square. His eyes got big and he stumbled back. I pushed him against the cage and started punching him until the ref pulled me off. It was over in eighteen seconds.

From there, I caught what they call the "fighting bug." I craved the rush that came with testing myself each time I stepped into the cage. I desired the whirlwind of emotions I felt from getting my hand raised. With fighting came the initiation into an exclusive group, and with that, I was sucked into the fighter lifestyle. That can be a good or bad thing, depending on the fighter.

At local events, fighters were "big shots" or VIPs. Fans wanted you to sign autographs and take pictures with them, totally in awe of what fighters could do in the cage. Fighters were treated to alcohol- and drug-fueled after-parties. Everyone wanted to party with the fighters.

I tried cocaine for the first time in Dallas after my fifth fight. It was my first time in a strip club, another pit stop on my downward spiral. VIP section. Owner's table. Alcohol flowing. Cocaine on the table, lined up in rows. At first, I was the only one not doing it, but a voice kept telling me, *This is where you're supposed to be. This is part of the lifestyle now.* I took a "key bump" first, then a few more bumps before graduating on to full lines. I don't think I could have felt as jacked-up with one hundred energy drinks. My pulse beat through my neck. *I could get used to this*, I thought.

A big plastic bag of cocaine rested in front of us, a wad of cash close by it. Both were tools for luring the strippers in, which I found downright demoralizing. I squirmed in my seat as the others reveled in their false sense of power. One of the club owner's friends wanted to exert his dominance a little more, so he grabbed a stripper's arm and pulled her forcefully into him. She was wearing a yellow dental-floss bikini and already had bruises on her arm.

"You just have to tell these girls what you want," he instructed our table.

"Let me go," she cried, jerking her arm away and slapping him across the face. He shoved her to the ground and I instinctively stood up.

"Bro, think about the next thing you do, because if you touch her again, I'm going to touch your chin with my fist," I said, my confidence soaring from the cocaine. The stripper got to her feet and hurried away.

I'd outstayed my welcome. Bouncers flocked to the owner's and his friends' sides and escorted me out. Outside, I immediately regretted having gone in there in the first place. I felt like my mom had caught me doing something dirty, and I felt like the women were being exploited. If I'd had the power to shut the place down and let these women walk out without ever having to do it again, I would have done it.

I wasn't much for the strip clubs, but cocaine was another story. I tried cocaine again on several occasions: on a lake Jet-Skiing with some friends, at some nightclubs, and at other social events. After a night of drinking, a bump or two would sober me up enough to where I wasn't sloppy driving home.

Following each of my fights, I could go to one of my many doctors and stock up on my pain pills. I just blamed all the pain on the last fight and previous surgeries. I didn't have to drink as much when I had four or six pills beforehand, and I'd take more as the night wore on.

The scholarship opportunity with Cael Sanderson and Iowa

State faded into the background and eventually went away. Fighting was the life I'd chosen and it was going quite well. My strong wrestling background allowed me to move up the ladder quickly, and I earned the nickname "The Viking" because of my Nordic looks and my ground-and-pound style, which is a bit reminiscent of plundering and pillaging. Some told me I got my nickname for looking like the Viking in a popular Snickers commercial that was running at the time.

My fighting record was 9-1 when my manager, Greg Bloom, began speaking about me with UFC matchmaker Joe Silva. A few weeks later, Joe called with an opportunity to audition for *The Ultimate Fighter*, the UFC's reality series on Spike TV.

I missed the previous open tryouts to fight and had another fight coming up that weekend in Dallas, when a *TUF* producer reached me on my cell. If I could get to the airport in time, I'd make the second phase of auditions the next day in Las Vegas. But I'd have to leave right then and we were on our way to the weigh-ins for my next fight. Of course, the promoter said no; I was contracted to be the co–main event in my hometown. But he had no choice after my opponent called to tell him that he'd cut his hand doing some kind of metalwork in his shop. I left and went straight to the airport with what I'd brought to the weigh-ins: the clothes on my back and a spare outfit in my gym bag.

The second round of auditions lasted two days and consisted of medical tests (blood work, physicals, and CAT scans), background checks, and the fighter interviews, in which drama-sniffing producers grilled the candidates. I think the producers really tried to see if they could get a reaction out of us by pushing our buttons. I wasn't a Christian, but I had a cross on the Affliction T-shirt I was wearing.

"So, you're a goody-two-shoes Christian kid?" one producer asked. I was already offended. "You're just a kid. What makes you think you can fight on this show?"

That was true. I was the youngest guy auditioning. I told the producers I wouldn't drink on the show. I would stay focused.

"I'll gladly be an underdog," I told them. "Let me shock you and the other guys you select," hoping I'd sway a producer or two.

I knew I'd already clicked with at least one producer before the interview. The night before, I'd rescued a kitten from a dumpster outside the casino we were all staying at, and the female producer was the first one I thought of. I bathed the kitten because it smelled awful, then brought it to the producer's room. I got some milk from the Starbucks downstairs in the lobby, and she called a local shelter. Honestly, I wasn't angling to get a slot on the TV show. I just didn't want the kitten to die.

At home, a week later, I got a call from that producer.

"You're lucky that I'm a sucker for kittens," she said. "Welcome to *The Ultimate Fighter*." I was on the set less than a week later.

CHAPTER 8

The Ultimate Fighter

The cameraman squeezes himself into the bathroom to record our conversation, crushing me against the shower door. I'm twenty-one years old and the youngest fighter on the biggest season in history of *The Ultimate Fighter*.

I'd watched the show since its start in 2005, and had told everyone that I was going to be on it someday. The importance of *TUF* in its heyday could not be overstated. *TUF* was the *American Idol* of mixed martial arts, except you weren't dealing with sweet Southern belles or guitar-toting pretty boys, but a mob of very hungry fighters willing to climb into the cage on a moment's notice and beat the heck out of one another.

Much like *Idol*, *TUF* could shave years off of struggling on the bottom rungs of the biz. An unknown fighter could win a six-figure, multiyear contact with the UFC, the show's grand prize; an underestimated fighter could jump onto the radar; a sentimental favorite could be discovered and become a staple of UFC events for years to come.

The premise of the show was simple enough. Sixteen fighters were split into two teams led by UFC veterans. The fighters lived and trained together for three months in Las Vegas, competing their way through an elimination-style tournament that produced two finalists and the eventual winner. Each episode culminated with a fight, but the cameras were kept mostly on the drama, or lack of it, that built up in the fighters' house, which was about twenty minutes from the Las Vegas Strip.

The fighters' house was a two-story playground that any twentysomething would be ecstatic to live in. It had a pool, a hot tub, a pool table, and copious amounts of alcohol available at all times. The only catch was there was no contact with the outside world. No television, no radio, no magazines, no books. Cell phones were confiscated. Even the house itself seemed off the beaten track. If you hopped the wall, there really wasn't anywhere to go.

A spot on *The Ultimate Fighter* meant several things for a fighter. Either he'd win the grand prize and join the UFC ranks or he'd return to his hometown with enough notoriety to headline regional-level shows for the rest of his career. Of course, there were other options that fell between these two extremes. Some fighters wouldn't win the show, but would do well enough to earn a bout in the show's live televised finale and possibly be awarded the standard UFC contract that follows. I ended up falling into this category.

The tenth season of *The Ultimate Fighter* was quite special because of one particular contestant, Kevin "Kimbo Slice" Ferguson. The thick-bearded Slice was an infamous, bare-knuckle brawler on the street-fighting circuit in Miami, whose crazy fights made him an Internet sensation. Slice had been on the cover of *ESPN* magazine— that's how much interest his story received heading into *TUF*. Slice would be a ratings bonanza for the show and helped make it the most watched season ever in the show's twenty-plus-season history. As for Slice's mystique, up close, it wasn't all that mysterious. Around the house, some of us called the mellow Slice "Kevin."

Reality shows are about perception, and as the "young gun" on the show that season, I wanted everyone to see that I could hang and then some. That meant hiding my drug use in some creative ways. Painkillers were stored in a medicine bottle I had for cold sores. One Oxycontin could erase my entire day, if I needed it to.

On top of that, I had a healing staph infection. Even though it was at the tail end of the infection, I became desperate to hide it from the doctors. Staph is a highly contagious bacteria common in fighters who spend all day rolling on the mats, and it could have meant an immediate dismissal from the show. There were two alternate fighters on standby to take my place. That made me willing to do anything to hide my staph infection.

In the hotel bathroom prior to our pickup for the first day, I bit down on a rolled-up washcloth as I scorched the staph on my forearm white with a curling iron. I covered up the wound and made up a story that my arm had grazed the iron while I was brushing my teeth. The doctors didn't seem to flinch at that. I squeezed out a tube of Neosporin and filled it back up with my staph infection cream to hide it. I also brought garlic with me to help fight the infection. I was also on two antibiotics that I told the doctors were for bronchitis and getting over the flu. I wasn't going to let anything stop me from getting on the show.

There had been past seasons when the producers allowed fighters to bring a Bible into the house, so I brought one with me. I wasn't a Christian; I just wanted something to read. The Bible was promptly taken away. Some fighters were allowed to bring in family pictures; others were not allowed, depending on their story line. I wasn't allowed—I think the producers believed I was the easygoing kind of guy who would hang back and they needed to ruffle my feathers. A past contestant told me to expect oddities like this on the show.

"Expect the AC to conk out or the water to turn off without notice," he warned. "Whatever they can do to make you uncomfortable, they'll do it." And it all happened as he said it would. On the morning of my biggest fight on the show, I walked into the kitchen and realized the groceries I'd asked for weren't there. I had a routine of egg whites, steel-cut oats, and blueberries every morning, but none of those items or what I'd ordered for lunch were to be found. It didn't just happen to me. There were days when other fighters' lists weren't filled on the day of their fights—the most crucial day to have those items to fuel you. We all agreed that they must be messing with us. Anything to rattle the cage. I shook off these distractions.

My first fight on the show was against Wes Sims, a six-foot-ten mammoth of a man. When I was fourteen years old, Sims was already in the UFC, fighting world champions. Stacked against his experience, I was just a kid, like the producers had said.

At the opening bell, I got Sims down to the canvas, and began to work my submissions. I caught him in an arm-triangle choke. It's a blood choke that traps an opponent's arm around his head, applying pressure to the main arteries in his neck. It was the same move that Sims had gotten caught in and eventually escaped from in one of his more famous UFC fights. I flashed back to that moment and tightened the choke as much as I could. Instead of tapping out, Sims decided to go to sleep. I thought he was a nut, but to him that was showing his fighter's heart. Sims could give up and tap out or fight to the very end. Tap, snap, or nap. He took the latter. I heard him snoring in my ear right before the ref pulled me off of him.

One of Sims's signature moves was foot stomping, and when I went to get my foot X-rayed for a cracked bone, I came clean to the doctor about the staph infection. Already a few weeks into the show, he agreed to keep it quiet and I took my meds privately.

My quarterfinal bout on the show, against Roy "Big Country" Nelson, was a lesson in poor game-planning. Nelson and I had started the season on the same team, so our coaches, led by *TUF* champion and former UFC champion Rashad Evans, stepped away from our preparations entirely to keep it fair.

My teammates stepped in and insisted that I should stand and strike with Big Country. I wanted to take him to the ground. Every fight that I'd taken to the ground I'd not only won, I'd ended it. My team argued that Nelson was a black belt in Brazilian jiu-jitsu, but I argued that he was only dangerous from the top position and I could take him down first and stay on top. They told me taking him down was the worst thing I could do. Basically, I was guided to do the opposite of what I'd always done.

It was a close bout. Nearly everyone agreed that Nelson had taken one round and I'd won the other. Under the rules, that meant we would fight a third, deciding round, but when the scorecards came back, two judges had given Nelson both rounds, and only one had us split, 1–1. My journey was over just like that.

I felt so empty after the fight. My coaches told me I'd been robbed. My teammates told me I'd been robbed. UFC president Dana White told me I'd been robbed. And I believed them all. When I got back to the fighters' house, I popped an Oxycontin, hoping to wipe away the next eight to twelve hours. I washed it down with alcohol so that nobody would suspect anything out of the ordinary.

With no more fights on the horizon, I quickly sunk into a depression. I drank and popped more painkillers. A lot of the time, I stayed in my room, sometimes pretending I was asleep. I think that some of my teammates knew I was depressed, but that's something fighters don't really talk about with one another. As the show progressed, my hopes of getting back on as an injury replacement dwindled. Then rumors started that producers were looking for any way to get Slice, who'd been eliminated in his first fight, back into the competition to raise ratings. When I found out no alternate was needed, I gave up altogether.

Still, I did make some lasting bonds on the show. There was a reason why I'd wanted to be on Rashad Evans's team so bad— so bad that I'd flubbed the other team's tryouts so they didn't want me. Two of Rashad's assistant coaches were Greg Jackson and Trevor Wittman, two of the top-five MMA trainers in the country.

I had an instant connection with "Coach T." He took me aside for one-on-one training. We joked around together and I asked how his family was doing. I picked him up on my shoulder. He called me a turkey, because Wren is a bird.

When I'd lost to Nelson and was drowning in depression and boredom, Coach T smuggled a Bible into the house for me. Unfortunately, it was a King James Version, and I had to trudge through all of the *thou*s, *thee*s, and *thus*es. The producers found the Bible under my mattress and interrogated me on where I'd gotten it, but I wouldn't give up Coach T. When they reviewed the tapes and saw Coach T hand it to me, they pulled him aside and reiterated that he wasn't allowed to give the fighters anything from the outside. The production staff were all watchdogs. If a cell phone had been smuggled inside that Bible and the results leaked, it could cost the UFC and Spike TV millions of dollars.

On the final day of shooting, we went out for a celebratory dinner at an amazing steak house in Las Vegas, where nobody's meal could have been under $100. Afterward, Dana White had me jump into his Land Rover with him, while the other fighters piled into a limo and a party bus for a night out on the town.

On the ride over to a nightclub, Dana gushed about my future with his organization as he brazenly raced through red lights.

"Look, I know the show didn't end the way you wanted it to, but I believe in you," he said emphatically, glancing at me and then the road. My knuckles turned white hanging on to my door handle.

MMA's most powerful player and ultimate pitchman was in full swing. "Forget about a manager!" he said. "I'll give you the best deal every single time. That's what I do. We offer our best price first."

Yeah right, I thought, but overall, I felt encouraged by White. I did feel he was trying to steer me the right way.

"A lot of guys' careers have been ruined because they take fights they shouldn't take," he explained. "Great fighters but terrible businessmen, or the other way around. I want you to be both and to surround yourself with the right people."

This next part stuck with me especially.

"Whoever your friends are now before the show, those are your real friends, your real family, and the ones who really care about you," he warned. "After this, they're going to come out like leeches, suck you dry, and try to take everything from you. They'll only be friends with you for what you do, not who you are."

Dana, his friend, and I arrived at the nightclub first and settled into a roped-off VIP section. When the other fighters arrived, Dana dished out $500 in cash to each of us.

The next night, the show's other coach, Rampage Jackson, took the remaining fighters in town to another club. At his table, he had a shoe box in front of him, which contained maybe ten to twenty thousand dollars in cash.

Most of the fighters were willing to indulge in the perks allotted to new reality TV stars and Rampage was ready to show them the way to do it right. Shirtless, he stood up on the stage and started throwing money in the air to make it rain. Many of the guys happily jumped at the chance to join the former UFC champion. One fighter pegged a girl with a wad of cash like it was a fastball, but she didn't care. Without thinking twice, she was on her knees, trying to pick it all up from the floor like a starving scavenger. Honestly, this wasn't what I'd had in mind when I'd thought about becoming a professional athlete.

On my final night in Vegas, I went to the Palace Station Casino to try my luck. I had $65 at the blackjack table when Dana White laid down a $1,000 chip in front of me. He put his hand on my shoulder, interested in his spur-of-the-moment investment. I didn't win the hand, so he placed another $1,000 chip down. Then he placed $2,000 down. He tossed the final $1,000 chip into my hand.

"You can keep it. You can spend it. Whatever you want to do," he said. "I'm just passing through."

I took the coin and immediately asked for change as White walked toward the exit. Once White was out of sight, I pocketed my chips and left the table. I'd already lost my chance at being *The Ultimate Fighter* and there was no way I was going to lose any more money.

People began recognizing me before the show even aired that September because our identities had been revealed at UFC 100 that July. I flew home to Dallas for a premiere party at the biggest Buffalo Wild Wings in the country at the time and there was a line out the door. They had to turn people away to abide the fire codes.

Once the show started airing, people were asking me for pictures everywhere I went. On the streets of Vegas or New York City. Running at Red Rocks in Denver. Inside Costco at the deli counter. Everyone wanted to take a picture with a reality TV star. But being a reality-show celebrity is not all it's cracked up to be. There are pitfalls everywhere, and I was about to fall. Hard.

CHAPTER 9

Quest

Sitting in my car at the gym's parking lot, I'm on the brink of a panic attack. I'm twenty-two and I've just been kicked off my team. I have a fight in four weeks, I just lost my band of brothers, and I have nowhere else to train. I've hit rock bottom.

I knew something was up that morning when I walked into the gym. My teammates stopped their warm-ups and their eyes followed me across the room into Coach T's office. Coach T looked disappointed.

"Justin, you've put me in a really tough position," he started somberly. "We've taken a vote and everyone has voted you off the team, everyone but me." He paused. "However, I can't go against the other guys. We just can't have your name attached to ours . . ." His voice trailed off.

They all knew I came in to train hungover, alcohol sweating from my pores, but they didn't know I was sometimes buzzed and high—not the safest conditions when you're punching and choking out teammates.

"Hey, but I'm winning," I quickly retorted. It was true. My record was a decent 10-2 in a weight division that promotions struggled to fill. My manager had recently started talks up again with the UFC.

"But the way you're living," Coach T said. "Why don't you look into getting some help, some kind of rehab program."

And with that, a door closed on me. I apologized to Coach T and we said our good-byes. I raced out of the gym so no one could see the tears welling up in my eyes. As I sat in my car, crying, confused, and feeling my lowest of lows, I wondered how I'd gotten here in the eleven months since joining Grudge.

I'd used the money I'd made on *TUF* to move to Denver to join the fight team at Grudge Training Center right after the show wrapped. I'd gotten my own place on Lininger Mountain on the second floor of the Lininger House, a four-story home that had been remodeled into separate apartments in the forties. I'd invited my buddy Josh Copeland, also a fighter, to come live with me. The house overlooked the famous Red Rocks Amphitheatre, and on some nights, the concert music wafted up to our windows.

Denver was a big fight city, and as the reality show aired over its twelve-week season, more and more people recognized me at local fight shows and on the street. *I'm finally getting there and it's going to be worth it one day*, I kept saying to myself, needing the self-affirmation.

My Grudge teammates were a talented group of guys. I'd met Shane Carwin, a former interim UFC champion, when Coach T had brought him onto the *TUF* set as a guest coach for a day. Brendan Schaub and Demico Rogers had both been on the reality show with me and I knew my roommate, Josh Copeland, who'd eventually be the best man at my wedding and become a UFC fighter himself. Because MMA demands so much of the body, heavyweight fighters (good ones, at least) are rare, and it was even more rare to have this many competitive heavyweights all together in one gym.

The life of a mixed martial arts fighter can be a strenuous game

and Grudge was known for producing results. At the Olympic Education Center, I'd trained five days a week, one to two times a day.
For MMA, we trained six days, two to three times a day, two to
three hours at a time. As MMA is a multidiscipline sport, we had
a variety of skills to drill, from sparring to wrestling to Brazilian
jiu-jitsu. Then there was strength and conditioning and cardio. On
Saturdays, we'd go to the Red Rocks Amphitheatre and run the
bleachers. Downtime was filled with recuperation, nursing injuries, and keeping a strict diet.

I balanced life as a professional athlete-slash-drug abuser pretty
well for a while. I had a routine down. I'd wake up, start my day
with steel-cut oats, blueberries, and agave; eat my egg whites and
take a pull from my vaporizer (the healthy way, of course). I'd wash
it all down with pills and liquor. Then it was off to training.

I openly flaunted my drug use. My autographed headshot from
The Ultimate Fighter hung proudly in two pot shops in Denver. I
got free weed from time to time, and one dispensary even gave me
a $400 vaporizer just for visiting their shop. Sometimes I'd go in
and get high with other customers. I was even going to get sponsored by a dispensary and have their pot-leaf logo stitched onto my
shorts for a future fight.

My fight with Jon Madsen at the *TUF* finale that December
was quickly approaching. I followed my "regimen," piggybacking
my drugs all the way up to the fight. I was high all of fight week
and popping pain pills up to a day or two before the bout. If they'd
drug-tested me before the fight, I definitely would have failed.

On fight night, I lost a split decision to Madsen, which sent
me back into a depression. Reeling from my second close defeat
in two fights, I rushed back to my hotel room and grabbed a
bunch of pills. I went straight across the street to the Golden
Nugget, because it had a liquor store inside, and bought a bottle
of Jack Daniel's to drink and drug myself to sleep. Then I moved

to another hotel room so my coaches and cornermen couldn't find me.

Three weeks later, my parents came to Denver for the holidays and they knew something was wrong with me. At their hotel, I finally sat down with them and told them about the marijuana. I didn't mention the pills—the pills were too bad to mention. I told them I needed medical marijuana for my elbow and minor back surgeries. What I really wanted to tell them was that I'd seriously been thinking of killing myself. I was so ashamed that I couldn't be transparent. I just couldn't come clean. So I only told them I'd been sad and depressed, and in that depression, I'd had thoughts that my life might not be worth living.

My mother began to cry. It looked as if a knife had gone right through her heart. Once I saw that I'd broken her heart, I frantically tried to backpedal. I told her it was going to be okay, that I just needed to get back on track. Once I got a few wins under my belt, I'd be back in the UFC and have a good job. I said that by me fessing up I was already turning it around—any excuse I could come up with to dry my mother's eyes. My parents left me, skeptical and worried.

I continued to train and party, and woke up one morning next to a stranger. I had a very serious, long-term girlfriend at the time and it crushed her. It was a common practice for fighters to cheat on their girlfriends and wives, especially on the road. I'd watched one of my fighting idols leave his hotel room arm in arm with a woman who wasn't his wife and vowed I'd never be that way. I'd despised this behavior in other fighters. Now I was just a hypocrite and no better than any of them. It was one of the few times it dawned on me that I was an idiot. I was a drunk. I was a drug addict. I was so selfish and depressed that I would do anything to fill the void at that point, even at the expense of others. I hadn't reached the top of the top in MMA yet, but after every fight I'd ask myself, *Is this it? Is this what will make me happy?*

The length between me getting high got shorter and shorter and shorter, to where I was waking up to it or using my vaporizer to go to sleep. I was always high because it made me feel happy. When I wasn't high, I don't know if I was more depressed, but that high feeling was gone, and I recognized that.

The more depressed I got, the more I used. I rotated cocaine back into the mix and the wear started to show. On the morning of my next fight for Ring of Fire, a prestigious Denver promotion, I was in the emergency room throwing up. I'd had some issues with my back and had gone heavy on the pills of late. The doctor thought I had a stomach virus, but I had no doubt it was from the drugs. The doctor gave me three bags of IV fluid and urged me not to fight that night, but that didn't stop me. During the fight, a wave of anger overtook me and I violently slammed my opponent to the mat. I was this irate person. After I won, I raced back to my hotel room to celebrate with my drugs. I didn't know it at the time, but this would be my last fight with Grudge in my corner.

The next two months of my life remain a blur. I get cloudy flashes here and there, but nothing concrete. I started skipping Grudge sessions and really plugged into the drug community in the mountains where I lived. I hitchhiked and caught rides from drug house to drug house, drinking, smoking, and taking hallucinogens like mushrooms and Ecstasy. I don't think I've ever done meth, but I really couldn't tell you, to be honest. It's possible I tried it while in this blurry fog. I woke up in some strange houses, usually one of the worst of the bunch. The other druggies would end up having to take care of me. On one night, I remember I made a concerted effort to end my life with a mix of pills, pot, mushrooms, and a half bottle of 190-proof Everclear. I remember my disappointment when I woke up the next day, still alive.

By design, I'd made it difficult for my friends and family to reach me, including my parents. My cell phone rang and I ignored it. I didn't want to hear from anyone. I just wanted to be numb. It was a selfish decision that ended up costing me a great friend. In the fog, I missed an extremely important phone call; when I finally got around to listening to the message, I realized it was from my friend Justin McCorkle. The recording was eight minutes long.

"You missed my wedding," it started. McCorkle paused and sighed. "My best man missed my wedding. How could you miss—" I hung up my phone midsentence, reached for some pills, and washed them down with some booze.

My mom got so worried that she came out to Colorado to check on me at my house. That's where she got a good look at my drug paraphernalia. There were bongs, a large vaporizer, rolling papers, a slew of empty pill bottles, and baggies of who-knows-what strewn everywhere. I even had baggies of hash blocks lying around. My mother didn't know the difference between hash and heroin. It all looked terrifying to her.

When I made it back into the Grudge gym a few weeks later, everyone knew I was out the door except me. And that's how I ended up in the gym's parking lot, bawling uncontrollably, my hands tightly gripped around the steering wheel. There was no way I could find a new gym in time to train for my next fight.

As I contemplated training with the local high school wrestling team, my cell phone buzzed in my pocket. I had a new email in my inbox. Maybe it was Coach T with the name and number of a rehab program? No, it was this persistent youth pastor from my hometown. He'd been bothering me every day for two straight months with phone calls, texts, and emails. It was Jeff Duncan.

Jeff was a man on a mission. Through the grapevine, he'd heard about my mom's surprise visit to Colorado and what she'd found at my house. He'd heard I'd missed my best friend's wedding. He said that God had told him that he was supposed to love me—that I was in the biggest battle of my life and wasn't going to make it without Him.

I'd ignored Jeff for months. I never answered when his number popped up. I erased his voicemails without listening to them. When I did respond, it was to rudely tell him that I wasn't in a good place, and to leave me alone.

Maybe it was just in that desperate moment, but this email seemed different. The subject line read "Game Plan for Victory," and it immediately took me back to my wrestling days. This was a language I understood, so I clicked on it. Inside, it said, "The best thing you'll ever do in your life." There was a receipt attached for a paid trip to a men's retreat of some sort called Quest.

I called Jeff. "What is this, bro?" I asked, irritated.

"It's a Christian men's retreat," he said.

"No, no, no. I can't," I said abruptly, and I quickly hung up.

Jeff called back, left messages, and coaxed me into calling him again. He was very serious at this point and told me something I still repeat today.

"Life is a battleground, not a playground," said Jeff. "If you treat life like a playground, you will lose the battle."

Jeff told me that I needed to be around Christian men. I told him those two words didn't really go together. Christians were phonies and hypocrites. Jeff told me that God loved me, and I resented him for saying that.

"Bro, I need rehab," I told Jeff. "I don't need to sit around a campfire singing 'Kumbaya,' holding hands with a group of punks and sissies and hanging out with a bunch of emasculated, castrated dudes. I know what religion does. It castrates men and I don't want to be a part of that at all."

He promised it would be different. Jeff fought me like his own life depended on it, while, in reality, it was my life on the line. I was three weeks out from a fight and had nowhere else to go. When I told him I needed to train, he offered to fly a training partner out to Quest with me.

"Just come. We'll hit the pavement in the mornings," said Jeff. "There's a pool. We'll get you in shape. You can hit mitts. I'll buy mitts."

This guy had two kids. Why was he trying to spend this type of money on me? What was his angle? What did he want from me? I couldn't answer these questions, but with nowhere else to go, I hesitantly agreed to the plan.

THE FELLOWSHIP OF the Sword's Men's Quest retreat was a five-day program held on the secluded, yet expansive Rio Ranchito Ranch in the hill country of south Texas. The ranch had five hundred acres of land, some of which rested along the curvaceous Guadalupe River. There was an outdoor pool and a hot tub, and miles and miles of trails to walk in the woods. The main house was a bona fide mansion, where about thirty of us stayed together, two to four in a room. It resembled the Alamo with its Spanish-style archways and other intricate architecture. The river ran directly behind the main house.

The retreat's purpose was to help us connect with God in a way that worked for us, one that wasn't forced and in our own time. There were counselors, called *facilitators*, there to speak to and guide us.

As promised, Jeff flew me and my training partner, Josh, out to Quest with him and supplied us with training mitts. I made sure to pack my own necessities—marijuana tootsie rolls, a THC dropper, and an abundance of pain pills in a smell-proof bag, tucked into my checked luggage.

There was a schedule you could follow at Quest, if you wanted to. In the mornings, after breakfast, we'd be sent out with a packet of devotionals (Bible verses followed by an explanation and ways to apply them to our personal lives) to complete for the day. There were other activities like fishing and hiking. Every now and then the house filled with worship music you could listen to, and there were cookouts with campfires at night, where a lot of the guys just sat around talking to one another.

For the first two days, I didn't participate much at all. I didn't try any of the devotionals. I was always the last one out of the house and the last one back in. When I wasn't training for the fight, I'd just walk around and skip rocks on the river and watch the fish. I would sneak in my fixes whenever and wherever I could.

There were guys there from all walks of life. Some wanted to find a real connection with God. Others wanted to strengthen their existing relationships with Him. Then there was me, the guy who wasn't buying into any of it. I'd been involved in some small conversations with the other men, but most of them wanted to know about fighting, so I showed them some moves.

By the third day, my eyes began to open up to what was happening in front of me. I'd watched the facilitators and other attendees and realized that there was something different about them.

These men seemed real. They didn't have an ulterior motive. Sometimes I was so jacked up on drugs talking to them, but they didn't judge me for it. They just loved on me. They wanted me to get better and they weren't looking to take credit for it. Even though I'd been an Ultimate Fighter, I suddenly felt like a boy among a group of grown men. I needed to man up.

When I finally opened up and asked if I'd always be this screwed up, the other men said they'd messed up, too, but when they let God reveal His love for them, their lives changed.

So on the third day, I completed that day's devotional along with the previous two. It encouraged me, talking about how God loves us and has given us each a passion and purpose to live out. Afterward, I walked back into the house and approached Jeff, who was speaking with a facilitator.

"Today feels different and I'm ready for my life to change," I told them. Jeff and the facilitator could see something was building up in me and asked if I'd ever submitted my life to Christ before.

To submit in MMA means to quit or give up, and that's something I couldn't do. Wrestling and MMA had instilled that in me.

"In the world, if you give up, you lose," I said. "Why would God ask me to give up?"

"Submitting to Him means He will give you your life back," answered Jeff. "He wants to bring you alive in Him and in your purpose. When you surrender, you are born again. You're giving your life over, and you're given a new life back, and that's the true life that God intended you to have."

Jeff must have read the skepticism on my face and changed tactics.

"You know that there's a God," he proposed.

I nodded my head. "Yes. Absolutely. There's no doubt in my mind that all of this didn't happen by chance."

"Well, if you don't doubt God, what are you doubting?"

I doubted myself. I doubted that God had actually given me the strength to live my life. I doubted that God created me for a purpose and that the Creator of the Universe could love me.

Jeff went on to explain that all my past, present, and future failures were already forgiven because of Jesus's and God's grace.

"Real people, with real problems, *really* need a real God with real answers, and a real solution," he said. Those words hit home. Jeff looked me dead in the eye and promised me that the answer I was looking for was found in a relationship with Jesus, and the God that made me.

It happened right there. Jeff and the facilitator had placed their hands on my shoulders and bowed their heads with me. They told me to pray whatever came to my mind and heart. I fell on my knees and prayed. I don't know why I did, but it felt like my body was conveying what my heart was feeling. I needed to ask for mercy and forgiveness for all the hurtful things I'd done. I needed to finally begin the main relationship I was created for.

God, I'm the best drunk, drug addict. I'm a liar and a cheater. I'm many things I've wanted to be and I'm everything I never wanted to be. God, I've hurt everybody. I don't want to hurt anyone anymore. I don't want to hurt. I need You in my life.

I asked God to show me how to trust Him. Then I told God that I *needed* to trust Him. Eventually my prayer changed to *I do trust you. I give my life to You, and today I start my relationship with You, God.*

As I knelt, I felt God just lift me up. It felt like something finally released me. All the emotional chains of depression, all the bondage, just broke and fell off me. At the same time, I felt God's arms envelop me, the way a father bear-hugs his son.

Instantaneously, things changed. It wasn't magic, but suddenly my heart was flooded with peace. It was the greatest gift I could ever be given. I just had one of those moments when I knew everything was going to be okay. I was crying with overwhelming emotion, but they were happy tears, because God had taken me, broken and alone, and put me back together again.

I know you're thinking, *All from one prayer?* Yes. I was desperate to feel God in my life, and when I asked for Him, He answered. That was the moment I experienced my Father's love for the first time, my Father in Heaven. He lavished love on me and let me know that I was forgiven and that He had a plan just for me.

I stood up and the three of us laughed and hugged. I thanked Jeff for stopping at nothing to get me there. Then I reached into my pocket.

"So, I just had that moment and I want to be real with you guys," I said, pulling out my pain pills and THC dropper. "Here's some drugs I brought on the trip with me. What do I do with this stuff?"

"What do you want to do with it?" they asked back, which I

thought was a strange response. "Do you want to keep them or get rid of them?"

"I want to get rid of them." It was nuts hearing myself say that.

There was a bonfire in the backyard that night. I threw some of my drugs into it, but I knew that I had more in my room. I was planning to throw what was in my pocket into the fire and keep the rest. But then it hit my heart and I knew that I needed to get rid of it all. I went to my room, brought the rest down, and watched it catch fire and crackle as I tossed it into the flames.

PART II

CHAPTER 10

Kairos

What do you mean you won't take me?" I snapped at the two ladies sitting behind the counter. I couldn't believe I was getting turned away from rehab. Couldn't they see in my eyes that I'd been through a rough time in the last few months?

Nineteen days following Quest, I fought at the Hard Rock Casino in Las Vegas. Spiritually, I was in a better place, but the drug use had taken its toll on my body.

During the last two rounds of the fight, I swallowed my own vomit. Demico Rogers, a fellow *TUF* castmate, had shown up to corner me. He kept asking me why I was drooling between rounds. I won the fight by decision, and at the hospital a couple days later, an endoscopy revealed a small ulcer forming in my stomach. I fought again in July and bulged two disks slamming my opponent to the canvas.

I thought I'd come back from Quest a changed man, but things were continuing to go wrong in my life. Staying away from drugs was still a constant struggle under stress—if I hit any kind of tough times or hardships, like injuries or money issues, I'd want to reach for them again. I was waging a war against my old self not to use.

I'm confused, I prayed. *I'm fighting clean for the first time in my career. I'm doing this the right way. Why aren't things falling into place?*

My next fight put me in the hospital with my eyebrow split open from a head butt. When the doctor offered me pain pills, I accepted them. I needed them. I had back pain. My face throbbed. When I returned to Denver, I immediately scored more pain pills and went back to the medical marijuana dispensary. I began drinking heavily, and life started to slide out of focus once again.

I questioned that moment I'd had with God almost three months earlier at Quest. Had it been real or fake? Was *I* what I hated the most? Was I a big phony? This dreaded me the most, because I didn't want to push people further away from God.

I isolated myself in my Denver apartment, wrestling with these negative voices in my head. On the day I decided to end it all, I woke up with my normal regimen of pain pills and weed. Weed usually masked my depression, but today it wasn't doing the trick and I was crying. *Today's the day*, I thought. *Today's the day I stop hurting people and stop hurting myself.* I envisioned suicide as something neat and tidy, like pulling the ejection seat on an airplane. I sat on my deck, contemplating how I would do it, when I heard a familiar voice behind me.

"You're worthless. You're stupid. You're a failure. You should just kill yourself."

I was horrified when I placed the voice. It was my own. I felt it over my shoulder, making the hair on the back of my neck stand up. I heard my own voice whispering in my ear; a very real, tangible voice coming from behind me.

I was so petrified that it took me a few seconds to get up the courage to slowly turn my head around. No one was there, but I felt some kind of presence, hiding in the shadows.

I grabbed my keys and some clothes, jumped in my car, and

drove all the way back to Dallas to join the nearest rehab program I could find. But now I was getting hassled by these two ladies, who didn't want to accept me into their program.

Somehow, in the one hour it had taken me to find a bank and withdraw $8,000 to pay for the program, the ladies had changed their minds about me. I'd passed the entire screening process, gotten approved, and had the cash in my hands, but the two ladies were steadfast. This wasn't a Christian rehab center, but these two women were Christians. Weren't Christians supposed to help those in need?

The ladies asked me to sit down in the lobby with them. They told me that while I'd been gone, they'd prayed about me and come to the conclusion that turning me away was the right thing to do. It was the first time the ladies said they'd ever done this with an addict seeking help. I was livid.

"Are you literally going to turn me away, a depressed, drunk drug addict who has the money to pay you up front? Can't you see how much I need this?" I pleaded.

The lady on the left answered.

"Justin, we really feel you're supposed to pray about this, that God is going to show you what to do," she said.

"Listen. I gave Jesus a shot and it didn't work out," I answered. "What I need now is rehab."

"What you really need to do now is pray to God," said the other woman. "If you listen and look, He will show you the way."

The decision had been made and these ladies weren't going to budge: that's how strong their convictions were about the message they'd received.

As we parted, they told me to come back in twenty-four hours if God hadn't answered my prayers. I could see by the looks on their faces that they didn't expect that to happen. I left feeling desperate. I absolutely doubted my salvation, but what else was there to do? I started praying for guidance, and a few hours later, God showed up in a mighty way.

I received a text from the Pickerings, a family I'd met attending Gateway Church before my relapse. The Pickerings didn't know what bad shape I was in; they had just felt the urge to text and check up on me. Scott, the father, met with me after I left the rehab center and I explained to him what had happened. He brought up Kairos, a two-day conference that helped people find breakthroughs, freedom, and healing from their struggles. Gateway Church just happened to be sponsoring the event in two days.

"Justin, you might have had a heart change, but for your life to change you have to make certain decisions and you shouldn't be affected by your surroundings," said Scott. He said I was like a crab in a bucket, and that took me back to my early childhood in Gulfport, Mississippi, where I'd go crabbing with my family. We'd snatch up some crabs in a net and throw them in a bucket. As soon as one was close to getting out, the others would turn their focus on him, grab him, and pull him right back in. From what I remember, none of them ever got out.

It had been like that for me in the months following Quest. I hadn't surrounded myself with positive people, not to mention other Christians. I'd surrounded myself with the same fighters and friends I'd partied with. I was still hanging out in clubs, and the drugs were still there. I think some of those friends didn't want me out of the bucket, so they'd pull me back down with them. I needed a way out of the bucket for good.

Scott called Gateway Church and they told him that Kairos was full with a waiting list. I was panicked to hear that, but Scott somehow remained confident and told me not to worry. It was as if he knew something was coming that no one else did.

Not twenty minutes later, we got word that someone had

canceled, a slot had opened up, and I would be offered it. As long as I watched all of the prerequisite freedom ministries classes videos in time, I was in. The next day, I watched the DVDs for eight hours straight. And the day after that, I went to Kairos.

In Greek, *kairos* means "God's time." Gateway Church describes its Kairos program as "a time for inner healing and breaking strongholds as well as physical, emotional, mental, and spiritual healing." I'd be standing among people with all kinds of addictions, or other circumstances that weighed them down and prevented them from loving themselves and others.

Kairos teaches us that freedom doesn't come from the absence of something. It comes from the presence of someone. It comes from Jesus. It comes from a relationship with God. Whenever you have a relationship with God, you can be free. Whenever you're closer to the light, the further you are from the dark.

At my Kairos experience, there were special speakers, presentations, and a lot of heartfelt prayer. But the part that moved me the most was the testimonies of others. A rape victim feared she'd never be free of her hatred and mistrust in men, including her husband of twenty years. A reformed drug addict spoke about his journey to break free of substance abuse. There were other testimonies about past incidents and situations that'd held people down like anchors, but not anymore.

Hearing story after story that I could relate to, something started to stir in me. I realized that I was going to mess up, that problems would arise and I wouldn't be a perfect person. During the most suicidal time in my life, I was a Christian. I didn't have to strive for perfection. I just had to strive to be close to the One who is perfect, who is God. If I got close to Him, He was going to love and nurture and guide me in the decisions I'd make and it would change the desires of my heart. If I had a relationship with God, and I saw and felt His heart, if I knew His heart had love for me, then I wouldn't need drugs to escape. I could turn to God in both the good times and the bad.

I told God that I didn't want to struggle with addiction anymore. I needed help. I felt like I was fighting battles bigger than what I could handle on my own.

I'm giving it all to You, I prayed to Him. *I'm placing everything in Your hands. Lord, instead of me holding on to it tight and saying I need to overcome this, I'm going to give it to You because You're stronger than I am and You can win it with and for me.*

In that personal moment with God, I could feel the chains that bound me to my drug addiction begin to slide right off me. I opened myself up to trusting God with the areas of struggle in my life where I'd shut Him out. I let my guard down, and God replaced that part of me.

After Kairos, I felt like I was going to win this fight. I had to learn that whenever temptations came up or my addictions started to flare or whenever I felt such a craving for alcohol, marijuana, and narcotics, I needed to turn to God.

There is one scripture that has stayed with me since I first heard it at Kairos. It's one of a handful of scriptures that refers to combat fighting, so it reaches me on a few levels. 1 Corinthians 9:24–27 (NLT) says,

> *Don't you realize that in a race everyone runs, but only one person gets the prize? So run to win! All athletes are disciplined in their training. They do it to win a prize that will fade away, but we do it for an eternal prize. So I run with purpose in every step. I am not just shadowboxing. I discipline my body like an athlete, training it to do what it should. Otherwise, I fear that after preaching to others I myself might be disqualified.*

A marathon runner has to build up to the twenty-six miles; he doesn't start out able to do that. Time and time again, the marathon runner punishes his body. He gets cramps and sticks in his side; he pulls muscles and gets shin splints. Still, every day he runs a little farther than the day before, so that on race day he can run the race to win. To become a fighter, you must be willing to sacrifice greatly. What makes a fighter able to punish his body two to three times a day, two hours or more at a time, six days a week, all in the hope of being tough enough to withstand a beating in an actual fight? It is the promise of victory.

I was the youngest heavyweight on *The Ultimate Fighter 10*. I was living my childhood dream and chasing the prize to one day have ten pounds of gold wrapped around my waist. But even if I'd gotten the shiny belt, it was only going to fade away in the end. It would sit on a shelf collecting dust, and it wasn't going to fill the void in my life.

I realized I could have an even deeper relationship with God than the one I'd started with Him on the Quest retreat. After Quest, I'd gone right back to fighting and had fallen into the same self-destructive habits. Now I understood it wasn't enough to go to church on Sundays and raise my finger to God in gratitude after a few fights each year. I couldn't compartmentalize my Christian life and my everyday one anymore. I decided I'd have to step away from professional fighting, on a three-fight win streak no less, to cement my relationship with Christ. I wanted to go after the only prize that really meant something: "the eternal prize."

Now, what does all of this mental introspection have to do with a physical drug addiction? How can a two-day seminar stop a drug abuser cold turkey? I've been asked about this a lot and all I can say is I've never touched narcotics or marijuana since Kairos. I drink occasionally, but haven't had the urge to use drugs. I've had moments where people around me were using and offered me some, but I turned them down easily because I was so free from it. I've stood next to abundant marijuana fields in the Congo and haven't gotten the urge to use again. I can't explain it other than to say that a hole, that empty place in my soul, was filled with His love for me.

Some time ago, I had a bottle of narcotics, a big 120-count bottle, sitting on my dresser. I hadn't taken a single pill from it since I gave my life to Christ. Still, I'd had them there in case of injury. Before Kairos, I saw those pills and I knew I could just reach my hand in and start taking them. After Kairos, the bottle became more of a trophy to me, because I knew I'd leave every single one of those pills right where they were.

God knew what he was doing when he told those two ladies at the rehab clinic to turn me away. A ten-step program wasn't going to be my answer, but a relationship with God was. At Kairos, I recognized my personal need for God. I needed to go deep with Him and not be a surface-level, "box-checking" Christian. To do that, I needed to look at the bigger picture—not just living for myself, but living for a higher purpose. I had to live to love God and love people. I had to find a way to make a difference in other people's lives.

CHAPTER 11

David

I t's a one-of-a-kind opportunity," my manager, Greg, pitched
from the other end of the call. "Three thousand graduates, and
they want you to speak at their commencement."

I watched a man in a navy blue business suit whisk by me one
way; a lackadaisical mom in a pink velour jogging suit pushed
her baby stroller the other way. I was in some airport flying back
to Denver and was having a hard time getting past the three-
thousand-graduates part. A feeling of dread washed over me.

"Bro, I'm a fighter, not a speaker. I don't have the ability to
do that," I told Greg, and wished him a good night. This was the
same answer I'd given him and others about eight other times in
two weeks. I was six months into being a Christian and I guess the
word had gotten out that a cage fighter had a testimony that he was
just dying to share with the world.

The only problem with that was it wasn't true. I was terrified of
public speaking. It was the Goliath to my David. My hands shook;
my voice cracked; the room got very warm. The thought of speaking in front of a few high school kids was more nerve-racking to me
than fighting in front of thousands.

Still, something didn't sit right with what I'd told Greg. I called Jeff Duncan, explained the situation, and asked him what he thought.

"It doesn't matter what I think," he answered. "What does God think? Have you prayed about it?"

"No," I said sheepishly. (I was still a novice Christian.)

"Well, go pray, you dummy," he said jokingly. Right after I hung up, Jeff texted me. *I wasn't kidding about praying . . . Pray about it RIGHT NOW*, he wrote. *Okay, okay*, I thought.

I reluctantly recited my prayer as I dragged my carry-on down the ramp to the plane. On the plane, I sat down next to an older gentleman in a suit with a briefcase. His name was Jack. Jack Murphy.

"That's an interesting shirt you're wearing there," he said, pointing to the Tapout logo. We began chatting, as many passengers do to pass the time on flights. Yet, the more Jack told me about himself, the more incredulous I got.

Jack was a public speaker for Bill Glass's Champions for Life ministries, and he shared his testimonial in prisons across the country.

"Have you ever been asked to speak, Justin?" inquired Jack.

When I told him I'd been asked to speak eight times in two weeks but couldn't because of fear, Jack just smiled.

"Why would God ask me to do something I'm scared of and not good at? I just don't think God would ever ask me to pursue my biggest fear," I said.

"That's the way God is," Jack said with a chuckle. "Of all the people in the world to sit next to on a plane, one of hundreds of planes that will fly today, out of thousands of planes that will fly this week, you sat down next to me. I train people to do this; our speakers have spoken to over three million inmates. Well, let me ask you this. Have you prayed or asked God about this?"

I nodded my head yes. I remember thinking to myself, *You've got be kidding me!* I felt like God Himself was setting me up.

"Tell me exactly what you prayed," he said.

"I said, 'God, if this is You, wake me up to it, please. If this is You, slap me upside the head with it.' "

"Isn't this enough?" asked Jack. Then, he reached over and gently slapped me upside the head. After we laughed, Jack reminded me of another notable speaker who'd doubted his purpose and abilities. This is what God told Moses in Exodus 4:11–12 (NLT): *Who makes a person's mouth? Who decides whether people speak or do not speak, hear or do not hear, see or do not see? Is it not I, the Lord? Now go! I will be with you as you speak, and I will instruct you in what to say.*

"God wants you to step outside your comfort zone, Justin," said Jack. "You have to depend on Him, so He can show up and let you know it's Him. God is looking for people like you, people who make themselves available to what God wants them to do." Jack pulled out a pen and pad and began scribbling.

TWO WEEKS LATER, I made my first speaking appearance at the Henry Wade Juvenile Justice Center in Dallas. I shared my testimony with five hundred troubled youth, many of them mixed up in drugs and theft and written off by the rest of society. I'd jotted down a few notes to try and prepare for the talk, but nothing could really ready me to confront one of my greatest fears in life. All I knew was that I was supposed to tell them what my life was like before Christ, how I'd found Him, and what my life was like now.

I was so nervous and very raw, stumbling over my words, but in a way I think that helped me come across as sincere and genuine to the kids. Afterward, one of them grabbed my wrist and asked me to pray with him. One kid turned into thirteen, all of us holding hands and praying together in a circle, some of us in tears. These kids asked me if they could do what I'd done, if they could give their lives to Christ. It was a great affirmation for me that I was on the right path and following the plans that God had for me. A lot of people would look at these kids and say they're in a hopeless situation, with no chance for change, but I felt like they were getting a new beginning—like the one I'd gotten. These kids were where I'd been just half a year before—I knew that if their hearts really wanted a change, God would give them a second chance. It was one of my first steps to having humility and trust in God. If you make yourself available to Him, anything is possible with Him.

With Glass's "Behind the Wall" ministries, a large number of my first speaking assignments took place in prisons. Sometimes I spoke in front of groups. Sometimes I spoke one-on-one with the inmates in their cells in maximum-security blocks. They called those people "lifers," because they'd committed murder and other heinous crimes that ensured they'd never see the outside world again. I even spoke on the same block where Charles Manson was housed in the California State Prison in Corcoran. (I didn't speak with Manson himself.)

During one of my first talks, I was still doubting myself as I made my way onto the stage. I'd forgotten what to say. My mind was blank. My mouth was parched. Then God showed up for me the way He did for Moses. Scrambling to find my notes I'd put somewhere, I reached into my coat pocket and found the medical marijuana license I'd misplaced some time before. I took the piece of paper out, told the inmates what I'd found, then ripped it up in front of them. I wanted to show them my commitment to my new way of life. A few of them stood and clapped.

Speaking with the inmates, I'd tell the guys I'd been in a 3-D prison of my own, maybe not like theirs, but I was a depressed, drunken drug addict, and I had tried, but I couldn't get myself out of it. My prison break had come on May 5, 2010, when Jesus personally delivered the key to my cuffs and cell. I made a life change and that was my relationship with God. He showed me how to love Him and to love others and to even love myself.

My background as a fighter gave me some credibility among the inmates—some prisoners said they could sniff out the phonies before they even got through the gates—but that was only an entry point. Many of these men believed that God couldn't and wouldn't forgive them, so why should they forgive themselves?

David was one inmate I talked to who couldn't forgive himself. Ironically, he used to be an MMA fighter like me, but he'd gotten involved with an Oklahoma drug gang and killed somebody. I read later that "somebody" had been six people: four adults, two of them pregnant. David eventually pleaded guilty to all six murders. But all that I knew at the time was that he was awaiting trial and was under maximum-security lockup for having threatened his last visitor.

With the inmates, I tried to avoid talking about what had gotten them incarcerated. Whenever others brought up what they did, it just made them relive it and they already thought about it every moment of every day in there. I wanted to be a more positive influence.

When I first caught sight of David, he was sitting on his cell bed with his hands cuffed behind his back. His ankles were shackled and he was strapped around his chest and legs, his back to the wall. Surrounding him at all times were four guards, who escorted me into his cell. Just add the mask and David could be Hannibal Lecter.

I sat down on the ground in front of David and introduced myself. After some initial conversation, David and I figured out that we'd nearly fought each other coming up through the ranks at the same time. I was actually supposed to fight David's manager. David joked that his manager backed out, knowing he'd get smashed, and David was going to take the fight himself. Then I got called up to *The Ultimate Fighter* and the bout never happened.

Ragging on David's ex-manager broke the ice, but it took me a long time to get through the hard exterior that David had up to keep love out. David wanted to do most of the talking, so I listened and commented when I could. I had to be patient and let David open up in his own time.

David was already reading the Bible and had a pile of journals stacked as high as himself in the corner of his cell. He'd been writing his own Bible commentary and prayers. David talked about how he'd never gotten as much as a speeding ticket before he went to prison. Life had caught him by surprise, he said.

An hour and a half passed before David really started to consider that he wasn't alone and that God was there for him. He said he wanted to turn his life around and asked if I would pray for him. With a guard's permission, I sat next to David on his bed, my arm around his shoulder, and prayed for him. David finally broke down and cried, maneuvering his shackled body so he could wipe away his tears on his knees.

When I left the prison that day, I thought about how alike David and I were as fighters and how drastically our lives diverged. I couldn't stop thinking about how that could have been me.

CHAPTER 12

Stranded

At my one-year mark of becoming a Christian, I entered a Kingdom Building Ministries discipleship program called The Experience. The program lasted for fifty-five days and took me to Haiti and the Dominican Republic for ten-day missions in each third-world country.

One of the first phases of The Experience was a three-day survival course called "Stranded." Myself and about thirty other participants boarded a bus for six hours from Denver to Franklin, Nebraska, population six hundred. A farming community, Franklin once swelled to twenty to thirty thousand people. Now all that remained was a small, nearly abandoned town square. Vacant and boarded-up buildings littered both sides of the main street, but standing tall among them was a two-story, redbrick building we would learn to call "The Bricks." The Bricks had been the once-thriving Franklin's public library.

Inside, the Bricks had a world-traveled feel. On the ground floor, hammocks hung everywhere and there were pictures of far-off lands and their people neatly lining the walls. A sturdy, beautifully wood-carved staircase—the kind you'd find in the 1930s—led to a second floor. This is where I met Caleb Bislow, the man who'd show me that I wasn't just a UFC warrior, but a warrior for God. Caleb was a missionary himself, having founded a high-risk ministry called Unusual Soldiers. He was also a speaker at Kingdom Building Ministries.

Caleb introduced himself to our anxious group and told us we were going to start with a prayer exercise.

"We're going to pray a little differently than normal," said Caleb, an unassuming adventure seeker in his early thirties. "We're going to ask and we're going to listen to what God has to say. Now, spread out and go listen to God."

To be honest, I walked away confused. Even with my Quest and Kairos experiences, I still had trepidation about reaching God. But I did as Caleb instructed and went downstairs to start praying.

Right before I'd left for Stranded, I'd gotten a fight offer by the Dream promotion and I was really excited about it. So I started praying about that. *God, should I take that fight?* I asked. A half hour passed, and I wasn't hearing an answer either way.

Then I realized I wasn't really doing what Caleb had asked. I took a deep breath and I cleared my head. I stopped thinking about the fight and prayed: *God, I'm Yours. Is there anything You want me to do? I'm all ears. I really am all Yours and I desire to do Your will, not mine. What do You want to impress on my heart?*

That's when the Pygmy vision flooded my head. It came like the ones I'd had at the Olympic Education Center, when the sports psychologists would have the team lay on the mat after wrestling practice. We'd play our next match out in our minds, move by move, visualizing our attacks and our opponents' countermoves as we went.

But instead of seeing my wrestling opponent in this vision, I watched myself weaving through the jungle and discovering these hurting people. I knew that they were hated and hurting and that they were slaves who were dying. I knew they were greatly suffering, probably more than any other people on the planet.

I was so overwhelmed, sobbing uncontrollably, trying to catch my breath, that I left the puddle of tears on my Bible. I'd never cried anywhere near that hard in all my life. The problems these people had seemed insurmountable. How was I going to do anything for them?

It took me a few minutes to come to grips with what just happened. My heart broke for them. I didn't know who these people were, but I suddenly knew I was supposed to go to Africa with Caleb. I scribbled down the words that came into my head, the ones that would match Isaiah 58:6–7: *Imprisoned. Oppressed. Poor. Sick. Hungry. Thirsty.* The thirty of us gathered back upstairs. Caleb looked directly at me and asked my name.

"What did you hear, Justin? Did God say anything?" he asked.

I thought this was crazy. I thought I was crazy. I'd shaken this guy's hand once, he'd told me to go pray, and I'd come back and felt God instructing me to go to Africa with him. I wasn't going to tell him right there, so I hesitantly answered, "No, I didn't hear anything."

"Really?" Caleb asked curiously.

"Well, maybe, but I have to think on it. I have to pray through it. It just feels crazy," I said.

Caleb smiled and said, "I understand."

He directed his attention to the rest of the group. "Who feels a life calling to do missionary work?" he proposed.

It felt like every hand in the room went up except mine. I didn't feel like I was supposed to be doing missionary work all the time. I still thought I was going to be a fighter. Caleb glanced over at me. *Quit looking at me, dude,* I thought. I didn't know who this guy was, but he looked at me like he knew something about me that I didn't even know.

We were divided into groups using questionnaires to determine our level of risk-taking. The white team was the non–risk takers; the red team the calculated risk takers. I was assigned to the black team, the big risk takers, and we were told we'd all have to survive and complete challenges in the wild.

All the teams were then blindfolded and piled into a van or the back of a pickup truck. I could feel our truck go off-road at one point as we drove farther and farther away from The Bricks and the rest of civilization. Along the way, the truck would stop and a group would be ushered off. Where you were dropped off was determined by which color group you'd been assigned to.

We drove for at least thirty minutes, maybe more. We eventually stopped and the black team's two female members were asked to climb out and take their blindfolds off after we'd driven away. On our next stop, the men were asked to get off, but as we stood up, someone grabbed my shoulder and sat me back down.

"No, he's coming with us," I heard Caleb whisper to his cohorts. I was grabbed by the arms and pulled out of the van and thrown into another vehicle. My captors tucked my head and body into it like I was a hostage, the door slamming behind me. I heard the van start up and drive away.

I started blurting out questions, but the driver wouldn't answer. We were on to another destination. After a few minutes, we stopped and my blindfold was removed. It was just Caleb and me left. He told me to get out.

"You're off the property," Caleb said. "You have to find base camp for the black team. I'd head in that general direction," he said, pointing and grinning slightly. "It's two hours until sundown. Good luck." Caleb climbed back into the truck and drove off in a plume of dusty earth.

I took in my surroundings. Behind me, there were cornfields as far as my eye could see, sprinkled with the occasional windmill. I knew I wasn't supposed to go that way. In front of me was a forested area with sharp cliffs and a river running through its center. There was not a sign of life in any direction. I really had no idea which way to go in terms of my left and right, so I followed my gut. I made it about a half mile down through the woods to the river and started following it.

I'd basically been dropped into my own personal episode of *Man vs. Wild*. The outdoors agreed with me, which was surprising considering my first and only other camping trip had consisted of fishing at Benbrook Lake, grilling hot dogs and making s'mores, then popping a tent in the truck bed until about eleven P.M., when my father and I decided it was too chilly and time to go home.

In the Nebraska wild, I began to think about what we'd need to survive. I didn't know what type of supplies, if any, we'd find at base camp. I spotted a brown rabbit not far in front of me and followed it with a big, thick stick in my hands, ready to nail him with it. I crept up on him, when he suddenly got spooked and hopped away. As I inched closer, I saw the four-foot-long snake, who, by default, got the brunt of my stick.

I walked up to base camp just before dark, the snake wrapped around the stick I'd clubbed it with, and joined my black team. I surveyed our limited supplies: a tarp, a pot, a knife, flint to make a fire, and a small bag of baby formula mixed with instant mashed potatoes for food. This was what we'd been given to survive on for the next three days. I was glad I'd brought the snake.

Most of the black team seemed into barbecued snake, so we skewered it with a stick and rolled it slowly over our campfire. We had been roasting our dinner for about two minutes when Caleb appeared out of nowhere to check on us.

"Did you get this?" he asked, looking right at me. I nodded yes, lifting my hard-caught meal out of the flames. Caleb swiped the stick away.

"The black team doesn't get to eat on the first night," he said. This was all part of Stranded, one of the many stressors that were thrown our way to break us down so we could build one another back up again.

While some of us held our own and even flourished under our new conditions, a majority of our group seemed blindsided by the entire setup. I think a lot of them thought, *I want to be a missionary*, but only a little time in the pressure cooker had changed their minds. I'd walked into this experience with no expectations, and was pleasantly surprised to learn that I had a knack for this. I didn't care that I was sleeping under a tarp. I didn't care that bugs were biting me, and it didn't really bother me that I had to pull ticks off me every night. I actually enjoyed the experience, curled up near the fire under the open stars. I was living it up and thought, *Yeah, I could really do this.* We drifted off to sleep not knowing what was to come the next morning.

Part of Stranded's purpose is to break you of your dependence of having to know everything: *I have to know what's happening next. I have to know what's happening next week. I have to know what's happening next month.* In different parts of the world, in varying circumstances, and in drastically different cultures, you might not *know* what's coming next, and sometimes you just have to roll with it.

Our next day's "challenge" was to make peaceful contact with "the tribe," somewhere off of the property, and bring them both aid and hope. The "Vulture Tribe" was played by a group of church members dressed up in traditional garb with their faces painted red and black, modeled after the renowned Maasai warriors. The Vulture Tribe "lived" on an island in the middle of the river, and each team was tasked with reaching them by building a successful raft from whatever we could find. We created a flimsy pontoon out of two plastic barrels and stacking sticks, and tied it down with rotting rope and vines. The black team's vessel split in two less than halfway to the island. My group swam the rest of the way, our supplies hoisted over our heads.

When we got to the tribe, the sun had already set. The Vulture Tribe was dancing and chanting around a bonfire, speaking to one another in a different language. To me, with no experience yet in this field, it looked and sounded like the real deal. Our instructions were to look for a person of peace that we could connect with, maybe through a game. We wanted to gain enough trust so that our "connector" would introduce us to the rest of the tribe. Once we accomplished this, the challenge was complete.

Throughout the three days, we'd had an ongoing exercise to give one another nicknames that reflected who we were. I was named Tender Warrior. Caleb's nickname was, fittingly, Crazy Blood. Caleb is one of the sweetest, most humble dudes I've ever met, but when it comes to spreading God's word, he's game for anything.

At the close of Stranded's program, I felt more than ready to embark on a mission trip to the Dominican Republic and Haiti with whatever challenges they would bring. Being torn down and built back up was both self-revealing and incredible for team-building before we set out overseas. When we boarded the bus to head back to Denver, we had only two days before our flight to the island of Hispaniola and the Dominican Republic. Sitting on the bus, I saw Caleb out the window and realized that this was my last chance to tell him about my vision. Something compelled me to get off and approach him.

"Bro, I'm supposed to go to Africa with you," I blurted out. "I know that sounds crazy. I don't know how. I don't know when, but I know God has put it in my heart to go to Africa with you."

Caleb looked me over. "I know," he said matter-of-factly. "Why do you think I asked you what you'd heard? God told me that you were supposed to come with me on my next trip. Why do you think I took you out the farthest? I had to see what you could do."

Caleb told me that he was heading to the Congo in a month. He said he knew the people I was describing from my vision and he had planned to visit them.

"They're hated and neglected and have even been cannibalized," he told me. "Justin, they're called the Pygmies."

THE DOMINICAN REPUBLIC, located in the Caribbean, was a five-hour flight from Denver. We stayed in a centralized village that offered outreach to a handful of smaller neighboring towns, all of them impoverished. I was taken aback by what little the Dominican people got by on, but at the same time, there was a vibrant culture alive among them. We spent time at a school for troubled youth and I was even invited to make speaking appearances with villagers eager to hear God's word.

I found myself drawn to those who were the worst off. In one of the smaller villages, I met a grandmother who was caring for her eight-year-old granddaughter, Wilicana, who was born with severe birth defects. She couldn't walk, or even sit up on her own, and would have to be cared for the rest of her life. Deep in the remote mountains where we were, the villagers were extremely superstitious. The rest of Wilicana's family abandoned her because she was crippled and therefore cursed. No one would touch Wilicana except for her grandmother and her little brother, Albert, so I scooped her up like the little angel she was and helped them shower her with affection. I called her "Princessita" over and over again because she was a little princess, and as deserving of God's love as anyone else. It was such a small gesture, but you could see by the look on her grandmother's face what a profound impact it had on her. I wholeheartedly believe I saw God's joy through Princessita's smile.

In Haiti, we worked at a mission house, visited local churches, and surveyed the earthquake's damage for the missionaries who'd come after us to help repair these unfortunate people's lives.

A lasting image I took from Haiti, which had been decimated by the 2010 Port-au-Prince earthquake, were the Haitians climbing through garbage piles as high as snowdrifts to reach brown, stagnant water for bathing and drinking. A lot of the street children I saw, some of them as young as five and six years old, carefully crawled through these jungle gyms of broken glass, open cans with razor-sharp edges, and hypodermic needles looking for food. Many of the orphans—their parents likely taken by the earthquake or diseases like HIV/AIDS—nestled into the garbage dumps to sleep at night. The street kids converted the mounds of trash into bedding. During the day, the sun bore down on the decaying waste, and the rancid smell in the dumps grew stronger. The street kids searched for glue or other inhalants to take the edge off the putrid odor, or get them high enough to make them able to sleep.

After twenty eye-opening days, our team flew back to the States. My mind drifted to the luxurious Las Vegas penthouse suites I'd lounged in as a professional fighter. I began reminiscing about all the decadent buffets I'd been able to gorge on and all the wasted food that gets thrown away every day. I got nauseous thinking about it. When I eventually met the Pygmies for the first time, I saw that they lived with even less.

CHAPTER 13

Stan

Upon our return from Haiti, the final leg of our fifty-five-day Experience was to spend a day working at a homeless shelter on the Fourth of July.

We got to the Las Vegas Rescue Mission at seven in the morning. I started cutting the chickens and got them all buttered and garlicked up. Then, we moved on to slicing cantaloupes and watermelon and making other preparations. The shelter knew it could feed 750 people that day and would still have to turn some away.

At six P.M., the shelter opened its doors and the line began to form. We were each given a task on the assembly line—mine was to take the finished trays, shake whatever was left on them into the trash, and hand the trays to the dishwasher behind me.

Each time I took a tray, I'd say, "Thanks and God bless." We got three, maybe four hundred people in, when I started thinking to myself, *Isn't there more I could do? God, if there's something you want me to do, let me know somehow through somebody or through inspiration in my heart or mind. Give me something and I'll do it.*

I continued collecting the trays, slamming two at a time, and handing them back to the dishwasher. Only a minute or two passed when I saw this skinny guy with stringy hair, who looked like he'd had a really rough life. He stuck out to me because he was wearing a red-and-blue Ole Miss Rebels cap. I'm originally from Mississippi and a lot of my family still lives there, so I couldn't miss it. When he got up to me, he handed over his tray and I said, "Thanks, man. God bless," as I had to the others. He mumbled, "Thanks," and in that split second, I suddenly knew that I was supposed to ask him if I could pray for him, but it felt too weird to ask a stranger that right there. The man walked away, joining the flow of traffic exiting the shelter. I continued my work, glancing back a couple times at him. He got about ten yards away when I yelled, "Hey." Ole Miss was the only one who glanced back at me.

What I wanted to say next was "Can I pray for you?" but all I could muster was "How are you doing?"

He stared at me blankly for a moment, then said, "I've been better." He turned around, walked the length of the cafeteria, and disappeared out the door.

I immediately felt defeated—that's how real it was for me that I was supposed to pray for this guy. I'd never had that feeling on my heart before, but I just knew it. I knew I was supposed to pray for him.

I started thinking I should go catch up to him. I gave my trays to the dishwasher and started to walk toward the exit.

"Hey, where are you going?" a woman said behind me. It was the kitchen manager, Shirley, a sweet and sassy woman, who'd delegated us all our jobs in the line. I told her I needed to take a break.

"Not until this is all finished," she said with a little bit of attitude.

I took a few steps back into the assembly line. *I missed that opportunity*, I thought. *Not only did I miss an opportunity, I'll never know what could have happened.*

A couple more trays came my way. I slammed them together and handed them back. Then I turned to a buddy next to me and said, "I gotta go." I just took off, Shirley's voice blasting behind me. "I'll be back in a minute," I yelled over my shoulder. I started walking briskly, then increased it to a jog, and was in full sprint by the time I flew out the door. Outside, there were homeless people clustered everywhere. We were in one of the roughest neighborhoods of downtown Las Vegas—the area they tell tourists to never go. I looked for my man in the red-and-blue hat and finally spied him across the street. He must have noticed me running toward him because I saw the look of fear in his eyes. I'm sure I looked like a linebacker coming to tackle him.

"What'd I do? What'd I do?" he asked in a small panic.

"Nothing," I said, putting my hand on his shoulder as I caught my breath. "Man, I don't know who you are. I don't know what you need and I know I'm going to sound really crazy right now, but it's so heavy on my heart that I'm supposed to pray for you right now. Can I pray for you?"

The man's eyes started watering and his bottom lip began to quiver. He glanced down at the ground and mumbled, "Yes."

His name was Stan. He'd moved to Las Vegas to wait for his death after his wife had cheated on him and given him HIV. This was Stan's first night ever being homeless. He said he'd picked the Vegas desert because it was so dry and humidity would kill him faster. Stan had gone through depression and drug addiction. He once had a normal job and a decent home, but then he'd found out he had HIV. Now all he could think about was getting to the Greyhound station in the next hour so he could empty his locker out before closing time.

"Can I pray for you?" I asked again, and Stan began to weep softly, then broke down into a sob. I just held him while he cried. My gray T-shirt turned darker from all his tears. Sometimes people just need a hug and some positive, encouraging words spoken over their life.

"This is the first time I've ever been able to cry about this with someone," Stan said between gulps.

I prayed for Stan as I held him and an idea came to me. I wanted to find the shelter's director, Matt, and get Stan a bed for the night. I coaxed Stan back into the mission by promising him that I'd drive him to the Greyhound station afterward.

"Nah-ah," Shirley said when I was back in her sights. "You get back here now!"

I threw Shirley an apology as I rushed past her. I had Stan wait at a table as I checked the kitchen and storage areas for Matt. I asked anyone who passed if they'd seen him. I checked everywhere, including the walk-ins, then started yelling out Matt's name. Finally, I heard an answer coming from the men's bathroom.

"Can't it wait?" Matt asked through the door.

"No, I have to tell you now," I answered excitedly. "I think God's doing something right now. I'm not trying to put pressure on you, but I think it involves you."

Matt emerged from the bathroom.

"This might sound really crazy," I started, as I recounted what had just happened with Stan and me. I could see Matt's interest start to peak as I continued. "Is there anything we can do for this guy?" I asked at the end.

Matt went to meet Stan. He asked him about his drug addictions, alcoholism, and any mental disorders, and once he was satisfied, Matt offered Stan a temporary room with a bed. Stan was in disbelief. His first night as a homeless man wouldn't be spent outside.

The next day, when I shared the story with others, it dawned on me that the Justin of old—the closed-off cage fighter hell-bent on destroying his life—wouldn't have touched that guy. The thought never entered my mind that this dude had HIV and I shouldn't hug him. I just hugged him because that's what he needed. It was motivated out of love, nothing else.

Six months later, I was in Las Vegas speaking at Central Christian Church and I shared a bit of that story with the audience. As I looked out at the group, I noticed that many of those who'd volunteered that Fourth of July weekend with me were sitting in some of the front rows. I'd remembered a few of their names and acknowledged them in my talk, especially Shirley. Afterward, they came up to me and asked if I knew what had happened to Stan. When I told them I didn't, they insisted I go see Matt. *Was Stan okay?* Thoughts of drug addiction and death ran through my mind.

The next day, I went back to the Las Vegas Rescue Mission. Matt was there to greet me with a big smile.

"Man, you're not going to believe what happened," he said.

Matt explained how the shelter had given Stan a bed, but couldn't keep him there for long because he was HIV-positive. Matt introduced Stan to a ministry for HIV patients and the ministry was able to get Stan back on his feet. Not only did Stan now have his own apartment, the ministry had given him a job to speak with others who had HIV. When Stan tells his story, he says that he came to Las Vegas a homeless man but God already had a place for him to live.

Matt put his hands on my shoulders.

"Remember how you told me you thought you were going to look crazy if you asked to pray for him?" Matt said. "Man, do you know how *not* crazy you look right now?"

I've looked back on that experience many times—it has increased my faith so much. If I hadn't been obedient to what God put on my heart, if I hadn't stepped out of the food line and my comfort zone, I would have missed the opportunity God had laid in front of me. I almost missed God's signal; I almost missed that nudge to get out of line.

My favorite scripture is Acts 4:13 (NLT), where the apostles Peter and John heal a crippled beggar panhandling outside the Temple. Angry and feeling threatened, the town priests, the police, and the town council meet to decide what to do with the apostles.

But other than threatening them, there wasn't much they could do to Peter and John. They couldn't arrest them for performing a miracle, and by then, the people had rallied at their side.

> *The members of the council were amazed when they saw the boldness of Peter and John, for they could see that they were ordinary men with no special training in the Scriptures. They also recognized them as men who had been with Jesus.*

I'm not saying that I performed a miracle or that Shirley represented the priests, police, or town council. Shirley was right to try and stop me; she was only doing her job. But it did take boldness from me to disregard her strict instruction and step out of line to follow Stan. Peter and John preached, knowing that the town officials wouldn't like it and they could be imprisoned.

I learned that if it's on my heart, even if it sounds weird to me, I am going to do it, because God will love people through that. And when I had my vision of the Pygmies, I knew that was another opportunity straight from God. I had to step out of line and get to them, no matter how difficult it might be.

A month after I met Stan, I was carving my way through the heavy foliage on my way to making First Contact with the Pygmies. At the end of that trip, I was ready to call it quits. I wanted to say, "Yeah, I did my part—now back to my life," but I couldn't shake this burden I had in my heart. It was an undeniable calling in my life. I knew I was the guy God had selected. I didn't necessarily choose it; it chose me. God had chosen the Pygmies for me to love.

CHAPTER 14

Emily

Flying back from our first trip to the Congo, I'd wanted to believe that we'd return to the States having made a big impact or at least some sort of difference. My vision had completely come true, so I'd waited the entire trip for some tangible challenge to appear. What huge giant were we going to handle or take out? What war would be won? What struggle would be overcome? God had brought us there and he wouldn't have brought us there without a reason and a purpose.

I couldn't have imagined that people lived in such extreme poverty and were forced into slavery until I saw it with my own eyes. You hear about Africa and how it's impoverished, and you know that they're a lot worse off than you, but you can't actually fathom it until you live it and see it.

Returning to the States, I definitely experienced culture shock. My whole world had been turned upside down and now I was stepping back into America's bubble of luxury and excess. At first, it didn't feel like reality at all, but some false, safe comfort zone. *The rest of the world isn't like this*, I thought.

I slept on my bedroom floor for about six months after I got back; I didn't feel guilty about having a bed, but I loved these people and they'd captured my heart. So, even though I was living in a mansion compared to the leaves and twigs they survived with, I decided to sleep on the floor like they did. It may sound silly, but I felt compelled to make my life more like theirs.

I returned to Grudge with a new perspective. I now viewed my MMA goals and dreams as something very self-centered. I loved my teammates and Coach T, but what I used to fight for was myself. That's not a bad thing, but why only fight for yourself when you could fight for others?

I trained during the week, but not as intensely as if I had a fight coming up. I couldn't get the Pygmies off my mind. I saw that a potential future loving them would be so much more important than what I used to do.

Seven months following my return, I approached Coach T in the same office where he'd kicked me off the team a year earlier. I'd been welcomed back with open arms, but I was turning it all down and moving back to Dallas. I felt like I should be doing something different with my life, at least for now. I told Coach T that I was going to take a year off from fighting and focus on God and getting my life back in order. Coach T and his wife bear-hugged me. Coach T encouraged me not to hang up my gloves altogether. I was only twenty-four years old and although he felt like it was "go time" now, he knew the door would remain open a bit longer for me.

I could feel God guiding my path back to Texas. But that wasn't the only thing tugging on my heart. I had met a girl who lived in Dallas–Fort Worth, and it definitely made moving back home a lot easier.

It began, normally enough, when I attended an engagement party for one of my church friends and I asked the newly engaged couple how they met. When they answered, "ChristianMingle," there were a few snickers around the room. *Who would need to go online to meet his future wife?* I thought. Still, my friends urged me to try it out, as there was a definite consensus—whether it be correct or not—that I was ready to date again.

However, there was also my calling for the Pygmies to think about. Most women wanted to live the American dream, not climb around the dangerous jungles of the Congo. What woman would ever want to give up American comforts to sleep in the dirt and eat caterpillars? The apostle Paul seemed to have lived a single life. Maybe that was my destiny.

Still, my friends wouldn't relent, and one of the guys made a profile page for me on the sly. I went into the page and fixed it up, making it less about being a fighter and more about my beliefs. Shortly after, I received an email with my first five matches. The first four women lived in the Denver area near me. The fifth one was from Keller, Texas. She attended Gateway Church, the same church my mom attended. There were pictures included, and when I saw Emily, I was blown away. Age twenty-one, curly brown hair just past her shoulders, sparkling blue-green eyes—and that perfect smile. Who was this beautiful woman?

In the "About Me" section, the first thing she'd left was a quote by Maya Angelou: "A women's heart should be so hidden in Christ that a man has to seek Him to find her." There was something so beautiful about it that it gave me chills. I was smitten by her picture and quote alone.

I found a button that said MESSAGE and clicked. Suddenly a default message popped up that said I had to pay $29.99 to activate my profile to begin messaging users. *Dang it! They got me*, I thought, but I instantly paid the membership fee to send Emily a note. We started conversing by exchanging each other's Facebook pages and gradually got to talking over the phone.

The first time Emily and I Skyped together, our conversation lasted for six hours. Emily and I shared our testimonies, and I felt like we were having a real God moment when she suggested I attend the Quest men's retreat when I got back to Dallas. Emily's father had attended the retreat and Emily had gone on the women's version, called HeartQuest. We were both astounded that we'd all attended the same retreat on the same horse ranch in the same big house a little less than a year apart from one another.

With what could have been "a little" (i.e., extremely) premature, I also shared with Emily something that had happened to me on Quest on my second-to-last day there. After I'd gotten baptized, I'd gone off to journal alone. I wrote down that the woman I would marry was going to have to experience what I'd experienced here at this retreat. Imagine how shocked and happy I was when Emily told me that she'd made an agreement with her father that whomever she married would have attended Quest, too. Sweet!

We officially started dating after I came to Texas to meet her that October, under the guise that I was visiting my parents. Trying to be as respectful as possible, I sat down with Emily's father to privately ask if I could date his daughter. Before I could ask, he called his wife and Emily into the room.

"Not only can you date her," he answered. "You and I gave our lives to Christ at the same place. I was in a very bad place like yourself, but God put on my heart that whoever I gave my daughter's hand to, they'd have to attend Quest—not that I'm giving you any ideas right now."

One of the many special things about Emily was that she didn't know what the UFC or MMA was. She thought I was doing Tae Bo in my garage or training cardio kickboxing in a gym with some friends. *She likes me because of me*, I thought. *She doesn't like me for what I do, but because of who I am.*

Emily watched MMA for the first time when Spike TV reaired the *TUF* episode where I fought Wes Sims, the six-foot-ten giant.

I actually sat down with Emily and my parents to watch the fight as a family.

At first, Emily wasn't too crazy about it. She didn't want to see me get hurt and didn't know what to think about all the punching. She also couldn't take my "mean face," meant to intimidate my opponent, seriously. She had only been exposed to the sweet, cuddly side of me and it made her laugh to see me look like a tough guy. She pinched my cheek and told me how my mean face couldn't fool her.

Along with the minor fame that came with being on *TUF*'s highest-rated season, I was up front with Emily about the underbelly of MMA and my past screwups. I wanted to get as far away from that life as I could and wanted Emily and I to start from a place of brutal honesty.

When I started talking aloud about going back to the Congo a second time, Emily was super supportive. She could handle a month of me being away, she said, and would start praying for me.

During this year, between my first and second Congo trips—from word of mouth only—I made more than forty speaking appearances at prisons, youth groups, men's events, Sunday churches, and even gave my youth camp experience another whirl as a guest speaker (it turned out much better this time around). In fact, I landed in Charlotte from the Congo and went right to a speaking event for a local ministry. After that, I was flown to another speaking event in Kansas City. Then I finally got to go home.

At these appearances, I shared my testimony and Congo experience. When asked how I reconciled fighting with my faith, I answered that God gives everyone talents, and my spiritual gift was to "lay hands on people." That usually got a laugh from the crowd. These events allowed me to share in some special God moments. I saw husbands reconcile with their wives, fathers reconnect with their sons, and siblings move past the past. The most exciting moments for me were when I watched people reconnect with God, or begin a relationship with Him. It made the trembling in my hands from my public-speaking fears more than worth it.

I don't know what it is about me and airplanes, but I had another powerful moment on one during this time. I sat down next to a young newlywed couple, who immediately recognized me from *TUF*. He was a tattoo artist and both were colorfully stamped from head to toe. We started talking about MMA and he asked what had happened to me—a fair question as I hadn't fought in two years by this time. While I shared my testimony, his wife overheard us and chimed in. She said it was crazy that we were talking about God because the couple had just discussed attending church for the first time together. The husband said he wasn't a religious person.

"Too many rules," he said. I agreed with him and responded with the first thing that came to my mind.

"Religion is absolutely bogus if it doesn't have a personal, tangible relationship with God," I said. "If its focus is rules for God instead of a relationship with God, run away; it's fake."

The wife told me that a pastor had come into their shop and encouraged them to visit his church. A pastor with tattoos in the Denver area? I knew exactly who they were talking about; that pastor was my pastor, and a friend of mine. I offered to go with them to church the next time I was in Denver.

I asked if I could pray for the couple and the man said, "Yes," and the wife said, "Please." I prayed for the man first, that he would have an open heart, so God could show him that He's real and that He really loves him. After that I saw his posture soften and his guarded walls come down a bit. Just as I began praying for the wife, I looked down and noticed that she was pregnant. We hadn't talked about that at all. I started praying for her and then I felt I had to pray for the baby's health. *God, will you just keep this*

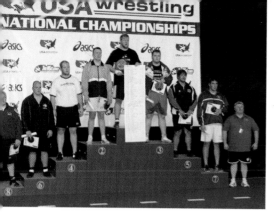

First Texan to win a Greco-Roman National Championship in wrestling
(Photograph courtesy of the Wren family)

Dream big. Win big. With my mama after Nationals.
(Photograph courtesy of the Wren family)

Childhood dream becomes a reality: my UFC Topps Card
(Topps trading cards used courtesy of The Topps Company, Inc. Photograph provided by Zuffa, LLC.)

Speaking at the 2013 Men's Conference for James River Church in Springfield, Missouri
(Courtesy of James River Church)

First Contact: I was
shocked and amazed to
see my vision come true
(Photograph © Colin J. Reed)

A common sight in the Congo:
children with machetes bigger
than themselves
(Photograph courtesy of the author)

Being a human jungle gym at an orphanage in
war-torn Goma, having fun with some kiddos
(Photograph © Colin J. Reed)

Ben leading the way in a snow
jacket, hiking through the
thickets of hot, humid jungle
(Photograph courtesy of the author)

Modern-day slavery: Namboli had a 120-pound bag of charcoal tied around her head, which she carried three miles for her Mokpala slave master
(Photograph courtesy of the author)

Ben checking on the orphans and widows' hut
(Photograph courtesy of the author)

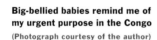

Big-bellied babies remind me of my urgent purpose in the Congo
(Photograph courtesy of the author)

The entire village attended Andibo's funeral, covering their faces in grief
(Photograph courtesy of the author)

The Beast! A miracle! Fight for the Forgotten's first truck.

(Photograph courtesy of the author)

Dancing is an integral part of the Pygmies' culture

(Photograph courtesy of the author)

Emily being greeted by Papa Way's beautiful daughters and friends

(Photograph courtesy of the author)

Emily's first camping trip: twig-and-leaf hut, mosquitos, roaches, rain, mud . . . She must really LOVE me!

(Photograph © Ben Liringa Koli)

Hunter boys: these little guys could already snipe running mice, hopping birds, and rolling passion fruit

(Photograph © Emily Wren)

Withering away: the first time I saw Kaptula

(Photograph courtesy of the author)

Kaptula on the road to recovery

(Photograph © Agung Fauzi)

Sitting around the fire in Tundu. This is what "Campfire University" would look like.

(Photograph © Agung Fauzi)

Chief Leomay and I before his hunt. That wicked-looking stick "chair" is actually quite comfy.

(Photograph © Agung Fauzi)

Sangee, Chief Leomay's grandson, and I pose with his second-ever kill, a large-spotted genet

(Photograph © Emily Wren)

The Tundu village I stayed with was one of my favorite Pygmy villages. They accepted me with open arms.

(Photograph © Agung Fauzi)

An inside look at Pygmy architecture, as the kiddos of Mpenda village grab hold of my beard

(Photograph © Agung Fauzi)

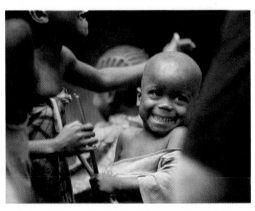

This cutie from the Kidogo village smiling after touching my beard. At first, all the kiddos were terrified of me.

(Photograph © Agung Fauzi)

My two favorite bears—EmmyBear and Pooh Bear (Bahjongee) on the new land acquired for the Mpenda Pygmies

(Photograph courtesy of the author)

Helping my Pygmy family see themselves for the first time in pictures was such a cool and easy gift to give them

(Photograph © Agung Fauzi)

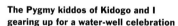

The Pygmy kiddos of Kidogo and I gearing up for a water-well celebration

(Photograph © Agung Fauzi)

The Beast making friends in Mpenda: we offered people lifts, many of them for their first-ever car ride

(Photograph © Agung Fauzi)

Working with Shalom Drillers to complete the water well in Kucheza village

(Photograph © Agung Fauzi)

An overhead view of the Shalom Drillers after finishing the first water well for the Mokpala (non-Pygmies)

(Photograph © Agung Fauzi)

The Kumi Pygmy water well. One of my favorite celebrations!

(Photograph courtesy of the author)

The perfect surprise on the most perfect day of my life

(Photograph © Agung Fauzi)

In Kucheza at its water-well celebration

(Photograph © Agung Fauzi)

baby safe; put Your angels around her womb and protect her and the baby from sickness and any kind of complications.

When we opened our eyes I noticed the man's arm was now wrapped around his wife, and both were wiping their eyes.

"How did you know that about my baby?" she asked. "We tried for one and we had a miscarriage. We almost split up over it."

I continued offering them comfort and talked about my relationship with God and how it had completely changed my life. As I did, both of them said their hearts were definitely open to learning about and beginning a personal relationship with Christ. I get so stoked when people see past the ugly side of religion and see the beauty of a relationship with God.

After we landed and parted ways, I saw the couple at the church a few times. They looked lighter than I remembered; not so heavy-hearted. Months later, I was overjoyed to learn that they'd given birth to a healthy baby boy.

I felt extremely blessed to be able to travel and speak to new people. Still, I couldn't shake my burden for the Pygmies. I couldn't go a day without thinking about them. I felt deep within my bones that God was asking me to put His love and compassion in action. I just had to discover how. I reached out to Caleb and he reached out to the network of missionaries in the Congo. A man named Way (pronounced "Why") was mentioned. Way worked for the University of Shalom in Bunia (Shalom, for short), one of the closest, decent-sized cities to the Congo's jungles. Way had close contact with the Pygmies. After exchanging emails, Caleb told me that Way had a heart for the Pygmies as well and I should really get in touch with him, yet all he could give me was his name.

I hunted Way down on Facebook and left a message on his page. I was elated that there was someone on the ground in the Congo who spoke the language and had just as much love for the Pygmies as I did. I waited for Way's reply for more than three months; Bunia's city power had been out, the Internet had been down, and he'd been in the jungle with the Pygmies.

When I finally got Way's response, I was in Nebraska with Caleb, game-planning the next trip to the Congo. I'd been pretty downtrodden that I hadn't heard from Way, but Caleb had told me not to give up. He told me to quit sweating it and to just pray about it with him. Caleb asked for God to give me a sign that this man was the one I should be pursuing.

I thought of Luke 10:2, which says, *The harvest is great, but the workers are few.*

God, I can't do any of this by myself, I prayed. *It's too big. I can't go there, not knowing anyone and not knowing the language. I need to know if this is the guy or not.*

Caleb and I were laughing when my phone pinged later that day with Way's response on Facebook. Way was cautious, but very supportive of me coming to the Congo. He would tell me later that he'd only checked Facebook a handful of times in his life, but our cool connection was one of the main things that prompted him to use it more. We started to exchange information and I found that I'd hit the jackpot. Way was virtually the local expert on the Pygmies. He'd been visiting them since 1987, the year I was born. With his Shalom University staff, he'd already been working for eight years on a plan to improve the Pygmy way of life in culturally acceptable ways.

It was now summer, and nearly a year since my first Congo trip. Connecting with Way hadn't been easy, but there we were, talking about our shared passion with 8,250 miles between us. Way and Shalom had a game plan and I was very interested in becoming a part of it. I'd already applied for the necessary visas, but had no idea how I'd pay for my airfare. I needed $3,500 and was shy to ask for it from others, but I sucked it up and emailed out a passionate plea to all of my contacts at nine o'clock one night. By 10:30, I had more money than I needed. Ten people had checked their email that night and donated. It was even more confirmation to me that I was supposed to be doing this. Send an email. Boom. It's there. And as an added bonus, Shane, a friend I met at the youth camp I spoke at, decided to accompany me.

I spoke to Way over the phone for the first time in those few days before we left for the Congo a second time. We agreed to meet at the airport in Bunia. I was hopeful that I'd be able to take in the true Pygmy experience this time and work with Way and his people in any way I could. This trip would be much different from the first. This time I was landing with another Pygmy freedom fighter waiting for me on the tarmac. This time I wouldn't be alone.

CHAPTER 15

Chibuseeku

There were three of us on the hour-and-a-half flight from Uganda to the Congo. Shane, a bold eighteen-year-old and fresh high school graduate, was a late companion to my team. The other passenger was a French female journalist coming to cover the conflict. Brave woman.

I'd only talked to Way once over the phone. I didn't really know what he looked like, so I had a little anxiety when our plane touched the tarmac. As I climbed out of the prop plane, I saw four men standing together, waiting for us. I would come to refer to these men as the "Original Four," and each one of them has blessed my life immensely in their own ways.

In his late forties, Way Alege, or "Papa Way," was the oldest and the father figure within the group. He and his wife, Sylvia, had five children and were raising three additional girls. Papa Way strategically oversaw the Faculty of Development and the Faculty of Agriculture and Sciences at Shalom. In addition to overseeing about half of Shalom's 1,200 students, Way had been working with the Pygmies since 1987. He'd won the Mbuti Pygmies' trust and friendship over the years, which would be crucial to our campaign.

If Papa Way was the coach of the group, Patrick Kisembo surely was his assistant coach. Patrick was the twenty-nine-year-old head of Shalom's Agriculture and Sciences Department, and worked under Papa Way. Slender, handsome, and a sharp dresser, Patrick rotated between black, brown, and gray golf caps, even in the forest. Patrick's lovable personality, combined with his teaching style, drew people into learning.

Jack Bokota, twenty-three, at the time a Shalom student until he became the youngest-ever Dean of the Faculty of Development the next year, always wore a big, sweet, bright smile. Jack was our expert driver on the treacherous roads, and would become a man who was often in the trenches with me, like a training partner.

Another Shalom student, Benjamin, age twenty-seven, was the most energetic of the group, and neatly dressed in a button-up shirt. You'd be hard-pressed not to see Ben, a former UN translator and master of seven languages, wearing a sports jacket—even in the forest. There would be times it was so hot and densely humid outside that I could see my breath and Ben would still be wearing a jacket; he was that immune to the heat. He told me he was afraid to ever visit the U.S. because it's a country with snow. Ben would become a confidant to me, a cornerman who I constantly listened to for input on the culture or translation or for support and encouragement. Ben was also a whiz on the motorcycle and engaged to a woman named Elnise.

Among the Original Four, we game-planned to visit nine Mbuti Pygmy tribes in just under a month. Sadly, six of them had slave masters who'd asked me what I wanted with "their Pygmies" or "their property." The other three would refer to the Pygmies as "animals."

On our motorbikes, we could hear the first tribe's music about two miles away. We got our bikes as close as we could to the noise, but it was dark under the forest's canopy. It had just been raining, so the trail was muddy and unruly. We pushed our bikes through the thick earth and over grounded trees and small creeks on thin handmade stick bridges, slipping, falling, and getting stuck along the way. When the rainforest became too much for our bikes, we ditched them and started hiking through the thick brush. It was such a challenge to get there, but once we could hear the Pygmies, it motivated us forward.

I had a few goals on this trip. I wanted to live with the Pygmies and get on their level, so I could experience and share in their suffering. I also wanted to listen to them, so I could learn from them. If I was faithful and did those things, I trusted God would show me how to love them. I didn't want to make the same mistakes other outsiders, whether well intentioned or not, had made. I couldn't go in there with no frame of reference and tell the Pygmies what their problems were. You don't go in with answers before you ask the questions. How do you gain someone's trust if you don't develop a relationship first? I had to understand their culture, make friends, and only then could we start a relationship.

What was special about this tribe was that they were the first to move onto their own land, purchased by Shalom on their behalf. In that land sale, sixty slaves had been freed, so I was seeing the beginning stages of Shalom's plan taking effect. (Right after I left, around sixty more former slaves would find refuge on the fifty acres purchased for them.)

We arrived sometime during the day, announcing ourselves to the chief of the hundred-person Moja clan. All four of my new friends spoke Swahili (the language of the Pygmies' slave masters). Ben also spoke the very rare Pygmy language, so they made the introductions. We broke the ice by playing Frisbee—for hours. The Pygmies had never seen this kind of contraption. It was all counter-intuitive to what they knew. The Frisbee would slip through their hands and hit their chests. Catching, they'd all bolt in different directions, or bump straight into one another, because they had no frame of reference to judge where it was headed. Even though it was so strange to them, we all laughed so much, and it was fascinating to watch them try to figure out the aerodynamics of the flimsy plate.

We didn't stay to eat with the Moja Pygmies that day—we saw that they had so little food among themselves, and we didn't want to take any. After it got dark, Papa Way and the others took Shane and I on a twenty-minute hike from the village to a building made of mud and sticks that was ceilinged with iron sheets. Shalom University had built this schoolhouse in a clearing on the Mokpala-Pygmy border. It had been intended for both people groups, but discrimination and practicality had prevailed. The school (like all schools in the Congo) couldn't offer a lunch program, so most Pygmy children reported to the fields in the hopes of getting a meal.

The two-room school had been laid out with two thin-foamed mattresses. I guess Papa Way and the others hadn't thought Shane and I could handle living the way the Pygmies do. After we had something to eat and were tucked in for the night, I followed Papa Way, without him knowing, to another part of the Pygmy village on our side of a creek.

"I don't know if you want to do this on your first night," he said as I caught up to him. "I don't have a mosquito net. I don't want you to get malaria. It's very dangerous. I would rather you just get a good night's sleep in the schoolhouse."

"I'm about to squeeze in there with you," I answered without haste, getting on my hands and knees to crawl in. "This is the only way I'll learn." With the mosquitoes' buzzing, Papa Way and I fell asleep, shoulder to shoulder, in the tiny hut.

The next day, we continued to get acquainted with the Moja village. There was one very sweet, middle-aged woman in the village named Chibuseeku, who'd fallen ill with an awful headache. I had some Tylenol back at the school building we were staying in. I knew I wouldn't sleep that night thinking about her suffering and knowing that it could be cured with something I could give her. So, once everyone was winding down for bed at the schoolhouse, I gathered the medicine and filtered a two-liter bottle of water mixed with fruit-flavored electrolytes. I thought Chibuseeku's headache might be due to dehydration.

I wasn't sure how to get back to the tribe, but I decided to wing it. I put on my headlamp and started in the direction of the tribe through the darkness. I picked between two or three forks in the trails and just prayed I was taking the right path. It had been raining again, and a creek we'd passed over earlier that day had risen dramatically. We'd walked over a board getting there and back, but now the bridge was submerged and lost in the muddy creek that was about ten feet wide and five feet deep.

Unable to find the plank or turn back, I waded into the water chest-deep with my headlamp, my phone, and the medicine raised above my head. I crawled through the creek and, once on the opposite side, I knew I wasn't that far away. Observing the Pygmies, I'd seen how they communicated by "calling" one another deep in the forest.

"OOH-ooh-OHH," I bellowed as soon as I thought I was close enough for them to hear. Thankfully, a Pygmy silently stepped out from the thicket and guided me the rest of the way back to their camp. When I peeked into the hut, Chibuseeku was lying down, her eyes tightly shut from the pain. She looked at me as I took the water bottle out of my bag. I took a sip and offered it to her. She sat up carefully, began to sip, and her eyes bulged with delight. She'd probably never tasted a strawberry-flavored drink, let alone in clean water. I then pantomimed taking the Tylenol pill until she understood and took one. I gave her a small banana I'd brought for her and we settled by the fire, my arm around her to comfort her.

Without Ben and Jack, I had no way to communicate other than with my eyes and hand gestures. Others gathered around the fire with us. I didn't know how to start a conversation, so I took out my small Bible (with waterproof pages) and read a short chapter aloud. Nobody knew what I was saying, but the village leaned in, enraptured by it. After I was finished, they nodded their heads, smiled, and gave me a thumbs-up. Some of the kids in the village had been so frightened by me earlier, but now a few were hanging around and laughing instead of running away. All the children would watch intensely as a few of the brave ones dared to step close enough to reach out and touch my bizarre yellow hair.

Two hours later, Chibuseeku pointed to her head, let out a smile, and gave me a thumbs-up. I patted my chest and pointed in the direction of my camp. Chief Jayloowah put up his hand and motioned for another Pygmy to come over. Everyone came to the end of the village to see us off, waving and smiling, as he guided me back to Shalom's camp. When we got to the creek, the Pygmy knew where the board was, so we were only waist-deep wading back.

The next day, Chibuseeku looked a hundred percent better. She'd drunk all of the water and was so grateful for it. Thus began my close relationship with the Moja tribe, specifically with Chibuseeku and her family, who'd eventually take me in as one of their own. Among the nine villages we visited, we stayed with the Moja the longest, for about a week.

We set up our tents within the Pygmy village on the third night. A big huddle of Pygmies crowded around, watching us assemble our dwellings of aluminum poles and vinyl. I offered my tent to the Pygmy chief and his wife to take and they both slept comfortably side by side on my air mattress, which was only wide enough for my shoulders. Whenever I blew up the mattress, the Pygmies hoisted it over their heads and passed it around like it was a zealous fan bodysurfing at a rock concert.

I enjoyed sleeping in the Pygmy huts, which were miniature igloo-like domes made of bent sticks, vines, and an assortment of jungle leaves. I still had to crawl on my forearms to get through the entrance and I could only sleep in the prone position, but I didn't mind. It was invigorating to wake up, sometimes sunken into the mud, with the Pygmies after a good rain. Yes, I'll admit the tight quarters could be extremely uncomfortable at times, but I was learning about living the way they did and that made it more than worth it.

On this trip, half of my gear bag was filled with about thirty pounds of food, a couple of water filtration systems, and emergency water purifying tablets I'd brought for the four of us. I'd brought fifty PowerBars, but I also tried some of the Pygmies' odder cuisine, like caterpillars. Our bathroom continually alternated among any choice of the millions of trees in the Ituri rainforest, and we cleaned ourselves and our clothes in the rivers with a bar of soap.

Soon after settling in, I and the other guys noticed a stick-thin girl named Fina who lived alone in her own hut. It wasn't extraordinary to see a girl, maybe age ten or eleven, living by herself; many children here were orphans. There was a community hut in the village for the younger orphans and the widows.

Fina's mother had died and her father had left, himself too mentally unstable to care for a child. Fina was a striking girl with a kind face and a beaming smile, but tuberculosis had left her a shell of her former self. TB is contagious, but when I looked at Fina, all I saw was a normal kid in need of a hug. I took her in my arms, and chose to believe God would protect me because my actions were motivated out of love. If not, then I considered it worth it anyway. Orphan kiddos already had enough struggles on their plate—being an outcast shouldn't be one of them. Papa Way, also a registered nurse, pointed out that Fina would need six full months of medicine to overcome TB. Being out in the wild and a victim of the harsh elements, Fina's chances weren't as good. Shalom and I pitched in for Fina's medical care, and she started her treatment just as we left the village. Papa Way and Sylvia agreed to take Fina in and oversee her treatment back in Bunia.

I tried to win over the other kiddos by letting them touch my beard. Whenever they were scared or skeptical or thought I was a ghost or spirit or half-man, half-animal because of my hair, I would squat down and let them feel my shaggy arms. As for the adults, many tribes had been taught not to look a white person in the eye if they ever saw one. If I noticed this, I'd drop down to their eye level and smile. I'd have Ben tell them that we are all God's children, so that makes them my brothers and sisters. We told the Pygmies that differences are beautiful, not bad, and we were all equals. I had to tell the Pygmies to eat when I ate. With Belgian colonization came some sad cultural rituals that were still alive in parts of the Congo. One of those was that the white man ate first, and when he was done with seconds, or thirds, they could eat.

Our translators, Ben and Jack, weren't around all the time, so the Pygmies and I found different ways to communicate. I learned their way of answering yes—a single head nod up accompanied with a big eyebrow raise and a higher-pitched *mmm* sound. I learned a lot about communicating with body language. I used the thumbs-up a lot, pointed, used head shakes for yes and no, and found myself acting out what I was trying to communicate. If that wasn't enough, we'd just throw up our hands, shrug, and laugh it off.

I felt a strong connection to the clan in Moja and I found out that they'd made one with me as well. The night before we left, Chibuseeku unexpectedly, but graciously, invited me into her family as her son. I had found my second family: my father, Manu; my brother, Biwanja; and my little sisters, Sumbalina, Priscilla, and Mado. Chief Jayloowah became my grandfather. There was no greater gift I could be given in that moment.

CHAPTER 16

Eféosa

From the moment the plane flies into eyesight of the luminescent chartreuse pools of forest below, its treetops as tight as broccoli spears, one knows they're about to enter a special place. With your own eyes, you can see rare, exotic animals like the antelope/zebra/ giraffe hybrid, the okapi, or the large-spotted genet, a crafty and supple mongoose–baby leopard mix that will eat nearly anything within sight. Have you ever heard a water drum before? It's the polyphonic sound that comes from eight or nine women splashing the water's surface with their palms a certain way in unison, each one hitting a different note to make a perfect harmony. Who knew that under so much beauty could lurk so much ugliness?

Ben and I (Papa Way and Patrick returned to Bunia after we left the Moja) motorbiked along the dirt road that winded adjacent to the nine Pygmy villages we'd travel to through the rest of the month. The slave masters' wives and Pygmy slaves also took to this road with the tasks given to them. We stopped to talk to a woman uncomfortably balancing a heavy bundle of sticks on her back, neck, and head. She was transporting the big branches for her slave master.

"What are you getting paid for this?" I asked through Jack.

"Nothing," she answered. "I've already been paid yesterday." I watched as the woman spoke to Jack and used her hands to show the small size of her payment.

"She said she was paid a patch of goat fur for this job. Maybe the size of a mouse pad," Jack told us, shaking his head.

This was plain cruelty. The slave master hadn't offered her meat, but the fur and skin of the animal, like the cowhide on my mother's office floor back in Texas. He'd also meant the gesture to humiliate the woman; Pygmies considered goats dirty animals that hosted evil spirits, and believed when a hunter consumed goat meat, that hunter would get weak in the knees and not be able to move swiftly through the forest. The Pygmy woman's slave master thought of her as his animal, so he felt it rationalized feeding her scraps like a dog. The slave master gave her just enough food for her to get by and to keep her coming back.

When we returned to Shalom University later, Ben had Papa Way show me a picture of the same woman, this time balancing about 120 pounds of charcoal on her contorted back. I took a snapshot with my iPhone so I wouldn't forget the image.

The charcoal woman's tale was one of many incredulous ones I heard in the next month. Moving from village to village, we found Pygmies slaving away from daybreak until sunset for ripped and tattered clothing, two small bananas, and sometimes even a broken piece of a soap bar or just a ketchup-packet-sized sprinkle of salt. And most of these slaves had to share these paltry items with their starved families. "Harry"—nicknamed that because he was the only Pygmy I'd ever seen with facial hair—worked all day in the fields and got paid two small minnows, maybe the size of my pinkie, for his time. He took the tiny fish home to share with his sickly wife. Some slaves weren't given food at all, but addictive drugs and Congo moonshine as payment to tend to the fields. They didn't have another choice. There were no options. Without land ownership and without sustainable hunting-and-gathering; with rebel groups mining around them for gold, diamonds, and coltan; with government soldiers poaching with automatic rifles and scaring away any small game; and with even some wildlife conservationists pushing them off the land, the Pygmies were trapped.

We got the most pushback from the Mokpala of the fifth Pygmy tribe we visited, called Kanisa. We'd looked for their masters to introduce ourselves, but it had gotten late and dark, so we approached the Pygmies without clearance. One of the slave masters bolted over to us as we tried to pick up a friendly game of Frisbee with our new friends.

"This is my land. What are you doing with my animals? You need my approval," he barked in Swahili. Ben raced to keep up with the translating. "If you're going to stay here with my Pygmies, you have to buy their land right now."

"But the Pygmy chief gave us permission to be here," we answered.

"But I own them," he said. The exchange went back and forth as we explained we were from Shalom University, that there were no strings attached, and that we simply wanted to live with and love on the Pygmies. When he saw no money to be made, the slave master finally stormed off.

The Kanisa tribe was congregated near the debris of some former buildings, a boneyard of a failed project of a nongovernmental organization (NGO), who, not knowing the relationship, had given money to the Mokpala slave masters to build the Pygmies' homes. When the NGO returned to check on its investment, the Mokpala had shuffled to erect a semblance of dwellings that crumbled shortly after the NGO left. It looked like a tornado had gone through the quick and careless construction—just enough work in order to steal from the NGO.

That night, around the main fire, we held the first of many

conversations we would dub "Campfire University," where we'd hear what was really going on with the Pygmies and their masters. I would literally pretend to go to sleep in a hut so that the slave masters monitoring us would leave for the night. Then I'd get right back and return to the low-lit fire.

We'd whisper about all the atrocities and indecencies the slave masters didn't want us to know about, while lookouts kept watch. In addition to hearing more testimonials of exploitation and abuse from the hands of their masters, we heard tales of the Pygmies being victims of cannibalism by encroaching rebels. We'd later hear a rumor that a rebel group was using Pygmy skulls as mugs. Could you imagine being part of a people group that is hunted down, cooked, and eaten? It was bone-chilling stuff to think about.

Sleeping in a Pygmy hut the next night, I heard chatter outside and then yelling coming at a frantic pace. I crawled out of my hut to see what the commotion was, not knowing a snake was moving only a few feet away from me. I walked over toward the gathering huddle and a Pygmy man shoved me back with his arm firmly against my belly. I looked down and saw the snake, its head still wiggling around after taking a maiming whack on its hindquarter with a big stick. It was gray with a white belly, but it had an entirely black mouth with a tongue and teeth the shade of midnight.

I wasn't told it was a black mamba—one of the most poisonous, fastest, and most aggressive snakes in world—until the next day. Had I gone a few feet to my right exiting my hut, this could have been an entirely different story.

We hiked through the jungle for hours at a time to get to the remote villages, which gave Shane and I lots of time to talk to Ben and Jack. We talked about the trivial—the Congolese didn't have such a thing as honeymoons—and the historical, as Ben would stop and point to an empty field that once flourished with five hundred Pygmies. Hopping over and ducking under trees, Ben and I started talking about the women we thought God wanted us to marry. Ben would go on and on about his Elnise, while I gushed about my Emily, whom I'd been dating for ten months. When we'd come across something notable on our hikes, I'd record a video on my iPhone. Ben and Jack always addressed the camera as Emily. We had a funny conversation about microwaves, an invention neither Ben nor Jack had ever heard of.

"You know, when you store your food for a couple of days and want to make it hot again, you put it in the microwave, turn it on, and it zaps the food," I explained.

"What does 'zap' mean?" asked Ben, followed by a why-would-we-be-making-our-food-cold, which then launched us into another conversation about refrigerators, which only the few wealthy ones in the Congo owned. It was uplifting to have these brotherly conversations with my siblings in the forest because the seventh village we visited didn't seem keen on hosting us.

This was one of the same tribes I'd visited on my first trip to the Congo a year earlier. I was embarrassed entering the village and cringed a little when I saw that some of them recognized me. I'd brought the crooked translators with me on our first visit and I was ashamed. Some of the Pygmies were happy to see me because they were friendly and forgiving. Others shook their heads and made no effort to welcome us.

I noticed right away that the women of the tribe seemed unhappy to see me. One woman had taken to drinking (a fermented concoction of corn and fruits) and began to get loud around me. She shook her finger at me and blurted out what I can only guess were obscenities. When I asked to explain myself, not even the chief could settle her down to listen to me.

I understood their hatred when the chief took me to the nine—yes, nine—infant graves they blamed on the hands of the translators I'd come there with a year before. In addition to my group, the translators had brought other foreigners to this same Pygmy tribe that sat closer to the main dirt road than most. One woman had visited the village and told them to sit tight; she promised to come back a month later with much-needed medicines. She didn't return and the sick had died waiting for her, among them the nine infants. So, when the Pygmies saw me, it sparked an instantaneous hatred.

We stayed with them for a few uncomfortable hours because the chief insisted. Shane was nice enough to find me this verse, so I could put things in perspective: "If you're not welcomed, not listened to, quietly withdraw. Don't make a scene. Shrug your shoulders and be on your way." (Mark 6:11 MSG) I wanted to respect the women's wishes. Although I pleaded for it, I couldn't expect them to forgive me on the spot. I was definitely guilty by association, and much of the Congolese culture says you're guilty until proven innocent. I wanted to come back someday and be welcomed. I'd just have to pray for an opportunity to redeem myself and clear my name. (I haven't made it back to this tribe yet. They left their spot, probably chased off the land by slave masters or the Congo conflict.) We were ushered off to the two final villages we'd visit. Both would define my second trip to the Congo.

In the eighth village, we backtracked to an area we'd already passed through but hadn't stayed at. I continued to find ways to put the Pygmies at ease. The Pygmies don't know their actual ages—they don't have ways of telling time, like calendars. And none of them owned mirrors, so the Pygmies had gone years, sometimes lifetimes, without seeing a reflection of themselves. When I flipped my camera's phone around, they could see their faces for the first time. Some of them shied away, others giggled, and some just stared in awe. It was funny to see some of the women primping themselves, just as any American woman would do. If they'd had makeup, they would have put it on.

At this camp, I heard a word being repeatedly whispered among the Pygmies that I hadn't heard before. When I sat down with the chief and Ben, I asked what it meant. The chief told me it was the name the Pygmies had given me—Eféosa, which means "The Man Who Loves Us."

The final village we visited was Andibo's. By holding his lifeless hand in mine, my life was forever changed. I walked deep into the forest, away from the tribe, and cried where no one but God could see and hear me.

Coming out of the forest, along the road in Komanda, I was quickly approached by a Congolese military officer in combat fatigues, complete with the beret. He had a machine gun resting on his chest.

"Where did you get that?" he asked in French. He reached for the wooden bow and arrows that my grandfather, Chief Jaloowah, had given me. "This is not yours. It belongs to the Pygmies." Instinctually, I kept hold of my gift while the officer gave it a tug, which tensed Ben and Jack.

"It was a gift," I said, patting my chest. The officer pulled over another official, who spoke broken English.

"Where did you buy this?" he asked. "Why would the Pygmies give away something that brings them food? You're lying!"

I tried to lighten the mood, but they didn't flinch when I said, "But I am a Pygmy" in Swahili. The two officers conferred, then told us we had to buy the bow and arrow back from them as a "traditional art tax." I'd already grown tired and frustrated with the blatant corruption that was everywhere in the Congo.

"No," I resisted. "Why would I buy it back from you? It's mine." Ben and Jack placed their arms on my shoulders.

"Let me see your papers," said the first officer. I pulled my identification papers out of my backpack. "These are only copies," he said as he reviewed them. "You must have the originals. You could have faked this document." The first man reached for the bow again and Ben and Jack nodded a signal for me to let it go.

Then my brothers intervened, explaining I was part of Shalom's surveying team doing on-field research. The officers scoffed at the idea that a mzungu would lower himself to actually live among the Pygmies.

"You must pay five thousand dollars for us not to arrest you for these false documents and theft," said the second man. It was let's-make-a-deal time.

I took my UFC Topps card out of my wallet. It had acted as my business card once on my first trip.

"Can we trade?" I asked. "I will give you my last card, and I'll show some of your military guys some wrestling moves. Maybe some Brazilian jiu-jitsu or choke holds? Some hand-to-hand combat so I can keep the bow?"

The first officer's whole demeanor changed. His hands dropped from their grip on his gun. The offer was acceptable. I showed some of the military guys some simple moves, like an arm drag and a guillotine choke. Then they let us go. It was way better than dishing out cash.

We arrived in Bunia on the evening before our departing flight to Uganda. Shane and I said our good-byes and headed to the small and shoddy airport for our seventeen hours of flight time back home. My plane ride was haunted by that same question over and over in my head. *If not me, who? If not me, who? If not me, WHO?* Finally, I decided. *Okay, God, I'm all in.*

CHAPTER 17

Gideon's Fleece

Two thousand emails. That couldn't be right. *I need a cup of coffee*, I moaned to myself, wiping at my morning eyes. But my eyes hadn't gotten it wrong. My email box had runneth over, overnight.

A quick scan of the subject lines told me that a charming ninety-second video clip I'd filmed with a group of Congolese little ones was getting some traction. Someone had pulled it off of You-Tube and posted it the day before on Reddit.com, a social media site, and the video went viral overnight. Unfortunately, this divine intervention that changed it all for Fight for the Forgotten wouldn't happen for another six months. In those six months, my attempts to get people to take an interest in the Pygmies would rock my faith's foundation and eventually fortify it.

I returned from my second Congo trip, exhausted and heartbroken, and found myself in the Dallas airport again. Andibo was still fresh on my mind.

While getting a bite to eat in the airport food court, I noticed a mother and her teenage daughter at the soda machine. They were both wearing shirts from their church for a mission trip to Haiti they were just about to leave for. What happened next left me both dumbfounded and utterly speechless, which was probably best. I watched them fight and argue over a Coke . . . Yes, Coca-Cola! The daughter wanted one before the trip; her mother wouldn't let her.

"I want a Coke before I get to Haiti, where there isn't any!" the daughter exclaimed. Their bantering escalated to the daughter being grounded upon their return to the States. Soon they were in a public, bitter quarrel that ended with the daughter yelling, "I hate you!" and storming off down the terminal.

I wanted to sit them both down and ask, "What are you doing? You're fighting over a lousy Coke?" I wanted to show them the pictures of the Pygmy slaves and Andibo's grave and tell them they both have bigger things to worry about than Coke, like respecting and loving each other. I doubted the women knew what they'd be getting themselves into in Haiti.

In America, we're very privileged and blessed, but I saw how much we take for granted. I felt trapped between two very different worlds: one where all you do is struggle to live and the other where every comfort you can think of is at your fingertips. Trust me, most of the struggles we think we have aren't really struggles at all.

I didn't have an answer for dealing with coming back this second time. At first, I had to stay close to God and not let people's behavior get under my skin. I just gave them the same grace that He gives me each day, even though I don't really deserve it.

Once I was home and settled in, I immediately uploaded my cell phone videos onto the Internet, including my team's argument with the Mokpala slave master as I stood over Andibo's freshly dug grave. I left videos on the MMA message boards and other social network sites, hoping someone of means and influence would jump in to help. I tried to come up with other ways to tell people about my family. Most of the feedback went something like this: "Never heard of them" or "You're crazy" or "Good luck with that." *Man, nobody knows them*, I thought. *Forgotten was an understatement.*

Honestly, I didn't have a real game plan. Starting an organization was a thing very far from my mind, as I'd feared I'd have to spend my time as a high-pressure salesman for donations. Instead of pouring my efforts into raising the funds that Shalom needed to ignite its plan, I started taking courses at the King's University at Gateway Church in Southlake, Texas. I wanted to deepen my relationship with God and my knowledge about the Bible. I also hoped to improve on my public speaking, and despite my religious scars from my childhood, I explored the idea of becoming a pastor. I told myself that Bible college was the answer for me in helping the Pygmies. God would show me how to help these people beyond sharing the Bible. How, I wasn't quite sure.

I enjoyed Bible college and everything it taught me, but I had a hard time keeping my eyes on the blackboard. While the lecturer spoke, I'd be researching for eco-domes to build in the jungle behind my laptop. I drafted a seventy-slide PowerPoint presentation about the Pygmies and discovered mouth-dropping statistics and learned about the Congo's greedy, inhumane past. I began putting this all together in an information booklet to show others. These were the blueprints for Fight for the Forgotten.

As I researched more and more about the atrocities the Pygmies endured, my sense of urgency increased. Bible college would take four years and I could feel that God wanted me back in the Congo much, much sooner than that. I had to find a way to love the Pygmies in a faster, more practical way. Against some of my teachers' recommendations, I left King's University that December, only one semester into the program.

It was a delicate time for me trying to acclimate back to my American ways after the atrocities I'd seen in the Congo. I hadn't really opened up to anyone about my second Congo trip until I got an email from Way days later. Mo, one of the little ones in Andibo's tribe, had just died from a waterborne illness. I'd spent ten days in Mo's village, carried her on my shoulders, and held her in my lap while she slept. Mo hadn't even made it to her fifth birthday. If she'd had clean water, this wouldn't have happened. It had started with Andibo and now a little girl had been taken. I was sitting and sipping coffee with Emily in a Barnes & Noble café when I got this news and all of these emotions came flooding back. It was the first time Emily had ever seen me cry.

I spoke openly to Emily about Andibo and the incredible impact he had on me. We started going through the pictures I'd taken of the trip on my cell phone. She was especially drawn to the picture of Namboli, the Pygmy woman who was forced to carry 120 pounds of charcoal on her back. The bushel had been tied around her forehead, and the woman balanced the load by leaning her upper torso about sixty degrees forward at an awkward and painful angle. A thin, leaf pillow had been placed between her forehead and the bundle tie to help prevent rubbing and bleeding.

I don't know if on my best day as a fighter I could tie a rope around my head, stack 120 pounds of jagged-edged charcoal on my back—digging into the back of my head, neck, spine, and shoulders—and hike well over an hour straight, wobbling under branches and scaling the slippery hills of the wild jungle.

Emily took my phone and gazed at the picture pensively for a moment. "Oh my goodness, that's terrible," she said. "This is God's daughter. She is my sister. I can't believe this is happening to her. I finally understand why you feel so strongly about these people."

I'd mostly told Emily the good things about the Pygmies, and I'd never opened up about my personal experiences with their hardships and how it ripped me up inside. I think I'd been trying to appear strong around her. Right then, she saw how real it was to me. And she saw the hope in my eyes that we could at least try something to make it better for them.

"How would we ever help them all?" my sweet Emily asked.

I winged my answer. "I don't know if we ever could, but even if we could just help Namboli, wouldn't it be worth it? If Shalom and we could make sure she had an option out—think how great that would be."

This was the first time I broached my intentions with Emily to return to the Congo a third time. I'd only told her that I'd been thinking about it.

"I don't know what God's asking me to do," I said. "Maybe he's asking me to go back for the rest of my life."

I'd been dating Emily for fourteen months and was deeply in love with her. I had already left her once for the place that author Joseph Conrad notoriously dubbed the "Heart of Darkness." As we drove home, Emily and I continued to talk, and she finally told me she didn't like the idea at all.

"Do you think I'm going to be your wife?" she asked. "What if something happens to you and you don't come back? What if you don't want to come back?" It was a subject that tested our relationship for many months to come.

By February, I felt alone in my crusade to be a voice for the Pygmies. I fretted over it with Emily. What did God want me to do? The Pygmies felt like my calling, but nothing had come from my efforts thus far. Still, I couldn't shake the Congo's beckoning, so I prayed on it.

God, if this isn't You, take this burden off of me, take this desire away from me to go back to the Congo. Show me something. If it isn't You, please make it fail. Please, Father. If it's You, show me, because if it's You, there's not a person in this world who can stop me.

That prayer was my first "Gideon's fleece." For those unfamiliar with the parable, Judges 6:36–40 tells the story of Gideon, whose name means "Mighty Warrior," by the way. He was once a terrified coward, hiding and trembling, when the Angel of the Lord appeared and told him he was to lead his army into war against an army ten times greater than his. The Angel continued to encourage the Mighty Warrior, but he was petrified.

Gideon asked, "God, if this is You, I really need to know." He took a fleece and laid it out and said, "When the morning dew comes, let the blanket be wet and the ground around it stay dry. Then I'll know it's You."

The next morning, Gideon woke up and the blanket was soaking wet, while the ground surrounding it was dry. Gideon wondered if it was just chance, so he asked God again, this time to keep the blanket dry, while everything around it became wet. It happened again as he asked, and that's how Gideon knew to go into battle. I'm sure, to his amazement, his army won, and gave God praise.

It took only three days for me to get the answer to my first fleece and, again, God showed up in a big way. That's the morning I woke up to the two thousand emails about the short clip I'd shot of some Congolese children meeting me—the first white man they'd ever seen—in their Mokpala village. I think it was their innocent smiles and giggling that drew people in. Or maybe it was the gentle, curious way the kiddos touched my blond hair with wonderment and joy, like a child petting a new puppy on Christmas morning.

On Reddit, the video caught the eye of a producer for *Jimmy Kimmel Live!* and the clip aired that night on Kimmel's late-night talk show. Kimmel also mentioned my name and the UFC, which allowed people to find and contact me. The *Today* show aired it that next morning as its "buzz clip" of the day. On those two appearances alone, the emails started pouring in. There were so many that Emily began sorting through them with me. Many of them were well-wishers and people offering to donate money or help in some other way. Quite a few came from the media and within hours I was booked for TMZ's popular TV show, Dallas–Fort Worth's NBC news, and a *Sports Illustrated* interview, among other appearances. TMZ host Harvey Levin decided to give our live interview prime real estate on the show, after America's beloved Honey Boo Boo and before some bursting Lindsay Lohan scandal. Deadspin.com, Gawker.com, and BuzzFeed.com also ran the video. A deluge of attention began that would keep rolling for three months. In that time, I appeared on TV news stories as far-reaching as Japan, Norway, and Brazil. The YouTube video itself had a million views in the first three days.

Despite this avalanche of support, I felt I still needed more proof that the Pygmies were my destiny. Like Gideon, I needed to lay out my second fleece. I'd already calculated that I'd need $50,000 to jump-start Shalom's project. On pure adrenaline, I launched a Fight for the Forgotten page on a crowd-sourcing site at four in the morning. I already had the name locked and an overabundance of Pygmy info to share, which allowed me to create the Indiegogo crowd-funding page so quickly. I'd been gathering information for six months, not knowing what He'd do with it. Now it was crystal clear.

I laid out my second fleece. *God, if this is You*, I prayed, *this site will collect the money I need to return to the Congo and implement the Shalom University and Fight for the Forgotten plan.*

When people asked me why I needed $50,000, I told them that this was my fleece. I was throwing it out there, and if it happened, then I'd know it was God and I could go bigger from there when we needed to. But there had to be a starting point.

Over the next few months, I did every single interview I was asked to do, no matter how big or small. Each one directed traffic to the crowd-funding page. I was flown to Las Vegas, Los Angeles, and New York to meet with potential supporters and documentary filmmakers. I was simply overwhelmed by the number of responses I got. I received an email from a doctor who wanted to donate medicine and volunteer his time in the Congo. I even received confidential emails from some serious Navy Seals who wanted to offer me protection on my next trip, knowing we could run into opposition from the dangerous rebel groups as we tried to implement social change. People came out of the woodwork, in a good way, and some surprising things happened that I could have never dreamed of.

It had been two years since I'd jilted one of my best friends, Justin McCorkle, and no-showed his wedding. We'd had virtually no contact since, but Justin called out of the blue and invited me to Oklahoma City to meet with him and his family. Luckily, Justin's wife had kept tabs on me, and seeing the new leaf I'd turned and believing my life change was authentic, she'd encouraged her husband to reach out to me.

I spent the entire day with Justin. I desired, needed, and asked for his forgiveness over lunch. He told me he'd wrestled with what had happened for a couple of years and that there'd been a dark cloud over his wedding and our entire trusted friendship. He regretted that I hadn't been there in person to see him marry. My regret was equally as great, or greater. I had let down and deeply wounded one of the best people I had ever known.

At Justin's house, I met his family, including his darling wife and three kids, and I got to see him as both a husband and father for the first time. We played board games and spent the rest of the night laughing and mending. I felt forgiven and relieved leaving Justin's house. A wound from my past that I'd feared might never close began to heal.

The video was a real blessing to me, and don't think that I miss its irony. Even though I had developed a vinegar-like bitterness in my heart for the parents of these Mokpala children, you can't see that in the video at all. I'd just buried an innocent child and crawled out of the jungle. I wanted nothing to do with the Mok-pala, but here were these smiling kids coming right up to me. They didn't know hatred or discrimination. They held my hands and I let them climb on me like a jungle gym. It instantly softened and humbled me. It wasn't video of a starving Pygmy child that caught people's attention; it was this video of pure, unexpected love from the people group who oppressed them that lit the fuse.

I decided to really test out this second fleece; I chose the "all or nothing" course of crowd-funding. If we met our goal, they would issue the money to the FFTF nonprofit account. If we failed to reach 100 percent of our goal, the entire sum of money went back to the accounts of the original contributors. In the first thirty days, 764 people contributed $53,596 to Fight for the Forgotten. Justin McCorkle had made the final donation that tipped us past $50,000. Life Outreach, a Christian ministry focused on international aid, generously donated another $12,000 after the fact. With this money, Shalom and I estimated we could legally purchase three hundred acres of land, drill multiple wells for clean drinking water, and hopefully and prayerfully see one thousand Pygmy slaves begin to transition into a life of freedom. From there, we hoped to start a farming program that would sustain their newly found freedom and way of life. Then we wanted to introduce alternative housing that could withstand the rainforest's worst.

From December, when I'd told Emily that I planned to return to the Congo for a year, she'd run the range of emotions. At times she was supportive and excited to see the traction. Other times she was angry, confused, and frustrated with me. She was angry with God. She couldn't figure out where her place was in all of it. Emily tried to hide it well, but it would come bubbling to the surface. She hated the fact that I was going to leave her and didn't feel like anyone understood or could relate to what she was going through.

When people heard of my plans, they'd approach Emily and say, "It's awesome what Justin is going to do. Aren't you happy for him? It will be so good for your relationship." At church, people would congratulate me on my efforts, and Emily would cry on the way home. She was torn because she wanted to be supportive of what I was doing—it was a good thing and a God thing. However, she still struggled with the idea of me being away from her and feeling guilty for feeling the way she did.

Once the money was secured and my trip was a 100 percent go, I became a high school kid cramming for his SATs. I had about three months to prepare for the trip, so I started researching water-well drilling and crop farming. In August, I attended a one-week Cal-Earth program in Hesperia, California. Founded by Iranian-American architect Nader Khalili, Cal-Earth teaches students how to use available natural materials—in this case, the earth below your feet—to create durable dwellings. Of special interest to me, Khalili had created an architectural plan for "Super-adobe homes" (often referred to as "Eco-domes" or "Earthbag homes") using rolls of sandbags, barbed wire, and earth. The models I saw looked a lot like the domes the Pygmies built in the jungle, which was important to me. When I'd asked the Pygmies what type of housing they'd wish for, they wanted to keep their dome framing as a part of their culture.

During all this madness, I found the right time to propose to Emily in the mountains of Denver. We'd wait till I got back to marry, and everybody joked that I'd found the most inventive way to dodge a wedding yet.

The most important piece to my Congo puzzle came twelve days before I left. That's the day I reached out to Water4.org. Not knowing anything about water wells or anyone else who knew anything about them, I'd tried to find a tutorial online that I could

make work in the Congo. I literally went to DrillYourOwnWell
.com, printed out a picture, and handed it to the guys at Lowe's.

"I need all these pieces," I said. "This is what it looks like."

I started putting the wobbly model together in my backyard.
The system relied on a jetting method with two garden hoses and
needed water fed into it to work. My mentor, Jeff Duncan, was the
first to point out my glaring error.

"Where are you going to get all the running water to get the
jetting to run?" he asked. I thought about the rivers closest to the
Pygmy camps and spent the next few days trying to figure it out.

A few days later, Jeff called me to check on my progress while
he was sitting on the couch of Marvin and Mary Sue Beard, a
friendly elderly couple in their eighties from Oklahoma City.

"What were you talking about, Jeff?" asked Mary Sue, after
he hung up.

"My friend's trying to dig water wells in Africa. He leaves in
two weeks and he doesn't have the right tools and he doesn't have
the right training. So, please keep him in your—"

"Hold on real quick," Mary Sue interrupted. She went into another room and came back with a newspaper clipping, which she
handed to Jeff. "I didn't know why, but I saw this and just felt I had
to cut it out and save it for something."

The clipping was an ad for Water4.org, a nonprofit that sent
crews to construct water wells for in-need communities around
the world. I went to their site and watched their demo video. *Now
THAT is going to work*, I thought. I looked at my plastic contraption and thought I could just snap it in half right there. But
Water4 was the real deal. I emailed them right away and that's how
I connected with Steve Stewart, the cofounder and inventor of the
Water4 method, and eventually met Matt Hangen, Water4's director of implementation. The first response I got was from Steve.

"If you can get up here to Oklahoma City, we'll train you," he said. Two days later, Jeff and I went up there. I had goose bumps entering the office, and have every time since.

Jeff and I sat in Steve's office and we shared our testimonies of how we each got to those three chairs. The anticipation among us mounted as we began to realize that God was doing something big here. Jeff and I had already watched the training video series on numerous occasions and Steve took us through a long training session. Together, we dug our first hole. It went maybe ten feet down. Steve was eager to teach me, but one day of official training couldn't make me a well driller.

Three days before I left for the Congo I drove back up to the Water4 headquarters in OKC. I met Matt, who had just come back from Africa the day before. Matt and his wife, Grace, had tremendous experience and success training numerous drilling teams throughout Africa. Their goal was to train teams within the local communities so they could function on their own. Using this method, they'd completed hundreds of water wells and provided more than thirty locals with beneficial jobs. Meeting Matt was so encouraging. He had a bushy beard, just like mine, and was a straight shooter. At one point, he pulled me aside and said, "I don't know if this will work. You haven't had enough training. You know a ten-foot hole is a lot different than a fifty-, one-hundred-, and one-hundred-fifty-foot hole, right? There are a lot of obstacles you can't see as you navigate deep down. You haven't had enough training and you're going to start a team?" All we both could do was laugh and pray.

Matt offered to train me some more if and when I returned to Oklahoma City. Seeing the promise in the locals at Shalom, they very generously donated $15,000 in tools and equipment, including eighteen new water pumps to more than cover FFTF's audacious goal of twelve working water wells in our first year.

The night before my departure, we had a dinner with forty close friends and family. A small group of people showed up to the airport the next day with signs to see me off. I've never felt that much encouragement all at once. It took three cars to get the equipment to the airport. I checked in thirteen tough black canvas bags, each carefully measuring out to forty-nine to fifty pounds each, with enough mechanical parts to build my own Transformer. For myself, I packed a hammock that rolled up into the size of a fist, a blow-up mattress less than two inches thick, a tent, five shirts, five pairs of pants, and twelve pairs of socks and underwear. Jeff completely surprised us by calling United Airlines ahead of time and getting clearance for my mom, my dad, Emily, and him to follow me through security to my gate.

My mom had just taken up guns and had a license, but wasn't thinking about that when she went through security. She'd left a ten-bullet magazine clip in her purse and TSA pounced on her.

"It's not a gun! It's not a gun!" she explained. "It's a magazine. I forgot it was in my purse." They took the magazine and the whole situation became a bit of comic relief.

Everyone took turns saying their good-byes. My mom told me I could come back sooner, if I wanted. Emily was tearing up at the gate. She handed me a journal she'd written, full of inspirational quotes, scriptures, and sweet letters to me. I wore my future wedding band around my neck after she surprised me with it the previous night. I held tough and gave her a hug. I wouldn't see her for a year.

"Come back and let's get married," she said through her soft tears. As the plane took off, I couldn't fight back tears of my own, but I thought if I didn't do this, I'd forever question myself. I had a choice and I didn't have to do this, but I felt like God was lovingly asking me to embark on a wild adventure of trusting Him. If I didn't go, I'd never know what could have happened.

PART III

CHAPTER 18

Malaria

Am I dying? I asked myself while the doctors argued with one another as if I weren't in the room at all. I was bedridden in my Shalom dorm room only three weeks into my yearlong trip. Was it malaria? No one could seem to agree.

How did I get here? That's actually a long story for only three weeks' time. I remembered landing on Halloween at Uganda's Entebbe International Airport. Tom Cox, a Water4 representative who lived in the capital city, Kampala, about forty minutes away, was waiting for me with Patrick from Shalom University. Tom was tall like me, with brown hair and a salt-and-pepper beard. He and Patrick helped me load my fifteen bags into Tom's truck and we were off to his house.

OCTOBER 31

Made it safe to Uganda! I boarded a midday flight from Dallas to Chicago (two hours), Chicago to Qatar (over thirteen hours with a four-hour layover), then Qatar to Entebbe, Uganda (five hours), where I'll stay a few days before heading into the Congo. I checked in thirteen bags and carried on two, and I think we'll need a bunch more with enough PVC and steel pipes to drill eight water wells! That's so many twenty-foot-long pipes! Despite the heavy lifting, I'm smitten by God! I get to go on a yearlong, WILD adventure into the jungle with my Dad, our Heavenly Father, learning to become Eféosa. Prayers please that driving through Uganda, around Lake Albert, and across the Congo border with so much gear goes smoothly.

KAMPALA'S A CRAZY-BUSY, vibrant city. In comparison to the Congo's cities, Kampala, Uganda, is a well-developed one. Parts of it are pretty modern and almost make you forget you're in a third-world country. You can see new-release 3-D movies in theaters, visit nice malls that have Kentucky Fried Chicken restaurants with waiter service (it's funny to see what constitutes high cuisine in different countries), and eat gourmet frozen yogurt with fresh fruit on top. You see many Mercedes-Benzes and BMWs—usually government vehicles escorted by military trucks. It's a bustling city with paved roads—potholed, but paved. Thousands of boda-bodas (or motorbikes) zooming by. Really nice restaurants and hotels, even ones that charge $200 to $300 a night.

The bags I'd brought from the States contained augers, single- and triple-prong chisels, a rock breaker, chains, screwdrivers, winches, and wrenches. I also brought handles for our drilling stems, and connectors and connecting pins, designed by Water4, for elongating the drilling stems of square tubing that would go in the ground.

For the next week straight, Tom and I searched for our materials. We needed around fifteen twenty-foot-long pieces of square metal tubing, which are very heavy. We also had to find several PVC pipes in different lengths, widths, and thicknesses. We looked for six-inch casing pipe, another heavy item, to protect the hole we were drilling from collapsing in on us. We collected hundreds of pipes for the first crossing over the Congo border.

These were extremely difficult materials to find, but we scoured the city for days. A lot of it was piecemeal work. We found a couple of places that could handle the bigger piping orders. The smaller items, like couplings and connectors, needed to be bought in bulk, but in most cases that wasn't possible. We'd ended up going to ten different places to acquire fifty of the same item. Quality was paramount, as the Water4 wells were built to withstand repeated use and time. We found items that would work, but only for a couple of years, so we passed on them. We didn't want to compromise the water wells in any way. Without Tom, shopping would have been a near-impossible task that would have taken Patrick and me ten times longer to complete. Tom and I bonded trekking up and down Kampala's crazy streets.

Our extra items brought the grand total to twenty heavy-duty, extra-long, canvas duffel bags added to all the twenty-foot piping. We rented a transport truck to carry the pipes. Patrick, Tom, and I piled into his truck with the bags and set out for the seven-hour ride to the Congo border.

We made it to the Ugandan border town Paidha (pronounced "Pi-da"). We got out of Tom's truck with our bags and said our good-byes. He wished me luck and told me how difficult it was going to be to get this whole project started, but to not lose hope.

"Corruption is an everyday thing in Africa, especially with its officials, so be ready and prepared for it," he said. Tom asked me to call him when we arrived safely.

"From Paidha to Bunia, it should be six hours, at the most," I said. "It's about one hundred and twenty miles in five to six hours, *as long as the roads are good.*"

It took about two hours to get over the border. Patrick and I hired a beat-up taxi to follow the transport truck. It cost our transport truck $600 to get into the Congo and that was "non-mzungu" pricing. It's sad, but if I'd been in the truck, they would have tried to charge around $3,000.

We traveled ahead in our navy blue, four-door sedan taxi, which only had rear-wheel drive and a trunk that wouldn't close. Every bump we hit, the car would bottom out. It was physically painful to ride in it, and the whiplash was brutal.

We got to the top of a hill, and I noticed Patrick look behind us a couple of times. "We gotta go. We gotta go," he repeated quickly.

"Why?" I asked.

He pointed behind us. As usual, the mountains were beautiful, but there were these clouds rolling in behind them. They looked dark and foreboding, yet wicked and almost unreal at the same time. A storm was rolling in very fast and we could see the rain falling and chasing us up the top of the mountain and down into the Congo countryside. We started driving faster, but the rain caught up with us. It got so violent that we had to pull over and stop. The rain pelted and the car vibrated.

In a half hour, the rain stopped, and we sat there with our windshield wipers swooshing big streaks back and forth. The defroster was long gone, so we wiped the windshield with our T-shirts. Now that the rain had gone, the real fun was about to begin.

It took us twenty-five hours to get from Paidha to Bunia. Not six hours. Twenty-five. Looking at the stats, we pushed ourselves out of the mud twelve times; we changed tires twice, while the bottom back right tire kicked out and rolled lopsided; we hit about fifteen to twenty roadblocks, about half of them government; and got asked for money well over twenty times. The soldiers would salute us, then put their hands out like beggars as we went by, because I was a mzungu and when they saw a white guy, they saw money.

Patrick, who'd been promoted to Dean of the Faculty of Agriculture and Sciences in the year since I'd seen him, was as stubborn as I was to the corruption.

"It's not his job to pay you. He is our guest of the university. Your corruption really brings a bad name to the Congo," he told one official who stopped us. "We shouldn't have to pay you off at all."

So, Patrick and I chose not to pay any bribes, which made the trip longer. The officials or gangs of townsfolk would stand in front of the car and demand money, and suddenly we were in a standoff. Only the taxi driver would give in and pay—he wanted his monster fare at the end.

We got stuck, and we got stuck often. Four-tires-submerged stuck. We'd take ten thousand Congolese francs, about ten dollars in U.S. currency, and split it up among ten people to help push us out. Patrick said that one dollar could easily match a day's wage in the fields or gold mines.

We got behind a whole row of cars that were stuck in the mud. About forty of us in a line. We started doing the only thing we could: helping one another. We pushed each vehicle out individually till we were all out. Then we finally started cruising, sort of.

In every town or village we went through on the muddy road, I had to have been one of the first white guys the locals had ever seen. By then, I'd already been knee-deep in sludge. My face had been thoroughly sprayed with the reddish clay from rotating tires. I'd breathed in enough exhaust that it had given me a headache.

We drove past a school where the kids were tending the fields, and more than a hundred of them dropped their hoes and rakes and ran after our car. "Yay-sue," some of them yelled to the bearded white man. Patrick said he'd never seen anything like it.

About eighteen miles outside of Bunia, our car's battery died and it took a while to revive it. Once we got the car running, the car died again. The gas gauge was broken and the spinning tires must have used more fuel than the taxi driver anticipated. It didn't matter, though. The engine was toast and smoke was rising from the car's hood. We were going to have to stay the night on that roadside, which made Patrick very nervous.

"We want to get towed or walk and find some lodging," he said, looking around him. Our car had given out right beside a gold mine, and shiny stuff attracts trouble in the Congo. Any kind of mines attracted rebels, gangsters, and clans of thieves that hopped around the countryside and jungle. Broken-down cars were always a target.

It was around three A.M., and the air was crisper in the mountains. The three of us huddled in our beat-down eighties sedan stuck in the mud. Patrick shivered and our driver held his red-and-gold letterman's jacket tightly to his chest. We all drifted off—until the sound of an approaching car jerked us awake. For some reason, Patrick and I got out of the car. The pickup truck drove past with seven or eight guys in the back, most of them carrying beers. As they passed by, loud music blaring, they sounded "rough," to say the least. I almost went to wave when I saw them, then realized what I was doing. Patrick and I took a step back together, partially shielding ourselves with a tree. The car slowed for just a second, then sped away.

"Maybe they weren't supposed to stop," I said.

"Maybe *we* weren't meant to stop here, brother," Patrick responded.

We slept for about two more hours. When the sun began to rise, we found some guys to help us pull our car out. They tied a rotting rope to the front of the car and it snapped on the first try. They tied another rope and that snapped, too. It took a dozen tries before we realized we needed to braid a few of the ropes together to stand the weight of the car.

Once we were back on the road, it didn't take us long to meet up with Papa Way. We'd been expected the day earlier and Papa

Way had called me about thirty times since then. Papa Way ran right up to me, both of us trying not to slip in the mud, and gave me a big hug. He was dressed nice, too, in khaki pants, a dress shirt, and shoes, so when he peeled himself off me, his clothes were filthy.

"It was worth it," he said, laughing. "We know God has sent you here with a big plan and a great purpose. We can't wait to see what that is." We put all the bags of gear, the drill kit, and more equipment for the water wells in the back of his 4×4, and headed off to Shalom University in Bunia.

I arrived at the university on Saturday, a muddy mess. I took a long, cold shower, rinsing and lathering up three times and still not getting the bright red clay out of my skin. I fell into my dorm room bed and checked my phone to see if there was any signal to call Emily and let her know I was okay. I'd told her the trip would only be six to eight hours. I passed out trying to reach her and left my key in the door—that's how tired I was.

I woke up to my brother Ben entering my room four hours later. My phone was still in my hand. I cleared away my mosquito net and leapt up to hug him. Since graduation, Ben had been hired as the field project manager of the Development Faculty at Shalom. Ben was one of my closest friends in the Congo and his faith was so huge. In the year since I'd seen him, his fiancée, Elnise, had been poisoned, and had recovered from a coma, but had lost feeling in her left side. Ben was visiting her in the local hospital every day. Like me, he had a big heart for the Pygmies.

Ben took me to see "Mama Jack," who'd cooked and cared for us so well on our last trip. Jack had also been hired by Shalom after graduation and was now its youngest-ever Dean of the Faculty of Development, stepping in for Papa Way, as he'd been promoted. We stayed for lunch and dinner, and our time was full of catching up and laughter.

The next day, we hit the road running. Papa Way, Jack, Ben, Patrick, and I met to discuss our plan for the Pygmies. We were excited to get to the water-well drilling, as we knew that would directly save lives, but there was something we had to tackle first before we could get to that stage. We had to buy land.

I cannot emphasize how important this first phase of our plan was. What good would it be to build a water well on Pygmy land, only to have them chased off it when we left? It was decided first that the land would be bought in the name of the Pygmies, not in Shalom University's or Fight for the Forgotten's name. That would give the people group claim to the land as their own, should any issue arise.

Papa Way and Ben lobbied with the ten local governmental chiefs, the local slave master chiefs, and local Pygmy chiefs for many meetings over many months. Shalom, the mediator, pitched the idea that if the slave master allowed us to buy land for their Pygmy slaves and let them go free to live on it, a water well would be built on the slave master's land as well. Both people groups had frequent funerals for children due to waterborne disease. At these "town hall" meetings, which could have thirty to three hundred attendees, Papa Way would begin his presentation with: "Who were the first citizens of the Congo?" There was no argument that the Pygmies were the very first, which opened the door to a talk about land ownership. Shalom wanted to partner with both sides in community development. In the end, Way and Ben were able to facilitate the purchase of 2,470 acres of land for less than $40,000. This process lasted through to January, when some of the Pygmy tribes began to move onto their own land. While we waited on this process, I started sitting in on and even teaching a couple of classes at Shalom in appropriate technology and sustainable development as a new staff member.

NOVEMBER 16

I just came across a cute picture of little Mo on my iPhone, playing with my beard during my second trip to the Congo last year. I can't believe she's dead. All morning, I've been fighting back tears, my stomach twisted up in knots. I guess I'm just flabbergasted that children dying is such a normal part of life for my family here. Little Mo was another victim of waterborne disease, something SO simple to prevent back in America, but SO devastating and out of reach to fix here. I couldn't imagine growing up drinking filthy water, having worms, amoebas, and parasites living inside me, having stomach pains, hunger pangs, and constant diarrhea that leads to malnutrition.

Why is this still happening in today's age? On days like today, it makes the statistics come to life and I can't wrap my head around it. Every minute, a child dies of water-related disease, like Mo did, because they don't have clean water to drink and bathe in. How much time have I wasted when I could have been making a difference?

Sometimes I think about the culture of American Christianity and parts of it really bother me. I've spent too much time inside a church for my own needs and I've spent FAR too little time being THE church for someone else's. God doesn't ask us to confine ourselves to our Christian bubbles or holy huddles, and Jesus didn't show us how to be a comfy pew-warmer or a bunch of lazy pew-potatoes. God gave us LIFE, which is an adventure to be lived, a time to make a difference, and hopefully becomes a legacy of love to be left for others. Jesus died to show us how we should LOVE God and how we should LOVE others. Jesus showed us how to find life, live life, love life, and also how we could add to, contribute, change, save, or even lay our own lives down for the life of another. In times like these, I pray that I won't shrink back, tuck my tail, and run away from this conflict zone in the Congo for the comfort zone I'm used to. I pray the Holy Spirit will teach me through this time and remind me how Daniel had courage in the lion's den, how Paul could worship from the pits of a dungeon, and how young David stepped onto the battlefield against a giant. To me, God, this journey feels like my Goliath. I have faith in You, that You brought me to this battlefield, and my team is praying for victory over this giant. Lord, be with little Mo's family, please. Comfort them by wrapping Your arms around them in this time of need.

THE CITY OF Bunia, a mecca for peace-driven NGOs with a UN presence, drew lots of missionaries, humanitarians, and aid workers from all over the world. News spread among us very quickly, especially when someone got ill. I was alarmed when I got word from Frank, a Norwegian missionary, that he'd come down with typhoid fever. We'd eaten lunch and dinner together a few times and had been drinking the same juice. To not be impolite, I ate a salad, a well-known no-no in the third world. We'd gone to a local, traditional Congolese place, where they could have made the juice without boiled water. When I went to visit Frank, the doctors had put a port in him for multiple IVs. I hoped I wouldn't get sick.

The first thing I noticed was the throbbing joint pain in my fingers. It felt like the sore knuckles you get the day after a grizzly fight, but this aching spread to my finger joints, knuckles, and wrists. At least it wasn't in my shoulders. Frank had told me that if the pain traveled into my shoulders, neck, and back, then I had malaria. Suddenly, my elbows felt achy. It was a Friday.

On Saturday, I woke up feeling off, but I tried to push through it. I didn't have a fever, just body aches. I seemed to be sweating a lot as well. We heard that some other missionaries had gotten some kind of a virus, and chalking it up to that, I spent the rest of the day in bed.

On Sunday, I slept completely through my alarm for church. I knew I had a fever, as my bed was soaked in sweat. I bounced from hot to cold sweats all of Sunday until the guys thought it best I head to the clinic. The Bunia clinic had four rooms all packed into a one-room building with a small reception area teeming with sick children and the elderly. The doctor weighed me: 286 pounds. He pricked my finger and let a couple of drops of my blood drip into a cartridge that worked like a pregnancy stick for malaria. It would only tell me yes or no.

While we waited for the results, a nine-year-old girl ran by and bumped the table and my quick test slid across it, but the nurse caught it before it fell to the ground. I'd been told that it took about five to ten minutes to get the malaria test results, but my answer came back in about a minute. "No." The nurse told me to sleep and I should be better the next day. I wondered if the bump could have messed with the results, but I left that up to the professionals.

That night, I couldn't sleep. I tossed and turned and sweated and shivered. It was uncontrollable. In fighting, I'd always been the only one to get in the ice bath without my teeth chattering. I could control my body from shivering. This I couldn't stop. It wasn't just in my teeth or hands; my entire body was shaking. I put on extra blankets. I threw them off later. I took a fever reducer and tried to get my mind off the shaking.

I woke up on Monday and Way, Ben, Jack, and Patrick were

standing over me in my dorm room. I told my team that I felt worse—way worse—and they prayed over me. They brought in a nurse, and from my symptoms alone, she could tell I had malaria. At this point, there was no doubt I was sick, but with the contagious virus that the other missionaries had circulating, they didn't really want me coming back into the hospital and making others sick. Throughout the day, I became extremely nauseous and started vomiting. By now, my Congolese guys knew—they'd all battled malaria many times. My temperature skyrocketed to 103.5 degrees Fahrenheit. I'd eaten two bites of a banana the whole weekend. My team would bring me three meals a day and I'd tell them I couldn't eat. I love my food, but every bite was like a chore. My body was telling me no. I was given a second quick test and got a second negative result for malaria.

On Tuesday, my team brought Dr. Jean to my room, who drew blood and started a port in my arm for multiple IVs. He started giving me a medicine called quinine, which fights and kills the malaria parasites in the blood. An hour later, I started vomiting violently.

To all of our surprise, the blood test results were negative for malaria, but I did have low-grade typhoid fever. Dr. Jean started treating the typhoid very aggressively. My guys insisted I had malaria, but Dr. Jean kept pointing to three failed tests that showed otherwise. Dr. Jean did, however, keep me on the malaria medication just in case, though I vomited brutally every time they gave it to me.

I couldn't keep anything down. My body felt like it was on fire; I was profusely sweating and was so, so thirsty. But I just vomited up any water I drank. The waves of hot and cold continued. The shivering and sweating continued. My temperature dropped from 104 to 95 degrees.

That night, I needed 24-7 care—I was that sick. When the nurses went to change my IVs, the power went out. The hydroelectric dam in Bunia had failed, which was a normal happening. My team stood around me with their cell phone lights. A doctor was holding a flashlight in one hand, trying to stick a needle in me with the other, and he wasn't very steady. I had already been told my veins were hard to find because I was so dehydrated. He finally figured out that he should put his flashlight in his mouth. The nurse, her son, Ben, and Patrick laid mattresses on the ground and slept there that night.

I woke up Wednesday to full medical care. They drew my blood and gave me my fourth malaria test, which came back negative. There were three different doctors rotating in on me, none of them in agreement on just what I had. One doctor told me to get the malaria out of my head. "It's only making you sicker." Each of them gave me different dosages of quinine, or none at all. I guess there was a discrepancy because I was twice the size of a Congolese man, so maybe I needed a double dosage. Anything and everything they gave me, I vomited back up.

You think I'd have been in a panic by now, but I wasn't afraid. I had peace. It's strange, but whenever you're somewhere you know God has sent you, you also know that really, really great things are about to happen. I knew there'd be obstacles and hurdles. Big things trying to stop me from what I was supposed to do. But the hurdles didn't matter—the victory is always worth it.

When I suddenly discovered I had dysentery as well, I realized I was battling three of the top sicknesses that killed the Pygmies, all at once. I realized it was another opportunity to connect with my family. This is what I'd come for. I came to learn, not with my mind and statistics, but with my heart, mind, body, and soul. I had to learn what they went through by going through it myself.

Papa Way came by Wednesday evening very distressed.

"I can't have your blood on my hands. I won't allow that to happen," he said. "I won't allow you to get sicker. I won't let you die out here. This would be my fault because I'm looking over you."

At this point, I was throwing up blood and bile. My mouth tasted like a rusty bucket of pennies. The smell was almost as sour as the taste. It got so bad, I could hardly swallow. Tears started streaming because my throat was so raw.

My team came to me and said there was spiritual blindness going on. In the spiritual world, there's good vs. evil, angels and demons, light and darkness. They felt that darkness had come over this situation to try and stop me from doing any of the good that God had brought me here to do. They believed the enemy of God was trying to kill me, that he was blinding everybody.

On Wednesday night, the room started spinning. I felt like a ship rocking on stormy ocean waves. I started to have a bad feeling. These doctors were going to kill me because there was no unity among the three of them. They all agreed I had some degree of typhoid, they had different beliefs about malaria, and all three disagreed on how to treat me. When each was in charge, they treated me differently. I pulled Way aside and said we had to get these doctors together. We had to come up with a new plan, one that didn't include treating me three different ways at once.

Am I dying? I asked myself again, because if I was, it was time to do something about it.

CHAPTER 19

The Beast

I hadn't eaten in four days. I hadn't urinated. I was completely dehydrated. I continued vomiting blood and bile. My head and hearing were buzzing like I had a beehive between my ears. And still, my team of doctors couldn't agree on a correct course of treatment. When Papa Way came by Thursday morning to check on me, I told him that we needed to look for new doctors as soon as possible.

"Let me see what I can do," he said in his calming voice, and then he was gone.

He came back an hour later and told me to pack my bags. I was leaving by plane for Uganda in an hour. It turns out that Way had a nephew working with the local Mission Aviation Fellowship, a group of Christian mission pilots who were willing to fly to the tough-to-reach places. Way had worked with the MAF himself for years and found a few ears that would listen to him about my story. It was Thanksgiving, so all the pilots were technically "off" for the holiday to spend it with their families. Jonathan, the only single pilot there, agreed to take me to Uganda on a moment's notice, which literally saved my life.

With only minutes to gather my things and get to the airport, I grabbed the bare essentials: my phone, laptop, chargers, three changes of clothes, and all the money I had on me. The airport was ominously empty; we might have been the only flight to leave that day. I handed my passport to the security post, got it stamped, and walked out onto the tarmac clutching a bucket I wouldn't let go of for the entire one-hour-and-forty-five-minute flight. There were only four seats in the plane, including the pilot and copilot, and a storm had just passed, so there was turbulence. I stared out the window the entire trip. I closed my eyes, hugging my puke bucket, trying to hold down the bloody bile that wanted to come up. My head throbbed as we made our descent. And then we were finally on the ground again.

An ambulance pulled right up to the plane door. Through Papa Way, Tom Cox had organized my transport to the hospital and my care on this end. As I lay down on the gurney in the back of the ambulance, my vision blurring and my peripheral vision tunneling, it dawned on me that I was really, really sick. Our ambulance sped and swerved through the Uganda traffic and at times came to a screeching halt, which wasn't good for my nausea. When we got to the hospital, the medical crew had a proper lab set up to test my blood. They immediately started me on an IV of quinine— they doubted I'd gotten the real thing in the Congo and wanted to check. I threw up the first treatment and was promptly switched to something else because I was allergic.

The Emmanuel Medical Centre in Entebbe, Uganda, was comparable to a tiny U.S. hospital: white walls, sterile rooms, and real toilets instead of latrines. I rested in a strong hospital bed with a mattress.

The test results came back and I was diagnosed with level-three malaria. I was on the borderline of level four. Four was the most severe grade, I was told, as a majority of those victims fell into comas or died. According to their tests, sixty-five to seventy percent of my bloodstream had filled with parasites. Another day and I would have gone comatose, the doctor on staff told me. The doctors started treating me accordingly. Tom had experienced malaria as well, so he called a friend who was a specialist and an American doctor living in Uganda, who recommended another malaria-fighting medication that was much better and that my body wouldn't reject. It took them six tries to start the new IV, as my veins had all but collapsed. By the time the doctors were done with me, I must have taken ten IV bags of fluid for hydration, but if my new physicians hadn't handled me the way they did, if I hadn't left the Congo when I did, I'm pretty sure I would have died.

When I finally urinated the next day (for the first time in five full days), I couldn't believe it. I'd peed out a pot of coffee, a sign of blackwater fever, another deadly stage of malaria that can lead to renal failure. Malaria sets up base camp in the liver and is constantly multiplying an army of parasites. These legions of parasites launch out in platoons to attack and kill your red blood cells, so my organs and white blood cells were working overtime, especially with the addition of typhoid fever and dysentery. It took me a few more days to tolerate the smell of food; I'd gone from 286 pounds to 253 in a week. I lost thirty-three pounds from vomiting, diarrhea, not being able to eat at all, and only being able to sip a few capfuls of water. I wouldn't suggest the malaria diet to anyone.

I stayed at Emmanuel (which means "God Is with Us," by the way) for two nights, and I left during the third day (costing me an incredibly inexpensive $150 out of pocket). For the private prop plane, the ambulance, and treatment it was less than a thousand dollars to save my life, but still, it's an inconceivable amount of money for the vast majority of the Congolese, and an impossibility for my Pygmy family.

Tom took me back to his house for recovery. I could move around once I left the hospital, but I was drained for weeks. I'd only have enough energy for a few hours a day before I'd have to rest. I occupied my time watching bad African telenovelas (soap operas) and Skyping with my EmmyBear. I was also waiting on paperwork from Kinshasa, the capital of the Congo, which is on the other side of the country. It took weeks to finally get the paperwork.

When I was well enough, we drove in Tom's Land Cruiser to eastern Uganda, a spot not too far from the Kenyan border. We crossed the Nile River to get there, observing the crocodiles and hippos. This part of the land looked like something out of *The Lion King*; elephants and giraffes spattered and grazed the countryside along the dirt road we followed.

What's really smart about Water4 is that they're adept at pinpointing places of real need. I've seen other NGOs build a well right next to another to make meeting quotas easier; I've also seen them place them in unsafe locations near fuel pumps, trash dumps, and pit latrines only ten to thirty meters away, an impossible place to prove the water is safe for consumption. Water4 targeted the hard-to-reach places, where the communities wanted to work with them.

During the tour, I got to see two wells in various stages of their building process, both strategically built near a church, a school, mosque, or other type of meeting place where people congregate. Water4 had just completed six wells in that area of rural villages, and word was spreading among the neighboring villages. I saw how thankful the people were. I'd ask them what life was like before they had clean, obtainable water close by and they'd slouch over and grab their backs, especially the women. The women were the ones who walked, sometimes more than four miles round-trip, to fill their twenty-liter jerry cans with suspect water and haul the forty-four pounds back to their families. They might make more than one trip a day, or carry two at a time; maybe two members of the family would have to go together. I'd carried one with the women one day and I can tell you it is the definition of backbreaking, spine-crunching work.

I saw countrymen helping countrymen in Uganda. This couldn't have been more pronounced than with the Young Men Drillers, a group of Ugandans who started their own well-drilling company. Many of the drillers had been child soldiers in the Lord's Resistance Army with Joseph Kony, or had their families killed by the LRA. The Young Men Drillers, many with inspiring stories of survival, had members from both sides of the conflict standing side by side for the common good.

Finally, I got to see the water wells in action, see that this system worked, and taste clean, fresh water that comes out of the earth, cold and crisp. (I clung to this memory in the harder times to come.) I knew we could do the same thing in the Congo and we could do it the way we wanted to. We wanted to live among the Pygmies as we drilled, our huts alongside theirs. Most NGOs wouldn't stay with the people they helped. They'd stay in a nice hotel that was two, three, four hours away and trek back and forth each day. Seeing these Ugandan drillers roughing it with their countrymen was just the confirmation I needed to know that we could rough it, too.

Illness brought me back to Uganda, but I knew I'd been brought back for many reasons. Watching the Ugandan team at work, a lightbulb clicked on. We needed a truck, not any ordinary truck, but one that could carry our team and a boatload of equipment all at once. I saw how hard it was for the Ugandan team to go without its own truck. They were paying a minimum of $300 to $350 on rental trucks each time they brought equipment to another well site. And once they were out there, they were stranded. What if they forgot a tool?

In the Congo, we were going to be roughing it in some sketchy locations. If anybody got sick, if gunshots started popping off, we couldn't be stranded out there. And we certainly couldn't spend $500 or more each time on just tool transport for every single well. The time, money, logistics, and traveling on dangerous roads with unreliable vehicles would have been a nightmare. With how hard we knew we'd be working, we wanted to make it as easy as possible on ourselves.

DECEMBER 7

I'm 364 days out from my wedding day, and that gives me one more year to grow. I wholeheartedly believe that our plans, our hopes, and our dreams can't even come close to the life God desires for us to live. Our biggest dreams birthed out of our greatest imagination can't even compare to the real life God has imagined for us to LIVE. I believe we can and will LIVE this life God has planned for us, even if those dreams seem to have a ceiling or limits, because we have an opportunity to latch on to Him and be given unroofed-unlimited-unstoppable dreams!

Danger is an ever-present reality, but fear is a choice! Jesus never promised us safety for following Him; He promised us fruit, fruit like LOVE for the unloved or even our enemies, true JOY even with little to nothing, and PEACE in the midst of insurmountable odds or extreme suffering. God is GOOD and there is no doubt about it! We need to get uncomfortable in our faith, step out of our comfort zones, depend on God, and lean into the arms of our Dad.

DECEMBER 19

All I want for Christmas . . . is to crawl through the jungle to see my Pygmy family, and to dig them a water well.

. . . .

OUR BUDGET WAS mostly spoken for already on land purchases and the water-well supplies. I was at the point of praying and hoping that people kept donating over the year because there was so much more to be done and too little finances to cover it all. Still, we needed a truck and fast, so I worked up the courage to post our plight on Facebook, and literally, within minutes, Water4 called, donating $4,000 to get the ball rolling. A friend donated $750, and another friend donated $2,000. An anonymous donor, a friend of Jeff's, I surmised, donated $12,000! (Thank you, donors. Without your generosity, the dominoes wouldn't have started falling!)

We were able to find a brand-new, white, four-cab Indian-built truck for the magic price of $18,000. We adorned it with FTFF, Shalom, and Water4 decals, so people would know who we were, and that we weren't up to no good, driving through the jungle. We christened our truck "The Beast."

There was a good $8,000 tax exemption on the truck, too. Since we were exporting the truck out of Uganda, the country couldn't charge us tax for the vehicle (which could be a ridiculous 50 to 70 percent of the purchase price). The truck was bought in the name of Shalom University because it was an educational institution, which qualified it for another tax exemption in the Congo.

We set out to make our truck Congo-proof, a near impossible feat. We welded together a mean-looking grille guard, not only to protect the front, but to lengthen the car by a few inches so we could also add a twenty-foot pipe rack up top. (On our many trips to Uganda during the year, we'd always buy and bring back our supplies to the Congo with The Beast; we couldn't afford not to pile on whatever we could on each trip.)

Once The Beast was ready, Tom's buddy Alan, a Ugandan driver, took me in our new truck to the Congo-Uganda border, where Jack met us. We also had a transport truck following behind with more pipes. We sat in line with the other transport trucks, waiting to be deeply scrutinized. Alongside the vehicles, people lined up, waiting to be processed. It was very disorganized, yet sobering, as soldiers walked around with machine guns hoisted to their chests, and RPGs (rockets) slung over their backs. On the Ugandan side, I counted about ten soldiers. On the Congo side, there were at least fifty.

Although I always smiled and tried to find a way to laugh with the soldiers and officials, I never enjoyed our crosses over the border. We were stopped every time for some minute detail. They never found anything truly wrong, but would make up the most outlandish accusations. The border had a scary and dangerous atmosphere, as the chance of a soldier grabbing you and dragging you off to jail to rot was always a real possibility.

On the borders, the corruption was palpable. Officials regularly shook down drivers, which is why border officials lived in big, brick mansions, while their countrymen greatly suffered. If you were using a taxi, the officials could find something wrong with the driver's paperwork and arrest you because you put faith in him as a driver and that makes you responsible for him. There were times when we'd be asked to unload our trucks for inspection, vehicles we spent hours unloading and loading—all to get us to cough up some money. Even with us being a charity, an official would ask us to help them and their family. "Well, you're helping our people, but how does that help me?" verbiage was commonplace. And if we did pay their bribe, we might be asked for a tip on top of that! It was an "every man for himself" situation on the border, and you could find yourself at the mercy of some greedy, greedy men.

When our turn came, I wasn't surprised to hear from the Uganda Revenue Authority that I hadn't completed the truck's exemption paperwork correctly, though I knew I had. We were asked to pay the truck's taxes—a cool $8,000—on the spot to pass through. They delayed us so much that we lost our chance at making it into the Congo that day, and had to sleep on the border at a $5 "hotel." I'm not the guy who ever complains to a boss. I'm the guy who doesn't send back the wrong food order, and powers through a poorly prepared, bad-tasting meal. However, this got me heated. I wrote their names down and Googled the names of their URA higher-ups. The next day, I threatened to go to their bosses (by name) to complain, and they backed off.

We drove over the border into the Congo and I was told again that I didn't have the correct paperwork. "I do have the right paperwork," I told the official.

"Then pay me thirty-five hundred dollars," he said gruffly, "or you'll be spending Christmas on the border."

We didn't have the money and I wouldn't have even thought of paying it if I did, so Jack and I were instructed to get out of the car. The soldiers took our Beast and its keys and we watched them drive it into a barbed-wire lot. Soldiers guarded the lot, machine guns at the ready. We had no choice but to stay in the border town that night and hope they'd release our truck to us on December 23.

We found another cheap hotel for a few bucks a day. It was the kind of place where you ordered lunch and expected it by bedtime. My bed was so tiny that my elbows fell off both sides and my ankles hung off the end.

The next morning, Jack went back to the border and spent all day, from nine A.M. to five P.M., bartering and negotiating to get the truck back with no luck. The next day, we ate some sweet goat meat for Christmas Eve. On Christmas Day, our dinner was chicken, rice, and beans. Jack spent his first Christmas away from his family, and missed his first Christmas with his fiancée's family. I'd missed the opportunity to celebrate Christmas for the first time with my Pygmy family.

DECEMBER 24

Stuck here on the Uganda-Congo border, I thought about Christmastime last year, and I remembered a chance encounter I'd had with a woman in a New Orleans casino.

I was staying in the casino hotel near my family and was strolling the floor looking for a late-night snack after midnight, taking in the flashing lights and inviting sound of coins spilling into the hopeful players' trays. I happened past a woman who'd just hit a jackpot for $9,200, our eyes met, and I instinctually gave her a high five. But something told me I needed to speak to her. Why was she in a casino on Christmas Eve, drinking and gambling alone? I knew it was very forward of me to ask, but I'm a man of instincts and mine told me that she needed an ear to listen.

She told me her only child, a son, had died seven years earlier from a drug overdose. God prompted me to ask her if I could give her a hug, all while she waited for her jackpot win to be paid out. That hug turned into a tearful exchange.

"I never drank alcohol until my son died," she said, sniffling, "so please love your mom dearly. Tell her you love her, show her that you do."

She cradled my face gently in her hands; I couldn't help but look her directly in the eyes.

"Your mother loves you unconditionally," she repeated, "even if you ever become a drug addict or anything else bad you could ever do."

I shared with the woman that I used to be a drug addict, that living the life of my dreams hadn't fulfilled me and it had all turned into a nightmare. When I asked if I could pray for her, she simply said, "Please," while I held her tight.

"You hug like my son," she said oddly. "I know I shouldn't cry because he's in a much better place now."

It turns out her son had passed away at age twenty-five. I was twenty-five. Her son had a drug problem, as had I. Her son was six-foot-two and had a reddish-blond beard, just as I did. Her son was her one and only child. I am an only child.

I felt SO BLESSED to be able to tell her how God obviously, right now, in this moment, in a hotel casino in New Orleans on Christmas, wanted her to know how much He loved her, how much He cared for her, how intimately He wanted to show her He was there for her by sending me unknowingly to her side. He wanted to begin healing her heart from the pain of losing her son. Against the odds, she'd hit a jackpot that snagged my attention and God wouldn't let me walk away until I knew why I was supposed to talk to her about Him. Wouldn't a young guy approaching an older woman who just hit a jackpot in New Orleans at midnight normally seem a little suspicious? Our conversation flowed so naturally. I hugged her a third time before I said good-bye and left to return to my room.

"My husband is going to think I've gone crazy when I tell him that our son came through you to tell us how much he loved us," she said as I walked away. "I need to look more into this God thing."

THE BORDER PATROL let us pass through the day after Christmas just to punish us for not abiding by their corruption. A "secret service official" followed us from the border so he could lock the truck up in a lot in Bunia that happened to be directly across the street from Shalom University. We found ourselves in a stalemate, losing the battle against corruption. We stared at our truck for six weeks and ended up paying $3,000 to free it.

What wore me out more than anything was the corruption. It would beat me down mentally every time because it was so out of our control. Corruption was a top reason why the Democratic Republic of the Congo was one of the poorest countries on the planet. Corrupt officials wouldn't care if they had a starving child in front of them—they'd take money from that child's hand. The few prospered and didn't care about the rest. They stunted their own country's growth and well-being—and they didn't care, even when you asked them about it. It was a contagious epidemic that was culturally acceptable.

CHAPTER 20

Moja

A few hours before sunset, we came unannounced, approaching them as they were singing and dancing around the main fire, as they normally do. When they saw me, they stopped, leaned in, and squinted their eyes to make sure it was really me. It had been over a year.

I squatted down, opened my arms, and they came at me a dozen strong: my mother Chibuseeku, my father Manu, my three little sisters Mado, Priscilla, Sumbalina, and some of my village family like Biwanja (Bye-wan-jah), and Rahmo, among others. I fell back onto my butt, then my back, as my family piled onto me. I'd never been hugged by so many people at once. It was a joyful family reunion.

It was one of the best feelings in the world. Better than winning a fight. Better than getting a present on Christmas. Better than ice cream. It was incredible. It was unlike any moment I've ever experienced, because we were worlds apart but our hearts had stayed constantly connected. I genuinely loved the Pygmies and my heart was overjoyed that they were equally excited to see me.

I always knew I would go back. But it was a hard, long road, and so many sleepless nights of wondering how I could help them. I took this seriously; they were my family. And they took it seriously, too. It was their lives we were dealing with.

When I stood up, some of them started dusting me off. They grabbed my hand and pulled me into a circle and we started dancing as the flutists and drummers assembled. Ben and I were dancing for the next thirty minutes while we waited for the rest of the Shalom team to arrive. (We'd been so excited, we'd left the rest of the pack on the roadside to catch up with us.) Papa Way, Patrick, and Jack arrived and went straight into the dancing as well. The rest of the team hadn't seen the Pygmies in a while, so they were also given a loving welcome.

The Moja tribe was a very special village to us all. It was the first Pygmy village to own its own land and move onto it, thanks to all the hard work of Shalom's Development Department. Thankfully, the village didn't look like it was worse off than when I'd left them. On a smaller scale, Shalom had implemented a successful farming project and the Pygmies had started producing corn next to the village. I hadn't seen the Pygmies grow corn before, or really much of anything, especially in a fairly uniform fashion. The first time I was there, they'd been so hungry. Now they could rip a piece of corn off its stalk and throw it on a fire. They could feed themselves. They weren't "fat and happy" by any means, but they were thrilled with the progress, and so was I. In Moja, the Pygmies were growing corn, beans, and cassava, and were better fed then they'd ever been. They'd also begun raising a few small, free-range forest chickens. Sometimes they grew enough corn to take to the local market, another big advancement for the Pygmies since I'd been gone.

Clean water was the big issue. Without water, little Mo and other children had died. There were more unnaturally bloated kids with tapeworms and other parasites wandering about the village. What was so brutal was that they lived right beside a river, but it was contaminated with bacteria and disease. About twelve miles upstream, the Mokpala had discovered gold, and then some Chinese businessmen, who greatly exploited the Congo, moved in. They'd approached the corrupt politicians in the Congo's capital with their lined pockets and gotten certificates for the mineral rights in land throughout the forest, which they proceeded to ruin. They tried to dam up smaller parts of the river. Then they dredged the riverbed's soil. They poured gasoline in the river, which had taken on a more reddish hue than the year before with all the clay getting stirred up. At times, you could literally see the pools of oil and gasoline floating on top of the water. It was pointless to go fishing. All the fish were trying to swim far away from that mess as fast as possible.

Despite the poisoned river, the tribe was super positive about the improvements that had been made. They'd learned generations earlier to live and be happy with nothing. But after the first couple of days, once the initial high of getting reacquainted faded and we started working on the first Pygmy water well, I saw how drastic the need was for water.

Our twenty-person team (the core guys plus fifteen Shalom students getting college credit) stayed with the Moja tribe for more than two weeks. It was where we all wanted the project to start. Key among us was Jacques, a tall, dark-skinned Congolese man who always wore jeans and a polo shirt. Working for Water4, Jacques had completed twenty-eight water wells in the Congo. Matt Hangen had personally taught Jacques how to drill great wells, so he sent his student to come teach us. Jacques trained us for a few days at Shalom before we headed into the forest.

You couldn't help but notice Jacques's incredibly strong work ethic. He woke up early and was always the first to grab the tools for cleaning to get them ready. Jacques was the one to teach me how to dig a proper well. I'd only had two short training sessions with Matt and Steve in Oklahoma, but I hadn't actually completed a water well. I knew the theory but hadn't had the practice, and was greatly inexperienced.

We got to it the very next day right in the center of the village. We set up our tripod, dropped our clawed augers into the ground, and drilled down three feet in three minutes until we suddenly hit a sizable layer of sandstone. Instead of being able to scoop it up like dirt or clay, our augers would just grind, screech, and slide around the coarse and slippery rock's top.

We then tried to pierce through the sandstone using our single-prong chisel with a weighted sliding hammer on the back, but we didn't even chip it. We tried to break it up with our triple-prong chisel, and finally we tried our rock breaker, but nothing could barrel through it. Jacques had never seen sandstone like this—it was uncharted territory.

We had worked on this first hole for two full days, so before anyone got too discouraged, we decided to pick up and move to another spot. Maybe if we moved a football field away, the geology would change. This time we cranked through eighteen feet before we hit the impenetrable sandstone again. We'd worked from sunup to sundown and decided to find a third site in the morning.

That night, as they did every night, the Pygmies wanted to share their homegrown cassava and corn, and we'd share the rice and beans we'd brought with us. While I'd been away, Shalom had arranged for the Pygmies to take their produce into the market to sell it for the very first time. It was so momentous, that a Congolese news crew had come out and done a story on it—Shalom had an agriculturalist living among and teaching my family, and the Pygmies' corn was deemed the best at the local market. After dinner, we would dance until our feet couldn't hold us up anymore, then return to our little Pygmy huts, sleeping just the way our hosts did. Other nights, we stayed up talking for hours about our respective customs.

JANUARY 11

Sitting around the fire tonight, I was asked if I'd ever want to marry a Pygmy, because I'd been made family, and I was questioning them about their culture, including marriage. They told me if I fell in love with someone, I'd have to bring my sister to the brother, in an exchange for his sister. Now he'd have a cultural obligation to take my sister, as to not deny me my right to love. Basically, you want to find your wife first and fast—you get no objections in the exchange, even if she isn't all that attractive, has a conflicting personality with yours, or is just not your type.

"Well, I'm engaged to be married, so I am not able to marry a Pygmy," I told the elders. Since we were already deep into this crazy conversation about marriage, I thought I'd ask.

"I don't have a sister, so what would I do if I wanted to get married?"

The elders sat around the fire and discussed this seriously for a moment. They all started nodding in agreement, and Chief Jaloowah turned to me and said, "We'd take your cousin!"

"Well, we are in another predicament," I said. "I only have two female cousins out of ten and one is already married, and the other is too young to marry." These old men looked around at one another like that was CRAZY and unheard of.

They sat around discussing this as I listened to the fire crackle and gazed at the sparks floating up out of the flames. I could hear one elder's tone change, and his cadence grew faster while he gave what looked like a peace sign. This time they all eagerly agreed.

Chief Jaloowah, my grandfather, looked over the toasty

campfire and said, "We discussed what we'd take in exchange
for you to have a wife if you don't have a sister or a cousin
to exchange. The brother would agree to settle for TWO
CHICKENS!"

I tried to fight back a smile, as I didn't want to disrespect
them. But as I nodded, just a hint of a grin escaped my lips.
It was well received by the elders, who had a big laugh with me,
until it was time to head back to our huts and sleep for the
night.

THE NEXT MORNING, we tried on the other side of the village, another football field away. We hit sandstone at ten feet, so we picked up and restarted again. We moved twice that day; at the second spot, we fought through some softer sandstone we could break up and it got us down twenty feet before our tools collided with our enemy.

We held our prayer nights off to our side of the village and anyone who wanted to was free to join in. We were delicate with this matter—the Pygmies had had a falling-out with the local church because they hadn't been treated fairly by the church folk. One of the five of us would speak or a student might perform a short devotional. Some of our Shalom students were great singers and all of them loved to dance. We would start our prayer-and-worship times by ourselves, but normally half or all the Moja village would show up and participate. They were always teaching us something new about their culture, and sometimes they'd ask us to teach them Christian songs and dances or read stories out of the Bible to them. On Sundays, we held an open church service around one of the water-well sites. We all prayed we would break through the bulletproof sandstone, but after a week of unsuccessful well-drilling,

I could see everyone getting disheartened. It was such hard work and we hadn't found a drop of clean water yet.

Luckily, a member of our board on Fight for the Forgotten had sponsored a satellite phone for me. I called Matt every day to report on our progress and he tried to navigate us past the obstacles we were hitting. On the fifth hole we tried, we moved closer to the river. The Pygmies standing around saw how tired we were and they started helping us dig and handling the winches and wrenches.

Altogether, we got twenty feet deep and finally hit water. When I went to pull the auger pin out, water spewed out onto some of us. We started jumping up and down like we'd won the lottery! The Pygmies began to celebrate, and we called it a day. We were excited, but knew we had a lot more work ahead of us. Once you hit water, that's good, but you have to keep digging through the water, and that's when it gets even harder, because the water is fighting against you. We celebrated with a good meal that night. Everyone had "bidi-bo"—corn and beans. We'd brought rice and also dried fish, which is a rare meal for the Pygmies. We all ate very well. The students were rejuvenated and remotivated. The Pygmies were happy and excited, and everyone went to bed that night with full tummies and happy thoughts.

The next morning, we woke up and got right to drilling. We realized very quickly how much harder it is to dig when there's water in the hole. Its sides can start caving in and the compact mud gets saturated and heavy. Everything we pulled out was so much heavier than it had been before, and believe me, it'd been plenty heavy before. We drilled all day, and by its end we found out we were about twenty-nine feet deep, with the bottom nine feet of it containing water. We'd also hit sandstone again, which meant that the nine feet of water was resting on a rock layer. Again, our team and the village got all excited. A nine-foot-tall column of water was plenty to start with, we thought.

The following day, Jacques instructed us how to get the next steps ready, like preparing the bottom pump and PVC pipe for the hole, but I just had this gut feeling from the little training I'd had in Oklahoma City that it wasn't quite right. I thought the water we'd found might not be safe. There was also only a certain amount of water in the well, and once you emptied it the well had to keep filling back up through the permeability and porosity of the soil. I didn't know if we could complete the well here.

I called Matt and he told us to try to empty the well. We started bailing the water out, and when we could look far enough down the hole, we actually saw it bubbling. Water was coming back in and refilling the hole, which was a good sign. When I notified Matt, he told me that tomorrow we needed to empty the hole as fast as we could. The next morning, we did what Matt said. It took us only twenty minutes to empty the hole, and the hole filled itself back up with water in about two hours. When I told Matt, he taught me the most valuable lesson I'd learn as a water-well driller. He knew that we hadn't hit clean water, but ground water that would continue to seep back into the hole once we emptied it. We'd essentially found a dirty bowl of water atop a sandstone layer—we needed to break through into a safe aquifer. Crisp, clean water was probably hiding underneath that stone layer.

"What you have isn't clean, and even if it was, it isn't refilling fast enough for us to put our Water4 stamp on it," Matt told me somberly. "We can't guarantee this is safe, good water that will last a long time. Jacques has been blessed with near perfect scenarios when it came to the quality and safety of water, and he has never dealt with this rare challenge. You're going to have to tell him and everyone else that you can't use that spot."

I discussed it with Jacques off to the side, and I could tell we were both feeling the pressure. We relayed the message to the student drillers that we'd have to move again, but they saw the water and some began to argue with us.

"It's refilling. It's deep," the students told me over and over. I had to explain to them and the Pygmies that the water wasn't okay to drink, and we had to abandon that spot. Patience began tethering, and heads began shaking. We'd spent four days on this one hole and had been at it for ten days total.

The next day, our reluctant drillers moved to a site even farther away from the village, but closer to the river. At this point, we were pretty far away from Moja, but we figured if they were willing to hike all the way to the dirty river for water, they'd surely come to our spot for the clean stuff. We drilled and found the same thing: some dirty water stagnating on top of a sandstone wall. The Shalom students were downtrodden, and in the coming days many of them gave up on the project. They were too tired and hungry, and wanted a bed to sleep in, or just a solid roof that didn't leak over their head. They wanted to get paid for such hard physical work and not just in school credit. Many of them just didn't believe in the Water4 technology. Only our core team still believed, but I sensed that they weren't sure it would work in this region in the Congo.

Some of the students suggested we go back to the fifth hole, where we'd had the most success, but I knew that was wrong. I called Matt again.

"I'm feeling a lot of pressure here, bro," I explained. "The students are insisting that we already have a working well. It refills, but it just takes a long time. They're saying the water has to be better than what the Pygmies have now."

Matt stuck to his guns.

"Just because it looks clear doesn't mean it's clean," he said. "It has to be clean for us to give it to them. They say it's cleaner, but cleaner doesn't mean safe. If it's still going to make them sick and kill them, I'm not going to put a water well out."

Water4 had its own safety regulations and standards to uphold and I was the one who had to enforce and protect them. I had to get firm with the students. "I love you guys," I told them, "but this is my family and I love them too much to hurt them." Hole number six was deserted, and we had to find a new spot.

After our seventh failure in a row, I called Matt back and asked him what to do next. He recommended going back to the very first hole, the one in the center of the village, and attacking the sandstone at full force there. A few of us went into Komanda and bought pickaxes, hammers, and hand chisels. We widened the hole for two days until it was about six feet wide, so we could climb down onto the sandstone and hammer away manually. We just knew that if we could get through that layer, there was a good chance that there was lifesaving water beneath it.

Still, our pickaxes bent and twisted. Our hand chisels dulled and warped. The wooden handles on our hammers broke off. The sandstone was really giving us a hard time. On the third day at that well was when the students protested and quit. I was working all alone in the hole when Chibuseeku walked up to me.

"You need to rest, my son," she said, intertwining my hand with hers to lead me back to the village. I acquiesced.

The next morning, the Pygmies helped me drop a fifty-five-pound rock-breaker from the tripod, but its pointed end couldn't crack the stone. We dropped it a hundred times, then measured how much damage we'd done. Maybe a centimeter of stone was gone and pounded down to sand. Nothing had chipped, splintered, or broken.

Papa Way suggested we take fire to the sandstone. The local gold miners would build a big fire atop rock layers, which would crackle and pop and break apart due to the heat. We started loading the hole up with wood and we set a massive fire. We could hear popping and crackling and our hopes began to rise again. The fire burned all night until it smoldered to a stop the next morning. Climbing down into the hole, we stood in a foot of ash, our foreheads perspiring immediately from the earth's heat. We shoveled the ash out and dusted up white and gray soot, which coated our bodies. We dug and brushed the ash away to reveal the fire had only taken an inch away from the rock. There were no other signs of damage. We tried the fire again the next night, then crawled back in again to find little progress. More than two weeks had passed and the disheartened students had to get back to Shalom University for other classes. It broke my heart to leave the Moja Pygmies and my family without clean water. I felt utterly defeated.

It was a long ride back to Bunia with our heads hung low. I've never been so sore and exhausted in all my life, and we had nothing to show for it. Everyday had been backbreaking work and every day we were eating rice, beans, and corn. For the amount of energy we were exerting, we hadn't put enough nutrition back into our bodies. My muscles were aching; my back tingled in pain. Jacques was perplexed. He had no idea why it hadn't worked. It was the first time he'd left a location without a water well completed, and he'd mastered twenty-eight water wells in a row. I prayed that this technology would work where we needed it to. I'd seen it work in Uganda with my own eyes. Now we needed it to work in the Congo.

CHAPTER 21

Sustainable Development

We returned to Shalom University and took a few days off to regroup. When we reconvened with Papa Way and explained the situation at Moja, he suggested we hire gold miners from the nearby refugee camps, guns-for-hire for any type of job you had. The refugee camps were swarming with displaced but able-bodied people groups trying to escape the conflict and its warring rebel groups. We drove the four gold miners out to Moja and got them to work on the sandstone with a group of Shalom student interns watching over them. They confidently said, "We got this," but a month later they still hadn't made any progress. The slew of brand-new, higher-quality pickaxes, chisels, and hammers we'd bought them were bent, broken, or dulled and flattened. The sandstone hadn't budged.

Meanwhile, back in Bunia, we got up on the horse again and enlisted a fresh group of students to assist with the next water-well attempt. Our first group of students had been in their final year of their master's degrees. These new students were in their first year and they were energetic and motivated to learn. They'd heard of the struggles back in the forest, but it hadn't discouraged them. We all decided to try digging a well on Shalom's campus, and selected a spot between the staff and student resident buildings. We worked from sunup to sundown, digging and digging. We got in a groove and hit water on the second day, forty-two feet down.

When we finally hit water, all I could think was *Hallelujah*. I was overjoyed. I knew that the people whom I needed to believe in this project were now going to have faith in it. Psalms 34:8 (NLT) says to "Taste and see that the Lord is good. Oh, the joys of those who take refuge in him!" After five more days of work, everyone would be able to taste and see God's good work for themselves.

What I loved about Water4's program was that it put the tools and skills into the hands of the people it was helping. We were teaching countrymen to help countrymen. The success of the project relied on the locals being involved, which meant they wouldn't be dependent on outsiders anymore. Even in Bunia, outside Shalom University, there'd been water shortages in the past that had incited fistfights, so the well at Shalom was well received. We had a yellow-ribbon ceremony with Shalom's president to dedicate the well, and it seemed the whole school showed up along with the rest of Bunia. The local media arrived, and about ten microphones suddenly popped up in front of Papa Way's face. Everyone took the invitation to taste the water.

When word got out about the well, more calls and opportunities came our way. Government officials, NGOs, communities, chiefs, everyone wanted a water well. And now we had more students wanting to learn how to drill for water.

En route to Moja to check on the gold miners' progress, we got word that another infant had fallen ill. Ben and I were walking up to the hut as the baby took his final breath.

Babo was eight months old and died from the combination of a stomach ailment (most likely waterborne disease–related) and an open wound in his side. His mother, my aunt Macho, had just brought him back from the hospital that day. With the history of the Pygmies and the Mokpala, who ran the hospitals, Babo's family firmly believed that he wasn't being given fair or proper treatment. So they opted to bring him home and try their best with forest medicines. Right as we arrived, we joined Macho and my little cousin Babo in her hut.

"*Poli Sana*," I said (meaning "I'm so sorry"). In shock and loss, she looked up at me with the most heart-shattering, tearful eyes. I just said, "*Poli Sana*," over and over and I placed my hand on her shoulder. I asked, "Can I pray?" She nodded and then placed Babo into my arms.

FEBRUARY 7

It doesn't ever get any easier, at least not yet. I think I need to be praying that it never does, or that'll mean my heart is becoming hard and callused. I held my cousin Babo's lifeless body today. He was the infant son of Chibuseeku's sister, Macho. This is the third Pygmy kiddo I personally know under five years old that passed away of completely preventable causes. I could go into all the heartbreaking details, but I don't feel ready. The thing that I'll talk about is how I felt like a complete fool. I learned a new, but brutal, lesson today, and if I'm honest, I was extremely embarrassed in the process. As Babo had just passed away, his mother Macho broke down. I asked if I could hold him and pray, so she passed him gently to me. I began praying my guts out, and at a sudden moment in the prayer, Babo, wrapped in a single piece of cloth, had a bowel movement. It INSTANTLY gave me hope. I thought he might still be alive, and I know everyone in the small hut saw the look of hope in my eyes. But they knew better. He was gone, and the very thing that had gotten my hopes up crushed theirs. Later, Ben explained to me that when a person dies, everything expels from the corpse. That's how blind I am to the harsh realities of death. I don't mean to be rude, but death

is something kind of pretty in the States, yet it's really ugly here.
In the States, there are only a few people that ever see the body
before it's been properly cleaned and treated with formaldehyde,
dressed nicely, then posed in a coffin with flowers all around.
People are given a schedule of when to come see the body, collect
their thoughts and then people poise themselves so they can give
their final farewells.

Here it is drastically different. Death is deeply painful
wherever it happens, but in the Congo it's really ugly,
unsettling, and unjust. With kids so commonly dying out here,
it's really rough for me to handle. I know I'm supposed to say
this will give me more motivation to drill more wells, to do more
good, and I'm sure it will, but not today. Today, this just sucks.
My heart's been crushed.

EVERYONE DUG BABO'S grave together. The crying was brutal. I
watched my grandfather, Jaloowah, get the news about his young
grandson just dying, and the look in his eyes instantly changed.
He covered his face and crumpled to the ground, crawling on his
forearms, weeping.

When we returned to Bunia to load up supplies for our first
Pygmy well, we found out there'd been a turf dispute over the
Shalom well between some middle school children and some high
school kids in the area. The high school kids had bullied their way
into using the new Shalom well, and told the middle school kids
they'd get beaten up if they tried to use it again. When the middle
school kids stood up to them, the high schoolers grabbed the well's
metal T-cross handle and smashed it up and down as hard as they
could. A teacher pleaded for them to stop, but they broke it. The
pump mechanism had been completely shattered. In their history of

water wells, Water4 had never seen this happen. And when they saw the picture, they immediately asked, "Who broke this on purpose?" which led Matt and me to an important conversation. Matt had seen self-destructive behavior like this before and knew what to do.

"Did you ask them for any money?" he said.

"No," I answered, a little confused as to why we'd be asking the incredibly impoverished to pay for something we wanted to give them.

"Communities have to invest in their own water wells, even if it's just a little bit to us," he told me. "Charity can be dangerous if you distribute it the wrong way. You can actually rob people of an opportunity to have something to be proud of, and a way of building themselves up with self-worth and dignity. Stealing opportunity from the people isn't helping them. Tell them you won't fix the well until the community pays one hundred dollars."

"Pump the brakes for a second, Matt," I said. "You're going to have to explain this to me. How am I going to ask people stuck in poverty for any amount of money, even a little bit, and how am I going to rationalize that to people back home? I'm not here to ask them for a hundred dollars."

"Brother, I'm talking to you from experience," he said. "I want to help them just as much as you do, and I promise you'll be helping more by showing them how to invest in their own well-being. Charity doesn't work when you just give it to people who could give something for it, even a little something. There is no need to cripple the spirit of a community who can help themselves. Creating an opportunity for people to help themselves out of poverty is normally a better option instead of charity, or a handout. That's why we at Water4 say opportunity is greater than charity. One hundred dollars won't even feed your team for more than a few days. One hundred dollars to a hundred people is only one day of work for each person there, and they get a water well worth three thousand dollars."

Matt's quick lesson in sustainable development started to make sense, and then he dropped the cherry on top. "An amount this cheap is more like a small token, or symbol to us, but to a community of Pygmies it might be a real sacrifice and could turn into a major confidence booster in life for them. I promise you that you'll see these communities rally together to protect their new well, and your hard work. It's a true win-win in community development."

I did as Matt said and told Papa Way that we'd need one hundred dollars from the Shalom community to repair the well. Papa Way completely agreed, and in his undeniable wisdom had already been thinking of something similar. Papa Way turned around and told the Shalom community that if they wanted the convenience of having clean water in their compound, they'd have to come up with the money. The Shalom community rallied and contributed their one hundred dollars, and we fixed the well in one day.

What happened next is a testimony to Matt's understanding of the people he helps. Having had to pay that one hundred dollars, Shalom decided to open the water well in two-hour increments throughout the day with someone overseeing. Shalom put a chain around the well with a lock. Each day, someone new was in charge of unlocking the well at the posted times. Now everyone benefitting from the water well was watching and protecting it, and making sure it was used properly. The community rallied around their well, and it became a meeting place where people had discussions and laughter while fetching their daily share.

CHAPTER 22

Faith

There was talk of Emily coming to the Congo before I even left for the Congo myself. It was something we both warmed up to over time because a year is an awful long time to be away from the love of your life.

Still, what kind of guy was I, letting my fiancée come to a country nicknamed the "rape capital of the world," where at least forty-eight women are raped each hour? My mom asked me if I really wanted to bring Emily to such a dangerous place. I assured my mom that the choice was Emily's, not mine, and I had a great, dependable team out here who kept an eye on one another. Emily and I both prayed about it, and sought guidance as to whether this all made sense or not. To my surprise, my Congo team was thrilled, and confident that Emily would be okay. Emily was also excited and felt like she had to do this to prepare for our future together.

Emily flew into Kigali International Airport in Rwanda. I hid behind a sign with two dozen red and white rosebuds (a hard-to-find item in Africa) and surprised Emily and her traveling companions. Emily had come with four other missionary friends, who had their own ministry and worked with orphans on the Gisenyi border of Goma, Congo.

On our first night, we stayed in an apartment-style hotel with the rest of the mission's team. The next day, we took a bus to Gisenyi and stayed at Presence Ministries Headquarters.

Emily's first week in Africa was a real challenge. She'd already gotten sick on the plane coming over, and the winding roads kept her queasy. We think she also got ahold of some bad food. And finally, we found out that she was allergic to her malaria medicine. It was a rough start.

Anything and everything that could go wrong and scare Emily did. When people would find out that she planned to go to the Congo, they'd say something that instilled fear in her.

"Aren't you scared for your safety?" "Wow, be careful there." "Don't go off anywhere alone because a lot of women get raped there." That's not something to tell a woman. When we crossed the Rwandan border into Uganda, even immigration said, "Do you have to go there? Can you cancel your plans? You should be really worried."

If you are a *mzungu*, in parts of Africa everyone stares at you. People gawked at Emily and she wasn't used to that. In the markets, people grabbed her arm and tried to pull her into their shops. I'd have to politely pull her away from the men. It was a huge cultural shift and change for her.

Before she came to Africa, Emily felt like her fear and anxiety were trying to stop her from going. Now everything was difficult for her, which only heightened her reservations. Still, she pushed on.

At the orphanage in Rwanda, I got to see how great Emily was with kids. They were attracted to her like a magnet, like a tractor beam. One little girl was immediately taken with her. She came up to Emily, gave her a big hug, and held her hand and wouldn't let it go. The little girl was so cute and sweet and melted Emily's heart. When we heard they were shutting down the orphanage, Emily's eyes watered up.

"This isn't fair," she told me. "That little girl is so beautiful and sweet. Where is she going to go? I want to take her home with me." But even if that were in the realm of possibility, Rwanda has strong antiadoption laws for foreigners that wouldn't make it possible.

We decided to take a bus from Rwanda to Uganda because we'd heard they were nice, and it was a whole lot cheaper than flying. We booked ourselves the first two seats and boarded the bus. It was a scorcher of a day, easily in the hundreds. The windows had been left open overnight, and our seats were completely drenched by rainwater. The seats were hard and uncomfortable; a beam along the bottom poked into our tailbones. There was a sour smell of mold everywhere. On top of that, our "eight-hour ride" took more than twelve hours, as we sat inside a humid oven on wheels.

On the ride, the windows were kept open; there was no AC. I was sitting by the window and some of my long blond hair was flying all over. Five or six times during the trip, Emily and I heard someone cough up one of my hairs. Emily chuckled and said I looked like a blond beauty from behind.

But when we got to Uganda, she reached her breaking point. "I thought I'd fall in love with the Congo," she said through her tears. "Everything just to get here has been such a battle."

The night before we left for the Congo, Emily had an even bigger breakdown. She didn't think she could go. She was scared that if she was struggling already with the cultural change, there was no way she could handle the conditions in the Congo, let alone the jungle. We started discussing how to cancel her ticket and get her on a plane back to the States. We went to sleep that night feeling beaten and discouraged, not knowing if Emily was going to make the trip or not. She woke up the next morning feeling a little more hopeful, but still not certain if she was supposed to go.

As we arrived at the Missionary Aviation Fellowship airfield, I looked at Emily and asked one more time, "Do you want to do this? We can cancel this. I don't want you to feel forced into anything. I'll love and support you regardless of your decision."

Emily started to tear up. She asked to go off on her own and pray. After a few moments she came back and said, "No, I'm supposed to go to the Congo. I cannot be held back by fear. God gave me peace about this trip and although it's been hard up until now, I need to continue to trust Him."

With this decision, something shifted in the atmosphere. There was a change in both our attitudes and our hearts. She got on this little-bitty prop plane, and we rode out some turbulence into the Congo. From there, everything went from bad to amazing.

Benjamin and Papa Way were hiding at the airport; they sprang out and gave us a big hug. We got through immigration the smoothest I've ever seen it done. We headed over to Shalom and the house where I stayed. My roommate Ben had taken a photo of us to a tailor and had gotten a dress made for Emily, and a dress shirt and pants for me in this really cool multicolored African print that read SHALOM UNIVERSITY. We went to Papa Way's house for dinner wearing our new clothes.

As we came down the red dirt trail leading to Papa Way's house, there were five girls waiting for Emily, each wearing beautiful purple and yellow dresses. They had flowers in their hands from their garden. Three of them were Papa Way's daughters, and they were joined by a couple of neighbors. They welcomed Emily in English and told her how much they loved her, and hugged her. They'd each gotten dressed up as if they were flower girls getting ready for a wedding.

Inside the house, Papa Way's family had prepared a delicious chicken dinner with fresh-cut potatoes that were fried like French fries. It was a really special welcome. They were overwhelming

Emily with love and blessing through smiles, laughter, hugs, and goodness. We stayed for so long that our hosts served us fresh-made yogurt and homemade biscuits for a late-night snack. Afterward, we sat around Papa Way's living room and shared stories.

"No wonder it was hard for me to get here," Emily said. "It's just like you. On your first trip, you never wanted to come back, but this is what you're supposed to be doing. These are the people you're supposed to be around. This is your family. I feel like I'm part of the family, too."

God answered my prayer. We'd been to the point where Emily was broken down and we were questioning if she should be here. But now everything was turning around.

Two days later, we went out to see the Pygmies. We made the four-hour truck ride on the dirt road, got out, and grabbed our bags. The truck drove away quickly to make it back to Shalom before nightfall, and it drove away with Emily's mosquito net. She too wanted to experience the Pygmy life, as long as she had a mosquito net to protect her. We wouldn't realize our loss until we got to camp.

We jumped on motorcycles, Emily behind Jack, me behind Ben, riding through itty-bitty trails in the rainforest. We rode about five miles, until we reached a river and had to push our bikes over a little bridge.

Emily had brought along a Go Pro camera, which I had strapped to my head. We'd been able to ride our motorbikes all the way to Moja's primary school. I saw her way in the distance, below the tree line.

"*Mama yango*," I yelled, meaning "My mother." Chibuseeku saw me, opened her arms out wide, and came running toward me. When she looked at Emily, she knew she was her new daughter-in-law. Emily bent down to meet Chibuseeku and got a big hug, too. As we dismounted our bikes, another woman approached, one I swore

I'd seen before. I knew I recognized her, but Ben had to tell me who she was. It was Namboli, the woman whose picture I'd taken on my second trip, the woman who had carried the heavy charcoal for a small piece of goat fur to eat. I'd inquired about her when I'd gotten to the Congo, but at the time Ben and Papa Way hadn't known where she was. She looked a lot better than I remembered, and she'd just moved to Moja a few weeks earlier.

If you remember, Emily had made a connection with the picture of "the charcoal lady" when she'd seen the poor woman hunched over with 120 pounds on her back. That was the first time Emily had a deep heart connection and felt the calling of us possibly having a life together that helped the Pygmies. That was the first time she accepted me going to the Congo and maybe considering that it might be part of her life, too. It was pretty amazing that the woman was now standing in front of us. God had winked at us again. Chibuseeku grabbed Emily's hand and escorted her into the village, proudly introducing her to everyone as her daughter-in-law. Emily got to meet the rest of my family, including my cute-as-a-button little sisters Mado, Priscilla, and Sumbalina.

The Pygmies in Moja wanted Emily to be comfortable, so some of them had started building her what I can only call a "jungle shower." It was a three-sided stall about seven feet high, made of twigs and big banana and palm leaves. To cover the open side, we hung fabric as a shower curtain. We'd bring a bucket of water from the dirty creek, boil it in a basin over the open fire, then use it to bathe. Voilà. Privacy in the jungle.

We put our supplies in our huts, then danced for three or four hours. Around the campfire, my five-year-old sister Sumbalina got tired of sitting in between us, so she crawled into Emily's lap and snuggled up tight, falling asleep in her arms. Emily was in heaven, and I was as well, just looking at the two of them.

We probably laid down an hour or so before midnight, seven of us in the one hut. I'd brought a two-inch-thick, two-foot-wide inflatable mattress for Emily, and everyone had agreed to not eat in the hut, which would attract bugs. The one thing Emily told me she wouldn't be able to do on this trip was overcome her fear of bugs. When she laid down, I turned on my flashlight for a second, and had to turn it right off. Next to Emily's head, someone had spilled a mound of sugar used for our morning coffee, and there was an army of ants that had already started a little river out of the hut. They were the big, vicious, biting ants, too. I told myself not to panic. I took a breath.

"You know what, Emily?" I said in a calming voice. "I think it would be easier if you turned the other way, in case anyone needs to get up during the night." She did as I suggested, and we settled in for the night. Crisis averted!

At about three A.M., Emily woke me up. The Pygmies were yelling, "Mzungu! Mzungu!" They had torches in their hands and were running around. Many peeked their heads out of their huts. We didn't know what the commotion was about until I heard the thunder. The Pygmies were warning us about an approaching storm. I'd packed a tarp to put over our hut to waterproof it a bit. The rain still got in, but it wasn't as bad. When we crawled back inside our hut, Emily's face said, "What did I get myself into?"

I had to give Emily the flashlight while I worked to move our belongings to the dry side of the hut that wasn't getting muddy. But the light kept floating away from me, as Emily kept pointing it to the roof. When the Pygmies make a hut with newly cut leaves, it attracts cockroaches, who feed on those leaves. She turned the light upward and, on every leaf, there were one, two, or three cockroaches. Roofs were made of hundreds of leaves. When it stopped raining, it still sounded like it was sprinkling because of the cockroaches' feet running over the leaves. One fell and landed on Emily's neck. For Emily's first camping experience ever, it was quite the adventure! What a trouper.

In the morning, we came out of our hut to get our tea, sitting around the fire again. Emily looked at me. It was surreal. I was here with the Pygmies, and Emily was sitting right beside me.

"Did I sleep in a Pygmy hut last night?" she asked me, a little excited. I nodded my head and brought her back to the hut to show her the circular imprint where the sugar had attracted the ants the night before. There wasn't a single granule left.

"Honey, thank you so much for not telling me," she said with relief.

We spent two days with the Moja clan. The Pygmies were having a feast to honor those who had passed in the last few months: four children under five years old, a teenager, and a mother.

Emily and I brought a pig, which was then roasted, and Shalom University brought corn, rice, and some chickens for the feast. I said a few words at it. There was a pastor there, and other people got up and shared. Emily got up and spoke as well, telling them how blessed she was to come to know and love the family I loved so much. We all tried to rally around their heartache, and the feast was a way to symbolize remembering the ones who'd passed. It was also a way for the Pygmies to get some closure.

The rest of our time with the Pygmies was super blessed. The next day, I took Emily to see the Pygmies of Makelele village. We hiked twenty minutes through the jungle until we came upon the river. We'd have to cross in a canoe carved out of a tree trunk. Emily was a lifeguard and a varsity swimmer, but that doesn't mean anything if you're crossing a body of water with a strong current that may or may not have crocodiles. The canoe was far from sturdy and extremely wobbly. We were also the only ones who knew how to swim, so that made the journey all the more nerve-racking. We got to shore just as dark rain clouds moved in. Pygmies from Makelele met us on the shore, and we all had to race to the village during a nearly one-hour hike. The rain caught us and came down for a full twenty minutes, as we moved through the forest as fast as we could. When we got to the village clearing, we were welcomed into their huts to wait out the rain.

Makelele was a special place. Emily got to learn some of the different cultural dances with the women, and held and played with some of the children. I got to play hunting games and set up different shooting targets for the boys. Makelele was very deep within the forest, and maybe that's why there was an immense amount of butterflies of so many different shapes, sizes, and bright colors.

MARCH 20

Like me since 2011, Emily is beginning to experience the pains of trying to learn a new language, one that is a hodgepodge of local languages, including French and Swahili. Because of this, Emily has had me CRACKING UP for the last two weeks. I have a big leg up on Emily because I've been here much longer, established relationships, and have already began to learn all their different Swahili and Pygmy names. Emily, though, is still in the mix-and-match, stumble-and-fumble stage, where she can completely mangle some of their names. It's great, though, because it can get us all laughing and teasing in such a playful way. Emily's a clever cutie, and in the last few days my EmmyBear has come up with a very fitting and endearing nickname for one of my favorite guys in the world, Bahjongee.

Every morning, Bahjongee is already sitting around the fire outside our huts in the communal area. He is a sweet, adorable old man who ALWAYS has a smile, and LOVES to contribute to the community in any way that he can. I can't put a finger on his age, nor can he, but he's old enough to need a walking stick when he has to hike long distances.

When we crawl out of our tiny huts in the morning, he normally has the local coffee we brought already brewing on the fire. He stands up, meets us halfway, and then gives us the biggest hugs he can. What a great way to start the morning! During our coffee time, he's normally working on a new handmade hunting net, or he's repairing a damaged net for the younger rascals who can still hunt.

Bahjongee is one of only two Pygmies that I've ever met who knows how to read. He's also one of the first Christian Pygmies out of the couple thousand I've met.

"I learned to read because I wanted to be able to read the Bible, so I could learn more about the God who loved us so much that He sent His son to save us," he told me.

One day, Emily was trying to point out how cute and sweet of an old man someone in the village was. I asked her to clarify, because there were several men that fit that description. She said, "You know, Ja-bo-jo," to which I chuckled and responded, "Who?!"

"Gosh... YOU know... Gee-bo-nee! No, that's not it! Is it?" she asked.

By this time, I knew she was really digging deep and trying hard to find the right name, but I couldn't help but laugh. I think she might have tried "Gee-bo-nee" again, and in her cute kind of frustration she might have even thrown in an Oscar Mayer "Bologna!" (I was secretly thinking, "Oh, Bahjongee!" but I didn't tell her just yet.) She then pointed her finger across the village and said, "Over there." She paused, then let out, "OH MY GOODNESS! It's POOH BEAR! Look how cute he is!"

At first I thought, "Why would you be calling anyone Pooh Bear?" But sure enough, I looked out into the distance and made a connection I'd never noticed before. Bahjongee ALWAYS carries his walking stick over his shoulder; it has a bag at the end he tied out of cloth, and he always has the biggest smile on his face and a bit of a pep in his step.

For the past few days, I haven't seen Bahjongee walk anywhere without his stick over his shoulder. Now, because of EmmyBear, I've had flashbacks of the Pygmies finding and digging in to get some honey from a tree (Pygmies love honey), Bajohngee being one of them! I don't think I could adore my two favorite bears any more than I do right now.

ON OUR LAST morning with the Pygmies, we got word that a Mokpala and Pygmy village less than ten miles away from where we were had been attacked by rebels, who'd killed a few people, raped women, and stolen all the village's valuables. I'd heard the pop of a few gunshots in the forest and in some of the towns in the past, but, luckily, I hadn't seen any rebel action. We'd be driving down the dirt road and see an abandoned lorry truck, its windshield riddled and shattered with bullet holes. If these rebels had ventured farther, they could have stumbled upon us, but thank God, they left the way they came.

Despite the sad and scary news, Emily had such a great time meeting the beloved Pygmies that she didn't want to leave. When we got back to Bunia, we took a trip to Nyankunde, an hour and a half away, and stayed with a missionary couple, Dave and Donna Jacobsson. They are very close and dear friends with Papa Way and his entire family. Dave was the Mission Aviation Fellowship pilot who had saved Papa Way and his family from getting killed by rebel groups. While all the other planes were getting the heck out of dodge (or Bunia), Dave chose to go find Papa Way and his family, even though that meant landing in a war zone with bullets flying. Papa Way is a man I greatly admire, so to meet the man whom he described as a hero was such an honor. The Jacobssons are truly amazing and brave, and such a loving couple.

We heard their testimonies, and Emily had the opportunity to speak with a missionary wife for advice. I went from thinking, *What kind of guy would bring his loved one to this place?* to thinking, *I know God wanted her to come to this place. What kind of a guy would I be not letting her come here?* God wanted us to love the people here and it didn't have to be as dangerous, if you're prayerful and make smart choices.

We wrapped up Emily's trip with a day of sightseeing. We took a tour on a riverboat down the Nile and saw crocodiles, hippos, and the Murchison Falls. Then we went on a safari and saw giraffes, antelope, hyenas, warthogs, and too many elephants to count on what our guide called "The Elephant Corridor." We said our good-byes at the airport and she was gone. Even though I knew we were almost halfway through the year, having Emily leave was even harder for me than when I said good-bye to her months earlier. I loved having my best friend there with me, and I was heartbroken when she left.

There was new hope on the horizon, though. Matt knew we were dealing with tough geological conditions not even Jacques could get through, so he decided to come to our aid in the Congo. We just needed that first well to show everyone it could work in the forest. If anyone could get our momentum going the other way, it would be Matt.

CHAPTER 23

Mpenda

W hen Water4's director of implementation agreed to come out to Bunia to help us prepare for our second attempt at a Pygmy water well, his timing couldn't have been more perfect. We'd found success with the Shalom well, but had yet to make it work out in the rainforest. Matt Hangen was the greatest reinforcement we could get. If anyone was going to get that first water well going it would be Matt, and hopefully he'd be the stick of dynamite we needed to get things rolling.

In anticipation of Matt's arrival, Papa Way, Ben, Patrick, Jack, and I decided to find a real team that would be committed to joining our Fight for the Forgotten–supported Shalom Drillers (or "Drillers for Peace"). We looked through the community-development graduation lists from the past three years, scanning for standout students who'd demonstrated personal excellence and a passion to help others.

The team we ended up with wasn't the biggest or strongest, but they sure were the smartest. I was blown away by how much they wanted to learn, how eager they were to be taught, and how they really wanted to prove that they could be one solution to their country's water crisis. We asked twelve; all of them said yes but one.

Most important, all of our new hires had spent at least one month living with the Pygmies as part of their graduation requirements. When we asked them about their experiences with the Pygmies, they all said they'd fallen in love with them.

To start, we took our new team through the training videos, then dug a hole with them until we hit water. We then sent them out to all of the ten Pygmy villages we were working with. We instructed the students how to go to the village elders to ask where they wanted their water well, so they could drill a test hole, survey the land, and collect samples of the dirt by layers. Then we'd know if we could dig there or not. Our new drillers surveyed all ten proposed water-well sites and came back with their reports.

In the meantime, Matt asked if he could bring in three men from the Young Men's Drillers (YMDs), the successful well-drilling team I'd seen with Tom in Uganda. It was like getting four instructors instead of one.

We handed our data to Matt when he arrived, and he took us through an intensive workshop on drilling water wells. We talked about geology, the rock cycle, land formations, and other clues the earth gives you to find water. He explained the different soil types, like sand, clay, and silt, as well as rock layers like gravel, quartz, laterite, and sandstone. We conducted initial training in Shalom's courtyard. Hydrology lessons included how to find water-bearing zones and quality aquifers, and we dove into the porosity and permeability of the soil.

Matt taught us how to make sure the water was clean by testing it for E. coli and cholera, and showed us how to test for iron and other elements. It was the first time Matt had addressed graduate students, and he found them inquisitive and able to follow along well. It was soon time to venture back into the rainforest.

We picked the Mpenda Pygmies because they were the closest to the dirt road, only a ten- to fifteen-minute walk off of it, which would allow us the best use of Matt's time. We didn't want to have to spend a day traveling to a spot, then a day hauling equipment in and out, another day hauling it back out, and then another day traveling back to Bunia. Starting at Mpenda gave us two extra days to get a well dug.

Our decision to choose Mpenda also went back to those land-purchase meetings Papa Way and Ben had had with all the tribes months earlier. The Mpenda Pygmy chief had been the first to stand up, even with the Mokpalas in attendance, and suggest that they trust Shalom's plan. Everyone in the room had been taken advantage of at one point or another, including the Mokpala, so it wasn't an easy request. But Chief Alondo was the first one who rose at his meeting and said his village was all in and fully committed. He'd caught the vision that Papa Way casted.

We'd had no previous relationship with the Mpenda Pygmies. They weren't among the original tribes we'd visited, but Chief Alondo had been such a key proponent at the meetings that we all agreed we should start there.

On the way to Mpenda, we stopped at the village of Kanisa, where we'd paid to keep a storage container behind its church to store pipes, cement, gravel, and other materials. A transport truck delivered eight wells' worth of cement, gravel, sand, and pipes. I drove in the Beast, along with Matt, Ben, and two of the Young Men Drillers.

The Mpenda tribe was so gracious and excited to see us. Chief Alondo insisted we leave our bags where they were, and the Pygmies carried all our gear for us. The Mpenda Pygmies had their $100 payment waiting for us. We ate and danced with them that first night, to mark our arrival. The next day we started to drill.

The drilling process started well. The dirt was a lot easier to get through. On the first day, we got thirty feet down. We were blazing. But we came back the next day and our hole was only twelve feet deep. We'd hit a mushy collapsing zone, which meant we'd have to redig the hole and add some big casing pipes to protect the twelve-foot hole that survived. We got back down to thirty feet and it started collapsing again. We put more casing along the walls of the hole.

On the third day, we were back to twenty-seven feet, but Matt said this was the first time he'd seen so much atmospheric pressure building up inside the hole. The mud and the sludge would fill our casing pipe and rise halfway to the top. It was like a straw in a cup of water, he said. No matter how much you try, the level of fluids and mud will fill the casing as you empty it out with the augers. This made Matt scratch his head. He huddled us leaders together.

"We need to talk about what our options are," Matt said. "We need to get on our hands and knees and pray, 'God, we need help. It's bigger than us and too tough for us.'" We knelt and prayed.

The next day, the well hole was still collapsing in on itself and the mud continued to stack up inside our protective casing, continually shortening our hole and shrinking our gains. Matt called Water4 back in the States, and asked for everyone to put their heads together to find a solution. We prayed some more, then Matt had an idea: What if we started dumping water down the hole to try and push the mud back down, to keep it from rising up? If we could steadily keep enough water inside our hole, it could theoretically counteract the mud from surging up, and hopefully it would allow us to continue advancing down. Matt explained it as being kind of like the Indiana Jones scene where he used a sandbag to swipe the gold idol from the scale.

The nearest water source was a creek—a forty-five-minute walk each way. How much water would we need? We brought Chief Alondo ten jerry cans, each able to hold forty-four pounds of water.

"We need to start with four hundred pounds of water to dump into this hole," I told Chief Alondo through Ben's translation. The water wasn't clean, but it would be blasted with chlorine later, then emptied, and clean water would replace it.

As we added water to the hole, we noticed the mud go down in the casing. So we repeated the process a couple more times. This provided me with the opportunity to walk the same distance the Pygmies had to do. No wonder the soles of their feet were tough and hardened. I felt like I lost a couple inches in height from the weight on my head. If I had to guess, over the next four or five days, we must have used nearly a ton of water. The water flow pushed the sludge down and we were able to continue digging again.

MARCH 20

Thank you, Lord, for Matt "The Lifesaver" Hangen! I know I always hear quotes saying "God's timing is perfect," but Matt coming at the time he did IS absolutely perfect. We not only needed his guidance, we HAD to have him here. We've been having SUCH a difficult time, we've been hitting SO many obstacles, and this manual labor is without a doubt the hardest, most gruesome, backbreaking work I've ever seen and participated in. No wonder we've had many run away from the hard work; even a few good people have given up because they don't think this will ever work.

I feel like Matt is saving this team and adding so much motivation to the project. He's got hundreds of wins (or wells) under his belt. With his knowledge and expertise, I think we're actually going to navigate around what are insurmountable odds to our team because of our inexperience. God, THANK YOU for lending us this dude's mechanical mind—it's unlike anyone's I've ever met. He knows how to make the drilling process come alive for us by vividly explaining what we need to do, how we need to do it, and why we have to do it with the highest quality and deepest integrity.

What I love most about Matt is his love for God, and I hope I can implement this more in my own life. It's a love so deep that he LOVES giving himself completely, even if that means he has to suffer a great deal, just so that others will have a better opportunity at health and life. He's hopeful they'll find their own personal love for God along the way. This guy's passion for drilling wells is second to none and it's contagious, just as is his love for God. I definitely know I don't have the same brain this guy has, but I pray that the team we've brought together can commit to learning, be coachable, and replicate everything he is teaching us.

With this first Pygmy well, I know we gotta get a win. Everything hinges on it. This is what will turn everything around for this team. Matt's bringing us up to our tipping point quick, I feel it in my gut, and now I know and pray that we are about to see a BIG momentum shift. Thank you for bringing this man into our lives, God. Full steam ahead! WOOT-WOOT!

WE HIT WATER at thirty-three feet and kept going. It had been a real dogfight. Matt said it was one of the toughest and most technical water wells he'd ever dug.

We started the second stage called "well development," which is the cleaning and protecting of the water well. We placed a sanitary seal on to protect our clean aquifer. Then we put a long cement plug (kind of like a cork) down into the ground. We blasted the water for three days with chlorine. While we waited for the chlorine to kill any contaminates that had snuck into our well, we drove Matt to the airport and he headed back to the States.

We went back to the hole and pumped out the chlorine water, so that fresh water could replace it. We hired and brought out a cement layer, who showed the team how to lay out a circular cement pad to surround the pump. We also cemented in an offshoot funnel that would let the rainwater drain away from the pump itself. The Pygmies named the well "Mungu Anatupa Maji!" (God gave us water!), which was etched into the cement forever. The women placed bright leaves around the well to decorate it.

As soon as the water well was usable, the Pygmies rushed to it. We took turns pushing down the T-cross handles and filling containers with clean water. There were cheers and hoots of joy.

Word spread that the Pygmies had a water well, and the local government took notice. The next day, we had our dedication and celebration for the well, and they showed up in an entourage. They came from Mombasa and some of the local forest towns along the way. It was a posse of government officials. They made their grand entrance like former Congo dictator Mobutu Sese Seko had, wearing exotic leopard-skin hats and vests. They were wearing suits with their leopard-skin hats (think Eddie Murphy's brilliant *Coming to America* costumes) and the chiefs all carried little whips with tails, or clubs—symbols of their authority. They wore these outfits to honor the event. A slave master chief even stood up and called for the equality of the Pygmies—something I thought my ears would never hear. Change was happening.

APRIL 5

Today I feel like I heard giants falling. To others, it would just sound like "Splash, splash, splash," but to me it was the sound of a huge victory on a treacherous battlefront. A battlefront that stood many giants. Maybe none of the giants were named Goliath, but they had names like typhoid, cholera, and E. coli, and they have been taking the lives of my Pygmy friends and family for generations. When we began the first Pygmy water-well dedication, I couldn't have imagined it would turn into such a celebration! I've been to the biggest UFC fights, I've been to the World Series, I've been to the Super Bowl at the Superdome in New Orleans, and I've been hooting and hollering for my Dallas Mavericks in game seven of the NBA Finals. NONE of those can compare to the pure satisfaction I got from today. Not a one. Not even close! It's fun to celebrate the accomplishments of a favorite sports team, it's satisfying to win a fight or claim a national championship, but I can't even put into words the incredible feeling of accomplishment that came with today. How do you compare anything in sports to conquering giants like waterborne diseases? I am BEYOND proud of my team! I am so excited for the Pygmies!

Today a government chief came out to the village with a governmental entourage and told us, "This is OFFICIALLY the first water well ever in history for the Mbuti Pygmy people. And from this day forward they should be seen as EXACTLY that—people, not animals." Looking into the faces of my Pygmy family I could see PURE joy in their eyes, and amazement at what they were hearing. I think they felt eye-level with me from how tall they were now standing. It was a deeper happiness than I've ever seen or experienced before. It really is indescribable!

When they saw the first splash of clean water, the whole village ERUPTED with shouts of joy, heartwarming laughter, and the singing of NEW songs. We literally danced around their new water well for hours and hours into the night. There aren't many days in life where you feel like you actually did something great, where you did something truly meaningful, but today is one of those days. I almost don't want to go to sleep and let it slip by. I wonder if the celebration I experienced today was anything similar to when the Israelites all came together and celebrated defeating Goliath. I know our victory didn't have bloodshed, or end an actual war, but all of us here know that having access to clean water is a huge life victory, and it's ending a war against waterborne disease that has lasted for centuries.

Thank you, God, for my team and me being able to fight on this battlefield. The Shalom Drillers didn't need weapons like swords, spears, or even armor. We just needed the right training and tools: augers, chisels, and rock-breakers. We weren't looking to spill blood, but water. Because of this, it brought two opposing sides together at a groundbreaking event for peace.

Taking a step back now, I'm amazed at the progress we've made. In the past, I'd had people from the slave master tribe come up to me with hate in their eyes, demanding an explanation for what I was doing with their property, or that I needed their permission before interacting with their animals. Now, to sit back and watch a leader in their tribe, a chief in the government, talk about how today is historic, and how the Pygmies shouldn't be considered animals anymore blows my mind. Second, and most important, it's shown me this battle wasn't just about water; it was about so much more. It's a great day, and it's another step away from discrimination, hate, and even slavery. You will always find God's heart and compassion among "the least of these" or "the forgotten."

"He will rescue the poor when they cry to him; he will help the oppressed, who have no one to defend them. He feels pity for the weak and the needy, and he will rescue them. He will redeem them from oppression and violence, for their lives are precious to him." (Psalms 72:12–14 NLT)

CHAPTER 24

Kaptula

I *f this man died tonight, no one would be surprised.* That was the first thing I thought when I saw him. Among the Mpenda celebrants, an old man named Kaptula (Swahili for "shorts") had come walking from the village to the water well. He was, hands down, the skinniest and weakest man I'd ever seen in person, and it was obvious that he was wasting away with some kind of illness. His thin bones were articulated everywhere by his taut skin and his ribs heaved up and down with every cough and wheeze. If I had to guess his age, I'd say he was in his mid- to late fifties.

Kaptula sat down among the buttressing roots of a sprawling tree and rested his arm on one of its grooves. I hadn't noticed him before because he'd stayed in his hut the entire time we'd been at Mpenda. But here he was now, taking in the celebrations, only able to watch the others sing and dance.

I saw a little girl approach the well and stick her cup under its spout. She took a few gulps, put her cup back under for a refill, walked over, and handed it to Kaptula, her grandfather. When he took a sip, I saw his eyes light up. He drank some more, then gave the cup back to his granddaughter, who guzzled down the rest. Kaptula lowered his head and started praying.

"He's thanking God that he and his family now have clean water," Ben said after speaking with Kaptula. "He said that this is now their land with their own water and, oh, how many things have changed."

"Asante sana. Asante sana" ("Thank you so much" in Swahili), Kaptula said as I joined him and his wife around their fire when the celebrations abated. *"Mutamo Sana"* ("It's so delicious"), Kaptula remarked of the water. I just had to know what was wrong with him, so I asked.

"I don't know, and the people at the local clinic don't, either," he said. "They don't have any medicine to give me." The clinic Kaptula referred to was not a good one. On the outskirts of Mpenda, the clinic's bed didn't have a mattress, so patients lay right on the springs. It had little medicine or medical supplies. A sort-of nurse tended to the patients, but he'd let Kaptula go home as sick as he was, and that didn't endear me to him too much. As we went to bed that night, Ben and I agreed to take Kaptula somewhere better.

The next day, we took Kaptula to the clinic about a forty-five-minute drive from the forest in Mombasa. The doctor said Kaptula had a simple cough, but he had no medicine to give him. On our next try, we decided to go to Mandima Hospital.

On the first visit, they had offered Kaptula Tylenol and some B-12 vitamins, so we brought him back again. This time the doctor only gave him cough syrup. On our third trip, after our strongest of urges, the doctor agreed to test Kaptula for tuberculosis. He gave Kaptula three plastic cups to cough in back home and said they'd test it when we came back with the samples. On our fourth trip, we brought Kaptula's first sample. The doctor said they would test one sample first, which would take about two weeks. He said that only after three positive tests (taken two weeks apart, with several more trips) would he treat Kaptula for TB.

Ben and I were getting confused and frustrated. I was furious. These first five trips to the hospital had already been over a two-week period. I was shocked by the callous responses to such a life-threatening sickness, whatever it was, and having a doctor tell me it was going to take a few more trips over several more weeks before they would start treating Kaptula. I guess the terrible doctor didn't mind if people died waiting for the test results.

When we found out treatment for TB is free and the doctors don't make a single dime off of the treatment, it started to make sense why we were asked to come back so many times. The doctor was charging us for each visit. I thought about my time with malaria, and how so many tests came back negative even though the parasites were multiplying in my bloodstream. I thought about how quickly malaria could have killed me had I not gotten to a good hospital in Uganda. Ben and I decided we really needed to go to a hospital that we trusted, where we knew doctors personally. It seemed like the medical staff we had been seeing just wanted to give up on Kaptula, the way a family makes the decision to put the dog down.

Kaptula was complaining about his chest. Surely they could have put him on an antibiotic for that. In the meantime, Kaptula was really sick, and wasting away. We just didn't have six more weeks to spare.

Ben and I decided our only other option was to drive approximately four hours to Nyankunde Mission Hospital and get them to check Kaptula out. Just like Papa Way with me, I didn't want this guy's blood on my hands. Surely, these doctors would give Kaptula the right treatment. I invited Chief Alondo and his wife, Alaina, to accompany us on our trip. Chief Alondo had begun feeling faint and weak at the time, which we would soon find out was diabetes. We wanted to knock out two sicknesses with one trip to Nyankunde.

If you think you are too small to make a difference, try sleeping in a closed room with a mosquito.

–DRC/African Proverb

Wow, this quote woke me up like a stiff jab! It makes me wonder about how many times people have held themselves back from being and doing something great because they thought they were too small to make a difference. What we think of ourselves can prevent us from tapping into our true potential. It can stop us from attempting something truly remarkable in our own lives and the lives of others. It makes us timid to dream, it stops us from taking the big leaps of faith, and it cripples the potential value each and every one of us can add to the world.

After battling for my life against malaria, I see how crucial of an effect even a little mosquito can have in my life. I think the average mosquito weighs around two milligrams, and now I weigh 265 pounds. In EACH pound there are 453,592 milligrams. World-class athletes have never knocked me out at my own weight, but a stinking SCRAWNY two-milligram pest can take out my 120,201,880 milligram body! It only took ONE tiny pest to push over the domino that started a chain reaction in my body that had millions of parasites overtake up to seventy percent of my bloodstream. The weight of the average human brain is three pounds (or 1,360,776 milligrams). That means each one of our brains is the weight of 680,388 mosquitoes! So we are obviously a lot smarter, right? Ha. I know that may sound goofy, but it reminds me that we should be smart enough to see ourselves for what we really are, and that's valuable.

We are more than adequate. We are able to make change.

We can all start, join, or fuel a movement. We are capable of tapping into an immense love that most of us can't even fathom, AND distributing it. It's possible for us to love the Hell out of this world in our own unique way. Pause, take a look, and assess who God created us to be. We have to push ourselves out of the deep ruts that we find ourselves in! God doesn't see us for who we are right now; He sees us as who we could be.

I need to keep my mind from focusing on my failures, shortcomings, and everything I can't do. I need to drift over to and focus on what I can do, and one of those is loving my family with everything I've got. My logic and my faith in God says that our small army of Shalom Drillers should be able to set off a chain reaction of people loving the Pygmies AND end the water crisis in the Congo.

You, me, WE . . . we're born to change the world.

WHEN CHIEF ALONDO and Alaina climbed up into our truck, they both put their feet on the seat and curled into a ball, holding their knees tightly to their chests. They hadn't ridden in a vehicle before and were at a loss as to where their feet should go. Without a translator in earshot, I tried to explain that it was safe to let their feet rest on the truck's floorboards.

"*Mapappa happa. Mapappa happa,*" I said in broken Swahili, which means "Sandals here. Sandals here." The couple carefully released their legs and began to investigate the modern marvel surrounding them. Kaptula, an expert at this point, having ridden in the truck for all his other doctor visits, showed the chief and his wife how to open and close their door and roll down the window.

On our four-hour ride, I'd prepared a special treat for the

passengers. The Pygmies were unaware that I'd recorded some of their beautiful polyphonic music on my iPhone. I'd also down-loaded Pygmy music from around the world—Cameroon, Gabon, the Central African Republic, and others. I hooked my iPhone up to the car speakers and the Pygmies were able to listen to their own music. I can't explain the look of amazement on their faces. When the Pygmy music from the other countries came on, I could tell that they knew the music. They didn't necessarily know the words, but the style was still theirs. They knew it was other Pyg-mies. During the parts where we could sing along, we all caroled, *"Iko mzuri sana,"* which means "It's so good."

As we entered Nyankunde, I watched the Pygmies look up in awe at the buildings, like the first time I went to New York City and saw Times Square. Nyankunde was a shadow of its former self, having barely survived a massacre in 2002 at the hands of a war-ring tribe of rebels that killed thousands. In the Nyankunde Hos-pital, patients, like the elderly and mothers with newborn babies, had their throats slit, were shot, or were butchered with machetes while lying in their hospital beds. A dozen years later, you could still see evidence of the carnage. There were masses of abandoned buildings with trees growing through them. You could see bullet holes in the damaged structures still barely standing.

When we arrived at the hospital, I asked for two rooms in their guesthouse, if they could spare them. I wanted to give the chief and his wife a night to themselves, since their grandchildren often slept with them in their six-foot-wide hut. However, the hospital was full and we only got one room for the lot of us. I went off looking for a second mattress.

The chief and his wife slept on a twin mattress that looked like a comfy queen-size with them lying in it. The chief's wife ab-solutely loved it—you'd think she was lying on a Tempur-Pedic mattress with Egyptian sheets and a duck-feather down blanket.

She loved it so much that she stayed behind while we went up to the hospital the next morning for the final checkup, making sheet-snow angels among the covers.

We found Kaptula a mattress. It was a cheap, two-inch piece of foam missing its bottom quarter on one side. The hospital had no sheets, so the Jacobssons, the lovely missionary couple we knew in the area, gave me bedding for the four of us and invited me to stay in their one spare bedroom. I was so thankful for the invite—the Jacobssons had given me and my team comfy shelter and warm meals on several occasions. However, I thought something special was going to happen if I stayed in the same hospital room as the Pygmies. I arranged with one of the nurses to have his wife prepare us rice, beans, and smoked fish for dinner. The four of us sat on Kaptula's mattress on the floor and ate. They loved the big fillets of fish.

Afterward, we sat around my laptop and looked at all of the pictures and videos I'd taken in their village since I'd arrived. They were glued to the screen, pointing and laughing. We watched until my computer battery died.

I laid my sheet out on the concrete floor between the bed and Kaptula's stained and mangled mattress. Kaptula looked distressed. He covered his heart with his hands and shook his head no. He lay down on his mattress and scooted his shoulders as close to the wall as he could. He then used his hands to show me how much room he needed, and how much room was left on the mattress for me. He grabbed my sheets and made my bed for me on two-thirds of the mattress.

I tried to speak in my broken Swahili. "This is fine, it's okay, I'm young, this is okay for me," I said, but Kaptula, mama chief, and the chief wouldn't take no for an answer.

Kaptula fell asleep quickly. I didn't. Listening to Kaptula's cough in the day was gut-wrenching enough—now I was trying to sleep while listening to his desperate breathing. He'd wheeze in, and every time he breathed out, his lungs would have to pop into gear, like they had a terrible transmission. And when it would pop and click, his whole chest and body would jolt. This had become his normal.

The next day, we found out Kaptula had TB. It had only taken us one clinic, two hospitals, and seven visits to get the correct diagnosis. The doctor said one of Kaptula's lungs was ninety-five percent dead; the other was working at seventy-five to eighty percent. I had feared as much. I could see Kaptula's breathing in his sunken trachea, and in the hollowed-out holes in between his collarbones.

Six weeks into his treatment for TB, a smiling Kaptula, Ben, and I sat around the fire talking. His face was a little fuller and his spirits much better. We talked for fifteen minutes or so before he stopped to ask me something. "Do you notice something different?"

"You look a little happier," I said.

"Yes, but what else?" he asked.

"I don't know, *mzee*, why don't you tell me?" I conceded. *Mzee* (pronounced "mm-zay") is an endearing term for an old man.

"I haven't had to take one single break to breathe in this entire conversation. I would have normally taken several breaks by now!"

Our efforts with Kaptula and preparing to drill the second Pygmy water well in the next village, Kumi, happened simultaneously. The Mpenda slave masters initially passed on contributing $100 for a water well, so we'd moved on to the next spot.

The Kumi water well took us ten days to complete, the fastest we'd ever completed one. We'd go on to average between ten to sixteen days per well. You never knew how long a well would take until you started hitting the obstacles.

We knew what we were doing by the time we got to Kumi, which had 120 Pygmy residents. We had two wells under our belts and everyone seemed to click. We were figuring out what each of us was good at and liked to do. There were ten of us on this well; we had people holding the ropes, cranking the tools, emptying the augers, and holding down the tripod. The last task was an especially important one. With too much weight to one side, the tripod could uproot at any time and go flying. It dug a hole into a tree on one occasion, like a giant hammer. It was dangerous stuff, and we had to do it right or someone could get hurt. So safety was paramount.

Kumi was another hospitable tribe. They built five huts for our crew—three for us to live in, another for break time, and one for our tools so they didn't get wet. For their contribution, they gave us a monkey, a wild hog, two bags each of corn and beans, and $200. They'd earned so much learning from the "community mobilizers" of Shalom Drillers—two Shalom graduates who went ahead of our drilling team and helped the Pygmies find paying jobs in their area. After the $200, we had to tell the Kumi Pygmies to stop, that they couldn't give us any more. Bale (pronounced Ball-eh), Kumi's chief, was extremely organized and had the respect of his people.

"The land we have now is going to change our history," he said to me one afternoon as we sat in the shade of a palm tree. I took a minute to think about what he'd said as he took another bite into a mango. I asked him to explain.

"My children's children will be able to say, 'This is my grandfather's land,' and in the next generation the children can say, 'This is the land of our grandfathers,'" he told me. "The land we have now, I think it was the land my grandfather took me to hunt antelope on for the first time."

Chief Bale told me how the forest in that area had always belonged to the Pygmies, but when people found out how rich in natural resources it was, they started stealing the land out from under them and started deforestation.

The Kumi tribe was one of the few to have a water-well celebration where none of the Mokpala came. The Pygmies always felt much freer whenever the Mokpala weren't around. For our celebrations, we started early, as nobody had gotten any sleep the night before, anxiously awaiting the next day.

Once we completed the Kumi Pygmy well, it was time to dig a well in their former slave master's village. I'll be totally honest; I felt awkward about it. I wanted to stay with the Pygmies at night and make the forty-five-minute walk to the Mokpala village every morning, but Ben said I couldn't do that.

"It's going to look like you don't like them," he said, and he was right. "We're going to build Pygmy huts right up there with the Mokpala." But as it turned out, the Mokpala had made special arrangements for me to stay in the schoolteacher's guest bedroom in his hut made of mud and sticks. "They built a cot out of bamboo that lifts the mattress off the floor a little bit," Ben added.

I realized I needed to stop being silly. The Mokpala were being very welcoming to us. As Matthew 5:44 (NIV) says, "Love your enemies and pray for those who persecute you." I prayed that providing water for both sides would help put out the burning coals of hostility between the two peoples.

My little guest room was big enough for my bag and cot—the room was about the size of my couch in the States. As I slept, dried pieces of mud kept falling on my head. I had to get up a few times during the night to shake the hard clumps of dirt off my sleeping bag.

We built two water wells for the Kumi Mokpala—one in the primary school's front yard and the second on the other side of the three-hundred-person town. The Mokpala had come to us and asked for the second well and paid for it.

A few days into the dig, Chief Bale came to me with a gift. He'd gone deep into the forest to get me a bottle of honey. Among the Pygmies, honey was one of their most prized treats. Pygmies would abandon hunts at the smell of honey. It was liquid gold to them. Chief Bale told me how much his village loved the water and how he hoped we'd be lifelong friends. I knew we would be.

CHAPTER 25

Tundu

A mong the 2,470 acres of land purchased in the name of the Pygmies, the Tundu tribe managed to find the most magical place in the forest. The Tundu Pygmies had found a clearing among the trees that opened up to the sky in a nearly perfect circle maybe fifty yards in diameter. They'd fallen in love with this anomaly in the rainforest. In Swahili, it's called *tundu*, or hole—the hole in the forest.

The hike to the Tundu village was one of the farthest and toughest walks we took in the rainforest. We'd hiked to one village that was two hours off the roadside, and another that was nearly three hours away, but this one was quite a doozy. We hiked about an hour away from the road, but the topography made it a much harder walk than it sounds. We were up and down hills and over, around, and under trees, and it was all mud until you got to the village. That made it feel much longer than a one-hour hike.

When we arrived, I got the standard first welcome: the women grabbed their young babies and dove into their huts and the children ran away into the forest screaming. The men weren't around, as they were off hunting.

We'd stay a month with the Tundu tribe, and it would become one of my favorite places during the entire year. What I liked about the Tundu was their authenticity. Of all the tribes we visited, this one was the most untouched from the rest of the world and more the way I imagined the Pygmies lived a thousand years ago. Also, it seemed they'd never been visited, hurt, or had their trust broken by any foreigners. It made it easier for them to warm up to us.

While many Mbuti Pygmies no longer had this choice, hunting was still the crucial component of the Tundu village. When the men went to hunt, none of them wore the clothing given to them by their slave masters. They went one hundred percent traditional, basically butt-naked with a little cloth or leaves covering them, carrying their spears handed down from generations.

Watching the Tundu clan, I learned how they made poison for their arrow tips. I learned how they cast their nets, at least three feet tall, among the foliage to ensnare the animals. These nets were so long, a few could be strung together to cover the length of a football field. The hunters knew where these nets were laid throughout the forest, and they chased the animals toward them. But the greatest hands-on experience I got was going on an actual hunt with the hunters. Despite my size, I felt I was a good runner. At the Olympic Education Center, I finished toward the front to middle of the pack every time. But with the hunters, I realized how fast these dudes really were. I was out there with them for half an hour and realized that I couldn't move through the forest the way they did. I couldn't move as quietly as they could. I was like an elephant plowing through and kicking things, while they were silent, sly foxes. *Crunch.* I didn't know there was a stick beneath those leaves, but they did.

They were obviously humoring me, because I could barely keep up with them. I was holding them back, and these guys probably wanted to catch some food. I asked Ben, who'd come along, to pass on a message.

"Tell them I'm so thankful, but they can go hunting for real now," I said. Ben relayed the message; the hunters all nodded and were swallowed into the forest.

JULY 2

I crawled out of my hut on my elbows this morning to find one of the grandfathers, Leomay, sitting on a log at the campfire with his grandson, Sangee. Little Sangee must be around twelve; his grandfather might be in his upper fifties. Sangee's parents died, so his grandfather took over caring for him and his younger brother, Toko.

There were about a dozen arrows laid out at their feet— not the metal-tipped ones, but the wood ones they'd carve spirals into the tips of and dip in poison, usually a mixture of toxic forest roots, berries, and a vegetable that resembles a rotting black potato. Leomay was bent over sharpening an arrow tip, Sangee looking on eagerly. Leomay also showed Sangee how to tighten the bamboo string on his bow and prepare his spear and the nets. I could tell it was a special bonding time for them, a rite of passage into manhood for Sangee, as he readied to head into the forest with the other men for his first day of hunting.

They returned as the sun set, hoisting an antelope over their heads like the Stanley Cup. Sangee had speared the antelope—his first real kill—with what was once his grandfather's weapon. I was told this spear had killed elephants, wild hogs, and virtually anything else that moved for many, many years in Leomay's grandfather's hands. Leomay proudly stood by as the entire village hooted and hollered in gratitude. That day, he'd laid out the nets for the other hunters

and they'd shaken the leaves together to try and scare an
animal into one of them. When the antelope hit the net, Sangee
immediately pounced on it and struck the animal with his spear.

The antelope was lifted up onto a tripod arranged out of
sticks, covered with leaves, and smoked over a fire. They shared
their kill with everyone, even me and all the Shalom Drillers, but
the meatiest part went to Sangee, whose chest puffed out and
whose smile wouldn't leave as he enjoyed his well-earned meal.

IN NEARLY EVERY village we'd visited, I'd eaten animals and organs of all sorts. I'd tried almost everything from monkey thighs (pre-Ebola scare, I didn't know better) to big lizards. On this day, the hunters had gone out looking for antelope and come back with two turtles. The turtles' arms and legs were tied together in such a way that it created straps, so the Pygmies could wear them like a kid wearing a Teenage Mutant Ninja Turtles backpack. If the turtles were found early in the hunt, they were tied to the hunters' backs as they continued to search. If they caught something better, the turtles would be released. If not, the turtles became dinner.

They cooked up the turtles over a fire, and broke apart pieces of the shell to eat carefully, like a hardened tortilla chip. They also ate the small field mice and the large forest rats, which gathered around the palm trees to eat the nuts that fell. These rats were as big as my size thirteens, but even the children loved them.

There were more details about the Tundu Pygmies that made them stand out from the other villages we'd visited. They had built a line of square houses and a line of traditional rounded domes. I thought maybe they were experimenting. In the other villages, families would congregate at their own fires. At Tundu, families had individual fires that they cooked around, but everyone would congregate at a massive, central fire.

For whatever reason, the Tundu village had the biggest population of creepy crawlies. There were so many of the dreaded tsetse flies. If those things get you, it hurts brutally. The fly bite can give you sleeping sickness, an innocuous name for a sometimes deadly parasitic disease. There were wicked-looking wasps, and huge bright-colored bumblebees the size of golf balls buzzing around. The ants in the U.S. are nothing compared to what I saw at Tundu. I saw vicious ants the size of small peanut shells, ants with such vicious pinchers that the Pygmies told me stories of how you can use their bites as sutures! You just let the ant bite you, then pop its body off, leaving the head and closed pinchers to seal your wound.

On my other Congo trips, I doused myself in repellent. I'd brought two months' worth for this yearlong trip, but had realized it was impractical. I felt I should get used to the bug bites the way the Pygmies get used to them, if I really wanted to live like they did. So I just stuck to long shirts and pants when it wasn't too hot.

Clothing could only protect me so much, though. One night, I ventured out of my hut in my flip-flops to relieve myself in the forest. When the moon's out, there's enough light to see shapes, but that night was overcast. I must have kicked some leaves because something stung my ankle. The pain was intense, as if my ankle had gotten injected with molten magma. My ankle was on fire, but I was so exhausted from work that day and decided not to wake up Ben.

The next morning, I had a fever, a killer headache, and was sweating profusely. A few of the Pygmies took one look and knew it had been a scorpion that stung me. They went into the forest and gathered herbs and roots, pounded them up in a mortar and pestle to make into a paste that drew out the poison and soothed the wound. The bite hurt for weeks, and it got so infected, a doctor (named

Doctor Happy) had to rip off the scab with jagged metal prongs. I literally bit down on my knuckles. I wasn't too happy about it.

JULY 9

Last night was special. Last night was spectacular. I have never experienced anything like it. I should have known that God had something special planned. The stars blazed through the hole in the forest. Not atop the Rocky Mountains, Russian mountains, or out on the open seas of Alaska had I ever seen the stars out like they were last night.

Starting from the sky down to the ground, stars were all in front of us. Where the night sky intersected with the forest, the trees were covered with lightning bugs. It was like a continuation of the stars. Then the vegetation on the ground was covered in something I hadn't known existed. It was the first time I'd seen this kind of caterpillar that glows, and they were blanketing the forest floor. I stood amazed by this one-of-a-kind starry night. In the background, I heard the Pygmy men begin to beat the drums, blow on their bamboo flutes, and the women and girls start to yodel and create a new song.

A little while went by and Ben came to ask me to join our well-drilling team for prayer before we went to sleep. As I got to our team, something struck me deep in my heart and I thought, Why do we go over to the side to pray by ourselves? We should include the Pygmies in our prayer tonight.

"Ask the team if we can pray around the fire tonight," I said to Ben, "and let's see how it goes."

It was already a near perfect night, but I think God loves to show us He is bigger and better than we think. We asked the

Pygmies if we could show them a few songs and pray with them before we went to bed that night. One of the elder women of the tribe promptly spoke up.

"Since your team came to stay with us, we've heard you singing your worship songs and praying to your God," she said. "We think that is the reason we have peace at night, we aren't having nightmares, and the evil spirits that usually come left whenever you came. We'd love to join you tonight."

Our team took turns praying around the fire, thanking God for our new friends and family of the Tundu village. After our prayers finished, Ben said, "Pika, cheza, dinga," which means "Clap, dance, everything." Suddenly, we all found ourselves in a sweet moment of spontaneous singing and dancing in what I would call an incredibly real and raw worship to/for God. A couple of minutes went by and the song developed into clap, clap, clap for our creator. Dance, dance, dance for Jesus. Everything, everything, give God our everything. For the next amazing thirty minutes, the whole village never took a pause as we made up new songs, drumbeats, and dances. I couldn't stop smiling, even when my cheeks began to hurt. Tonight wasn't like any other night. It will go down in my history book as something super special, a treasure in my heart.

As for the water well, our first attempt failed. The zones were semipermeable, but we'd have to get more depth to make it a sustainable spot. The water was steady, but it wasn't rushing in. Then, we hit a layer of quartz. We spent four or five days trying to bust up the rock, but we didn't have the weight or momentum because the water column in the hole slowed down the impact.

I called Matt from the satellite phone and actually got to him through the hole in the forest. There must have been a satellite overhead at that exact time. Matt told me what he'd already told me before: "If you don't think you're in a good water-bearing spot, move." We did as he said, and on our second hole, we got water, and a lot of it!

The former slave masters in Tundu were the most kind of those we met. I think it was because they never had complete control over these Pygmies because of their traditional way of life. Their interdependent relationship seemed more intact, like that of fifty years ago. There seemed to be a higher level of mutual respect from the Mokpala to the Pygmies. Maybe that was a testament to the leadership of Chief Leomay. This was also the first Mokpala tribe that hadn't dragged its feet on the $100 contribution. They provided housing for our team and their well went off without a hitch.

Sister villages Kidogo and Kucheza were the next two tribes we dug water wells for. We'd invited the twenty-person Kidogo tribe to the Tundu water-well celebration, and a few came over to see the working well and reported back to their tribe. With this group, there'd been an internal conflict among the Pygmies over moving to the new land purchased for them. An NGO had come to the Kidogo tribe five years earlier, taken pictures with the Pygmies, and promised a water well and a school, which had all proven to be a lie. The Kidogo Pygmies used their new land as a hunting reserve at first, then a few of the tribe trickled onto it to live. The majority of the village still lived on the old land and chose to stay with their masters.

When we arrived at Kidogo, there were only about thirty villagers there—only a few more people believed in the project and their new chief's leadership when they heard of Tundu's clean water. When we started digging, that number doubled to sixty or seventy. Once there was clean, running water, the population doubled again to about 120 villagers.

Tarzan was the chief of the Kidogo tribe. Tarzan's father had also been chief, but Tarzan had earned the role by being the first of his tribe to move to the new land. Tarzan was the youngest chief I'd ever met, and he'd never heard of the fictional character and didn't get the irony. Trying to explain it to him proved a funny undertaking.

Between water-well projects, we went back and forth to Bunia and Kampala as needed for rest and supplies. Whenever I stayed in Bunia it was with Ben at Shalom. He'd translate for me and help me with my Swahili. In Bunia, a much smaller city than Kampala at a hundred-thousand-plus, I could get online and Skype with Emily.

In the rainforest, we had to be mindful of black mambas, leopards, big, hairy spiders, and other deadly creatures like rebel groups. In Bunia, we had to keep on our toes for thieves, angry mobs, and corrupt military soldiers and officials—sometimes all in one day.

On one of my first mornings in Bunia, I'd gone to the bank to open an account for Fight for the Forgotten. Waiting in line, we all watched a military truck pull up outside. Soldiers jumped out, grabbed a guy on the street, threw him on the ground, unnecessarily beat him, and patted him down for something. The soldiers picked him up and threw the man in the bed of the truck. What was crazy was, the troops sat in the back, and they drove off with this guy under their feet. A dozen strong-armed soldiers with machine guns strapped across their chests drove off with a man as a footrest. We heard rumors that he'd been a deserter.

We had to be our most vigilant with our safety at night. Bunia is a strange place. The town is bustling and people will be all over the streets in the light, but whenever it first gets dark, the streets empty. It becomes a ghost town because of the Congo's history of never-ending wars and the militia-led Bunia massacre. Nobody walks alone in the dark. If I was at the UN café in town at night on the Internet, Ben would sometimes come back to walk me home.

One night on the way to dinner, Ben and I saw a scuffle in the distance. When we got close enough, we saw a guy's leg hanging out of the ditch, his limp body contorted and bloody. He was an accused thief; the mob had caught him, beat the mess out of him, and probably killed him. With the heated crowd still congregated, some with the smell of alcohol on their breath, Ben grabbed my arm and kept me moving.

Thieves were super slick in Bunia. They'd act absentminded, bump into you, and all of a sudden your stuff would be gone. But the mobs didn't take too kindly to thieves. All you'd have to do is yell, "Thief!" and anyone around you would come to your aid. And by *aid* I mean they'd, at minimum, beat the thief to a pulp or maybe put a tire around the guy and set it on fire.

We'd just finished up dinner when two motorbikes collided outside the café. Both drivers were okay, but they started fighting with each other, and suddenly a crowd of sixty to eighty people swarmed them, everybody shouting. We started to leave, and I noticed this guy behind us. He was young, maybe twenty-three or so, tall, athletic with short dreadlocks. As Ben and I walked home, talking along the way, I'd take a peek here and there and see him still on our tail. He got so close to us at one point that he was on our heels, right over my shoulder. Whenever I would stop, he would stop. We took four or five turns onto new roads and he still followed us. I moved my wallet into my other pocket, the one closest to Ben.

As we got to Shalom, Ben darted into the building past security, but I decided to stop. I'd realized the guy was trying to time it to where he could be right behind me to snatch my wallet as I entered. I started walking through Shalom's entranceway, but turned around. I was staring at him. A security guard told me to walk right in. Clearly, the guy was a thief. When I tried to speak to him, he started shaking and pretending he was mentally ill, I guess in case I tried to accuse him of something. Then he bolted away down the street. That was the last time we walked after dark.

CHAPTER 26

Mama Miriam

AUGUST 11

Yesterday, Laura Harkonen, my friend and a Mission Aviation Fellowship pilot, and I came up with a nifty idea. Right about NOW, Emily should be boarding her MAF flight from Uganda back into the Congo. And even though this is Emily's first time meeting Laura, in just a few moments, she should be hearing Laura on the intercom reading a love note I wrote for her.

Read over the loudspeaker during an MAF flight from Uganda to the Congo:

EmmyBear,

I love you DEEPLY and I love you DEARLY. When I see "the woman beyond my dreams" coming all the way to the Congo, to love the people I love, I have to ask God why He loves me so much. I don't deserve it, but it draws me closer to God and makes me want to love Him and you more and more!

I'm so blessed that Laura, your pilot, is so rad that she is reading this to you right now! She is about to hand you a letter that I gave you on Christmas three years ago. Those words are more true today than the day that I wrote them! I want the letter to remind you that you are an absolute masterpiece, that I adore you, and that I can't wait to marry you!

Also, I want you to pay special attention to the bottom of the letter. I wrote, "This is only the beginning of the journey!" The last three years with you have been the most incredible journey of my life because we are both trying to run after Jesus, side by side. I can't wait for us to be side by side, loving my Pygmy family, I mean OUR Pygmy family, TOGETHER!

Babe, our God is absolutely awesome and I believe He gave me the PERFECT, for me, bride-to-be! I still remember when my fears outweighed my faith and I was scared to let you come to the Congo. I told you that I didn't think it was safe for you to be here. And then God led you to a verse to show me. You told me it applied so perfectly to us and it ROCKED me!

But Ruth replied, "Don't ask me to leave you and turn back. Wherever you go, I will go; wherever you live, I will live. Your people will be my people, and your God will be my God." Ruth 1:16 (NLT)

I'm basically overwhelmed that my "Ruth" is following me to this faraway land! Today starts a new adventure! And once again, this is only the beginning of the journey! Inside and out, you are beautiful beyond compare! I love you!

Love,

Honey Boo Boo (inside joke)

WHEN EMILY LANDED in the Congo with Matt Hangen and his wife, Grace, and award-winning filmmaker Derek Watson, it had been six months since I'd seen her last. Having her in my arms again melted my heart, but on top of that, she'd brought three world-changers with her. Matt Hangen had brought his wife, Grace, the logistics coordinator for Water4, to introduce her to the people in the forest he'd fallen in love with. Derek had been hired by Water4 to capture a video to show Water4 supporters what great things they support and make possible.

Once we got everything loaded in the Beast, and once we got final approval from the corrupt officials to pass through, we were on "the road" to the forest. About three hours into our journey, we came upon a mangled pile of debris. There were literally tons of twisted metal and demolished wood sitting right in a rushing red river—the only "bridge" that would get us onto the only "road" into the forest. The 1920s-built, Belgium-constructed bridge had met its match with an overloaded lorry hauling illegally cut mahogany. Our guts dropped at the sight of it. There was no way we could cross this river. At the very best, we were going to lose several days both ways—that's if we could find an alternate route, and even then we wouldn't know if it was safe to travel. After we heard it was going to take weeks to repair the bridge, we called a huddle and began to pray. During the prayer, a name leapt into my mind: Laura, the MAF pilot. On our way back to Bunia, we were going to pass Nyankunde, where the Mission Aviation Fellowship pilots had recently reopened the hangar and grass runway. We couldn't call them, so we drove straight there. We were told all the other pilots were out flying around the Congo, except Laura. When I asked Laura, she joyfully accepted the challenge and began calling around.

She found out that there was an old grass airstrip behind Mandima Hospital, where we'd taken Kaptula the first several times. The only problem was, it hadn't been active in a long time, so Laura asked a contact to go out by motorbike to check the overgrowth. We hired some of the villagers to go out in the field with machetes to cut down as much tall grass as possible, in order to make it safer to land. We also gave the local authorities a heads-up—which we knew they'd see as an opportunity to ask for bribes, but that's better than them using it as a reason to arrest us. Then we unpacked the truck and loaded up the plane.

We took off, and in only a couple of hours' time, flew right over the same collapsed bridge that had stopped us in our tracks. Then the fun started. Laura took us on a direct route, but she turned it into a kind of joyride. We flew low over gold mines, and I saw everyone's faces light up when they got their first look at the incredibly wide and vast forest. When we got ready to land, we had to fly in a circle a few times and buzz the runway to scope out the landing strip. If I were the pilot, I'd have seen it as a massive challenge; there was a small mountain blocking one way to approach, the airstrip was smack-dab in the middle of 360 degrees of massive, one-hundred-foot-plus-tall trees, the runway was on a hill, and the villagers hadn't really gotten much done in clearing the knee-high grass. Laura made landing uphill with all those variables look easy.

Unfortunately, the plane parked directly on a massive hill of vicious army ants. Soon we were all covered. I rushed Emily into the passenger seat of the van we were renting, pulling probably thirty ants off her pants and her shirt along the way. Only after she had been taken care of did we notice that I was covered in ants up to my beard.

As the director of implementation at Water4, Matt had come back a second time to continue his formal and extensive training of the well drillers at Kidogo. This made it our fourth official training in the Water4 drilling method, and our second session with Matt as a team. The Shalom Drillers were still hungry to learn. Even after drilling ten new water wells, our team wasn't satisfied or complacent. They told Matt that they wanted to be the best darn well-drilling team in all of Africa, and then all the world! Matt used the two weeks to teach, encourage, and inspire our team to work toward that ambitious goal.

Emily and I were so thankful that Grace was able to be there. She'd come to support Matt, to meet the Pygmies, to see God's love and compassion in action, but also to help Emily out. Grace had spent five years in rural Togo (in West Africa) with Matt, and they'd become expert campers in Africa while drilling many, many water wells. Grace assisted Emily with her second camping experience ever, showing her how to cook over a campfire and all the rest that comes with living off the grid. Derek, the filmmaker, had grown up a missionary kid, and the dude was an absolute champ during the two weeks he was in the jungle shooting footage.

We started at Mpenda, where we made our base camp. I got to see Kaptula again, looking better than ever, and he was a funny companion to have at the campfire. Emily, Grace, and Matt also got to hear the Pygmies' firsthand stories of slavery and oppression.

We planned to complete the well at Kidogo before Matt, Grace, and Derek had to head home. This meant that they were going to be able to take part in all the festivities and see the massive celebrations we have in the forest with each new Pygmy well! One of the coolest things we all got to witness, though, was the immense but intimate personal impact we were making on the water crisis. That's when everyone got to meet Mama Miriam, a Pygmy woman who has suffered more, and lost more, than any of us could ever imagine.

After becoming very ill, Mama Miriam went blind, most likely due to waterborne disease and a sickness called "river blindness." When you have a disability in the Congo or other parts of the third world, you often become "untouchable." Mama Miriam told me about the disparity she faced and how she struggled with feeling like she was the lowest of the low.

Miriam had lost five of her seven children, as well as her husband. She and her two young children were completely dependent on the rest of the village for their survival. Her children would either scavenge for food, be forced into vigorous manual labor for the Mokpala—where they might be paid small portions of food—or they got tiny leftover scraps if anyone from their village had anything to give or sacrificed to share with them. For the family of three, Mama Miriam was given only two liters of dirty, contaminated water a day. That's to drink, cook, and maybe bathe with. Even if they could have discovered clean water, they didn't even have a real container to collect it in and to keep it clean. They had a couple of disgustingly dirty bottles, and only one cup to drink from.

The loving Pygmies of Kidogo and our Shalom Drillers team had collectively decided on a strategic but special location for the new well in their village. Mama Miriam and her children were only going to have to walk twenty steps from their hut to get a clean drink of water! She now had safe water at her disposal, and in abundance, whenever she needed it. The entire village would never again have to walk miles for filthy water contaminated by critters' feces and urine, or debilitating bacteria and disease. Miriam would be able to get her own water for the first time since going blind.

After the water well was dug, built, properly protected, and cleaned, we were ready to party and show everyone how to use it. The celebration was huge! The Pygmies brought us cassava leaves, a whole chicken, and tons of wild mushrooms they'd collected in the forest. Shalom Drillers contributed loads of rice, beans, and fish so that we could all feast.

During the dancing and singing around the new well, we started pulling people into the center to have them pump the water, one by one. I noticed that Mama Miriam had eaten, sung, and even danced off to the side, as to not get in the way, but she never took her turn pumping the water. I think she must have thought it was going to be difficult or that you had to be able to see it to do it.

Earlier, I'd noticed that our assistant leader of Shalom Drillers, Kakura, had made a sweet connection with Mama Miriam. He had served her food, and they'd sang and danced together. I saw them laughing quite a bit, and I watched him leading her around the village by hand. As things began to wind down, I snagged Kakura and asked him to come help me show and explain to Mama Miriam how to use the well.

Kakura hadn't even finished asking her before she sprang up and grabbed us both by our hands. We led her from her hut to the pump. We guided Mama Miriam's hands onto each side of the cross-shaped, galvanized handle. What came next brought happy tears to my eyes and immense gratitude to my heart. The Pygmies, as a whole, are a very expressive people, but this was one of the most sincere, deep, yet funny ways I've ever seen gratefulness expressed. When Mama Miriam pushed the handle down, she said, "Oh, oohh, oooohhhhhh." And once she heard the splash of water crash against the cement, she threw her hands straight up into the air and let out a shout for joy. I brought her a cup and was going to have her fill it, but she paused, lowered her hands enough to cover her mouth, and started to mumble. Kakura leaned in to hear what she was saying, but he couldn't make it out. When she finally did drop her hands she said, "I can't believe it. I just can't believe it!" in Swahili, and then she reached out for both our hands and pulled us in for a hug.

Then it struck her. She hadn't tasted the water yet! She pumped and I filled up the cup, and when she tasted it she said, *"Mutamo sana!"* ("So delicious!") After it had all sunk in, she grabbed both of our hands again for us three to sing and dance right there at the well. My Swahili is far from great, but I could make out that she was thanking God, a whole lot, and in many different ways! Then to culminate the moment (as if it could get any better), as we danced, I remember Kakura looking me straight in the eyes and saying, "This is why I love this job! God is so good."

AUGUST 31

I've never been given so many nicknames in all my life! Each week it seems two or three are added to the already growing list of names. The Pygmies call me two names: Eféosa ("The Man Who Loves Us") and Mbuti MangBO! ("The Big Pygmy"— the BO! is really annunciated). From village to village, even in ones I haven't visited yet, these different nicknames are HOLLERED out, while fingers point at me. In the Congo, Uganda, and Rwanda, I've been called Jesus, Moses, Abraham, Samson, Solomon, Peter, John the Baptist, Noah, Goliath, Jesus's brother James, and even one of the Wise Men. The Pygmies don't really have a reference for most of these names, but anywhere there is a bigger population or even just a single church in the area, someone is going to shout one of these names out to me.

Just yesterday in Bunia—which has a very large Catholic mission and Catholic population—a MAJOR rumor had spread that the Mother Mary had come to visit the city and propped herself on top of the big tree at the mission, like an angel atop a Christmas tree. Kinda odd, but I've asked around and people swear by it. Well, today we made a pit stop in Komanda on our way back into the forest. Benjamin went to find someone to put air in our tires while I looked out the truck window and saw a kid sitting on a huge log. Beside him, he had a jar of peanuts that he was selling. I went over and gave him a hundred-franc piece (ten cents) for a small bag of peanuts. I sat on the log with him,

started goofing around, and other children started curiously
gathering around.

One thing led to another and in no time at all I had ten
children to my left, ten children to my right, two kiddos climbing
up in my lap, another one up on my shoulders, and a small
audience sitting at my feet. I'm used to becoming a human
jungle gym once kids get over their initial fear of how big, hairy,
and scary I am to them. Benjamin had been gone for thirty
minutes and I just kept goofing off with the crowd of kids.
I snuck my hand up my shirt and waved my beard with it (by
now my beard was in ZZ Top Land and my hand was covered).
I'd look down at my waving beard with big eyes like I was
SHOCKED that it could do that. My antics drew a bigger
and bigger crowd of kids and adults, and suddenly I realized I
had a mob of people surrounding me, and growing. A few women
with palm and banana leaves began to fan me, which I also
thought was strange.

"Eféosa, we have to go NOW," Ben said as he broke his
way through the crowd to me. "I just heard them on the radio
at the car garage say that Jesus came to Komanda and is
playing with the children in the center of the market! This isn't
a safe town."

By now, there were about three hundred people surrounding
me, concentrated on everything I did. I put the kids down
and began to walk away with Ben, but some people started
grabbing on to my arms and tugging on my shirt. I told them
in my broken Swahili that I was sorry and had to go, but they
kept grabbing on to me, and Ben had to jump in and pull people
away. We got back into the truck for our escape, but I rolled
down the window to say one more thing.

"God bless you, everyone," I said in very broken Swahili, which made Ben crack up. What I'd actually said was, "God bless you, my children!" On the drive back to Bunia, the Komanda radio station reported that "Mary may have visited Bunia from the top of a tree, but Jesus came to Komanda to visit our children!" If only.

CHAPTER 27

Two Weddings

SEPTEMBER 20

The last two dreams I've had have really been quite vivid. It's strange, too, because I normally don't fall into that deep of a sleep in the humid huts here in the forest. In my first dream, I was training for a fight in a nondescript gym. In my body, I could feel that it had been a hard road back to get healthy, to work out the kinks, and to get back into fighting shape, but I knew I was having fun.

In the second dream, I appeared at two different weigh-ins before fights. The first weigh-in had only a few fans watching, and some family and fight teams standing around, so it must have been a small show. It didn't feel like my fight at the Boone County Fairgrounds, where I staggered out of the stands with beer on my breath, but it did feel small. As I stepped off the stage, I could hear my name being called and suddenly I was on a much bigger stage in front of hundreds of people. I stepped onto the scale, smiled, and then I woke up.

I guess it's not too odd to have back-to-back dreams

about the sport I love, but it did get me thinking. I stepped out of the sport of MMA with confidence. I couldn't handle the roller-coaster ride of the fighter lifestyle and I let it bring the worst out in me. Now I've found a new path to walk and a new fight to fight. I know I'd be completely content to live here in the forest, sleep in my tiny twig-and-leaf hut, and spend time with my Pygmy family. I know I'd be happy, too, for the rest of my life! God brought me halfway across the world to fall in love with a new family, and they are AWESOME. I thought I'd killed the desire in me to fight or at least redirected it so I could fight for people, not against them. However, if people are open to hearing God, I believe He will speak to us, drop little hints, show us signs, or send us a guidepost—even in our dreams.

AT SOME POINT, I knew the Shalom Drillers would have to fly without me—they wanted to keep digging wells way after I was gone. So, aside from checking in on the process here and there, I stepped back on the eleventh and twelfth wells at Mkuki and let our very capable team handle them mostly without me.

Emily and I had other work to do in the Congo before we left in two months. As part of our fund-raising efforts, we'd promised some special items for those who had given to our cause so graciously. We collected sheets of burnt-orange bark cloth and had the Pygmies make a handprint on the parchment with dye, as a way of signing their names and saying thank you. We decided to do this in three of the villages we visited and it became a fun way for Emily to connect with everybody. I also brought a portable printer I'd gotten from one of my Uganda trips, to print out photos instantly for the people group who'd never seen their own reflections. Their reactions were priceless. Our first stop was the Kumi tribe, where we'd dug the second Pygmy well.

On Emily's first morning in Kumi, the boys, about ages three to ten, were eager to show off their hunting skills. They had gone out at dusk and caught three forest mice. They released them all at once and the mice raced off in every direction. The Pygmy hunter boys quickly scattered and stalked the mice throughout the clearing in the village. The funny thing for me was that I could see they all had clear shots at the mice numerous times, but they wanted to make sure Emily was watching before they took it. One landed right between a sprinting mouse's shoulder blades, another to the head, and the final one was right between the eyes. Emily didn't know what to think! She was stunned, but told them, *"Mzuri sana"* ("Very good"), in appreciation of their skills.

The mouse race sparked the idea to make up more games, as we always did with the kiddos in the villages. We used anything we could find as target practice for the boys. Then an idea struck us. If we took rotting passion fruit, or just made a small hole in a good one and emptied it of its seeds, we could roll it past the hunter kids for moving-target practice. One kid would hit it, one might miss, then the next three or four kids would hit it while it was still rolling. Emily was amazed that these little kids were such masters of bows and arrows. Emily, the kids, and I had such a blast that we did this for hours until it was time to get ready for dinner and dancing.

That night, Chief Bale's wife gave us a gift the village had gathered for us; a very valuable and symbolic gift: two eggs from their two forest chickens. Ben told us it could have been the only two eggs they had. It gave Emily an idea to bless them back.

"Do you think they've ever had scrambled eggs before?" Emily asked.

"Honestly, I don't know," I answered. "I've only seen eggs a few times out here and they've always been hard-boiled."

Emily had two plastic dozen-egg carriers that we'd loaded up with Uganda-farmed eggs and brought with us. The next morning, she cooked all the eggs up for the Pygmies to try. She invited the chief's wife over to watch, and her kids came with her. From the look on their faces, I think they thought Emily was destroying, ruining, or wasting the eggs when she started beating them in a bowl with a fork. Emily taught the chief's wife how to stir the eggs in a pan with a spatula, something the woman had never seen before. The Pygmies lit up when Emily sprinkled just a little bit of salt in the eggs. When they began to taste and share it with one another, everyone was making sounds like *Yum* and *Mmm* and rubbing their bellies and telling Emily how great of a cook she was, and no wonder I was such a big guy.

That evening, Emily saw that we had extra pasta, so we invited the chief and his wife over to our hut for dinner. They brought their chairs made of sticks and parked them right out front of our hut. This was their first time trying noodles and they loved the pasta and canned tomato sauce. They asked what kind of food it was and I told them "Italian." Then I told them about a country called Italy and how they have their own style of food, but people all over the world now eat it.

For days to come, the new "rave of the village" was that Chief Bale and his wife had actually tasted "food from the land of Italy."

Emily became especially close to Mayasa, the chief's wife. Emily had heard that Mayasa had hurt her foot, so she took essential oils and triple antibiotic cream to her hut. Emily's a massage therapist, so she worked on the foot and dressed the wound. Although Jesus led his disciples, he also served them, and we can clearly see that when he washed their feet. It was a touching moment for Emily and Mayasa to share.

As our last couple of days in Kumi came to an end, we were

told that a woman was pretty ill, so Emily went to check on her. Emily saw that the woman was pregnant, but her caregivers assured her that she wasn't in labor and not due for another six weeks or more.

Emily came out with a frown and said, "Babe! She looks like she is so uncomfortable and in so much pain. We gotta do something."

Emily and I rushed over to our leafy abode and she grabbed some ibuprofen from her bug-proof tent (which we would set up inside our huts for Emily). I grabbed some of my supplements and an empty bottle. We went down to the well we'd drilled a few months back and mixed an electrolyte drink that we piggybacked with immunity support. Emily brought the drink and the ibuprofen into the hut to give to the woman, while us men stayed outside, discussing what to do. Emily poked out of the hut a few minutes later.

"She's dripping sweat now, Justin," she said.

"Does she have a bad fever? Is she moaning from the pain?" I asked.

"I can't tell for sure about the fever, but she is just lying there. Quiet . . . but grimacing."

I honestly wasn't sure what to do, but it wasn't even five minutes later when we heard a sound coming from the sick woman's hut. It was the women talking and saying my name, "Mbuti MangBO!" quite a few times.

"Maybe she's started feeling a little better now," I said.

"But why do they keep saying your name?" Emily inquired.

"I bet they're just saying that I better know and take notice of how lucky I am to have someone as sweet and caring as you to marry," I said. Emily kind of rolled her eyes and smirked.

But she was right. The women were repeating my name a lot. It was definitely unusual, so we went to check it out. When we got to the door, I was stopped from entering, but Emily was invited in. In a few seconds, I heard Emily call out, "Babe! She just had a baby!"

We were stunned. This Pygmy woman had given birth without making a sound, not even a peep. Instead of an epidural, she just had some flavored water and two ibuprofen. Now, that's tough. By the way, only the women are allowed in the hut during the birthing process—not even the husbands are allowed, which is cultural tradition I could support back in the States!

They named the baby Mbuti MangBO! Justin, which literally translated into "The Big Pygmy Justin." They'd named the baby boy after me.

Soon after the birth, the women, even the elderly women, gathered little leafy twigs and started chasing us men about and hitting us. All the men ran, so I kind of trotted along in curiosity. Later, I found out that it was a tradition for women to tease the men about how they caused women the pain of childbirth.

Emily was welcomed back into the hut to hold the baby. Then they led her outside to come over to me. Emily placed little Mbuti MangBO! Justin in my arms. I was so humbled that the Pygmies would ever name a kiddo after me. The father said it was because of how our team and I loved them and had found a way to get them land, water, and were developing ways for them to start farming their own food.

The women of the village had dropped everything for the birth. They moved their fires around the new mother's hut so they could make everyone's dinner and rally behind her. They sat around outside and sang soothing Pygmy songs.

When we made it back to the Pygmy village of Mpenda, Emily again got to experience how amazing it is to go back to a village you've been to before, and to feel the deep connection you've made. As we entered the village, Emily and I let out the biggest Mbuti forest calls that we could muster. All of a sudden I watched women of the village and a lot of their children run to Emily and give her the biggest hugs. The women grabbed our hands and sang and danced us into the village and over to our awaiting huts.

In Mpenda, Emily got her Pygmy name given to her by three of the Pygmies I had the closest relationship with: Chief Alondo, Kaptula, and Bahjongee. Her name was Lusume Kumateli. Lusume, given by Chief Alondo, means "chosen by us," while Kumateli, chosen by Kaptula and Bahjongee, translates into "belongs with us or belongs here." The naming was a big blessing for Emily and confirmed to her that she belonged here and wasn't a third wheel. Emily felt and saw that she had a real reason and true purpose for being there besides the fact that she was about to be my wife.

We returned to Tundu and our special hole in the forest. I'd asked Emily to bring this bug-zapper tennis racket from home, and I pretended I was in a home run derby with the buzzing golf ball–sized bumblebees. The women had also prepared beautifully painted bark-cloth art for us to take home with us.

Emily and I were incredibly excited that we'd be able to attend two African weddings before we went back to the States to be married. The weddings were especially meaningful because it was Jack and Ben, two of the Original Four, getting married to their lovely fiancées. These guys had added so much to my life and been such an amazing blessing. They are, without a doubt, two of the greatest friends I've ever had. When Jack, Benjamin, and I all first met, it had been before any of us were spoken for. Throughout our relationship, Emily and I watched these two tremendously influential men, friends, and brothers in my life go from thinking they'd found their true love to becoming engaged, and now about to be married.

As part of the family, we were able to contribute to Jack's and Ben's dowries, which needed to be paid to the brides' families before the wedding planning could commence. We personally contributed to the purchase of goats and cows for both dowries. This wasn't too difficult because Jack and Ben were both part of the Congolese Hema tribe, a goat- and cattle-raising group. We were so honored to be involved in it all.

Both weddings lasted two days each, over back-to-back weekends. Jack's wedding was a big gathering and hundreds of people came together to sing, dance, and talk with one another. On both days, the women from Jack's church sang about how he needed to care for Justine as a husband. Papa Way was an elder at the same church, which had petitioned for and gotten my five-year visa in the Congo granted.

One key difference between American and African weddings is that instead of having a best man or maid of honor, the bride and groom each have a married couple stand beside them who have been, and will continue to meet with and give marriage advice to the newlyweds.

At Jack's wedding reception, I got to see the pride in his parents' eyes. They were amazingly sweet people who had raised three terrific children. Jack's mother told Emily how she'd fed me well a few times throughout my year here and how she considered me her oldest, but only American, son. I don't think Emily and I could have expected how elaborate, how extravagantly beautiful, the wedding was going to be. It was so nice to see Jack get married to the love of his life, Justine.

For Ben's wedding the next weekend, we'd made special plans to send Anyole, our Shalom Driller and driver of the Beast, back into the forest to pick up some special guests. We'd invited the five chiefs and their wives from the first five villages where we'd completed water wells. As Chief Jayloowah has gotten too old for long travel, we brought the probable-chief-to-be, my father Manu, and my mother Chibuseeku. Can you imagine that eleven out of the twelve Pygmies we sent for had never been out of the forest? Vehicles were something so unfamiliar to them that their natural instinct was to put their feet on the seat, squat, and wrap their arms around their knees in a balled-up position. Knowing that they were on a six-hour journey on those terribly bouncy and treacherous roads, we were worried about them getting carsick, so I had instructed Anyole to try to keep them occupied by playing songs from each of their villages from my iPhone over the car speakers. Anyole said the combination of biscuits, water, and music did the trick!

The Pygmies arrived a couple of days before Ben's wedding. We'd made sure the Pygmies brought along all the sticks that they could, to build their huts. When they got to the Shalom staff residences, they had the option to sleep in a house, but like we'd predicted, they wanted to build their traditional homes in the front yard so that they would be comfortable, and display their culture for any visitors. We had helpers come to cook all of our meals, and during the day we'd go explore the town. By the look of awe on their faces you would have thought we took them to the Las Vegas Strip. It's crazy how different ways of life can be, even if they're only cut off by a rainforest and six hours of hazardous roads.

In the evenings with the Pygmies, we played movies on my laptop. They loved anything we showed them from Pixar, especially the movie *Up*. It draws me in every time, but the suspenseful roller-coaster ride captivated the Pygmies! There were big laughs, it evoked some hand-holding, and then drew out a few tears to be wiped. Needless to say, it was a unique experience for me to be able to watch that with them, and see the characters from a modern-day cartoon bring such humanity out in the Pygmies.

Ben's wedding went off without a hitch. Most of the Pygmies consider themselves fortunate, and are gracious if they even have one change of clothes, so Ben had gotten us all matching outfits that were tailored from fabric with a Congolese print, style, and design. At the ceremony, the fourteen of us sat right behind Ben's family. Our Shalom Drillers were in the row right behind us.

Another fun tradition you'll see at African wedding receptions is the presentation of your wedding gift by dancing! Anyone who's brought a wedding gift dances their way down front and places it on the table. The Pygmies grabbed their gifts—which included a forest chicken; a hand-carved, reclining wooden chair; a wood mortar and pestle; and a few other small items—and danced to the table. It was wonderful to see them so well received and to watch everyone try to learn and imitate the Pygmy dances. Emily and I were caught up in two gift dances: one with the Shalom Drillers presenting household goods, and another with the lead team of the Faculty of Development from Shalom University, where we presented Ben with a cow (we also did this with Jack). I spoke a few words at the reception and gave Benjamin and his beautiful bride, Elnise, many well wishes. I joked that Emily and I would come to them for wedding advice, since they'd have a two-month head start on us, then the four of us would go over to Jack and Justine's house, since they had a week or more on all of us. With all of the wedding festivities, I recalled the wedding advice I'd written down in my journal months earlier from one of my favorite Pygmy couples.

SEPTEMBER 24

Marriage Advice from the Mpenda Chief and His Wife

<u>Chief Alondo</u>: If you want to be a good husband you have to show her you love her every day. We have to eat every day, so do whatever it takes to feed your wife well. Don't let her go to sleep hungry, even if that means you go to sleep hungry for days. If you are hunting for your food, pray to God that He will help you and I believe He will bless you. If you don't get anything from the hunt, don't come back empty-handed

until it's dark so that you and your wife know you tried looking for everything you could. If you are farming for your master, work hard for him so that he may give you a big enough portion of food for both you and your wife to share. Also, start a little garden of your own. That way, if you don't get food from the hunt, fish from the river, or food from your master you will still have food for your wife. If you do everything you can to keep your wife's belly full, she will know you love her. If you can feed your wife well, then you are ready for children. But to show your wife you love her you must feed her children well, too.

<u>Wife Alaina:</u> If you want to make sure your husband knows you love him, you'll take every opportunity to tell him and to show him. When your husband knows you love him, you might see him stand up a little taller or stick his chest out a little more. Telling him isn't enough, though. You must show him you love him, too. When he brings back meat from the forest, you need to prepare the food well, so that he and your children enjoy it. He will be tired from the hunt, so he needs to relax, and if you have any food from your work of the day, you'll give him that to begin. Another way you can show your husband you love him is to be the best mother you can be to your children.

A COUPLE DAYS later, we had to say our farewells to the Pygmies and let them go back into the forest to rejoin their families. As we loaded up to go to Uganda, Papa Way brought me a gift. Earlier in the year, the guys had teased me that I'd gotten off easy only having to ask Emily's father for permission and not pay a dowry. Papa Way joked that Emily was his daughter-in-law and that I'd have to make the twelve-well quota to marry her back in the States.

Papa Way gave me a handwritten letter, acknowledging that, together, we had gone above and beyond the goal in securing land, drilling water, and were building a strong foundation and making headway in food security. He wrote about how we had a rough-and-tumble start, and at every turn for the first six months we'd hit obstacles like sickness and corruption, which had prevented the start of our work with water.

"Justin is a fighter," Papa Way read from the letter. "He has paid us, his Congo family, the dowry in full, and I would be honored if he took my adopted daughter's hand in marriage." I gave Papa Way a big hug for quite a while, but I knew another one would surely come again soon. The six of us (the newlyweds and the bride- and groom-to-be) headed to Uganda together to see Emily and me off.

CHAPTER 28

A Perfect Ending, a New Beginning

I locked eyes with my mom, ran up to her, and gave her a big, big hug. It was at the peak of the Ebola scare, and it had taken us much longer to get through customs. My mom, my dad, Emily's parents, and a couple of friends were waiting for us in the baggage claim area at DFW airport.

My mom wiped happy tears away. She is the most consistently positive person I've ever met. She instilled belief in me. She wasn't quite sure about me going to the Congo at first, but she still supported me.

It had been a tough year for my mother, too. In the year I'd been away, she'd been diagnosed with multiple sclerosis. I hugged her with everything I had.

One of the main things I'd missed in my year away, besides Emily, was ice. In rural Africa, there is no ice for drinks. We're practically on the equator and you can't get a cold, iced drink. And in the rare places you could find that did have ice, it was most likely made from contaminated water. I found the nearest Starbucks in the airport and ordered the iciest, "girliest" Frappuccino I could get.

We spent the night at Emily's parents' home, along with my parents and Emily's best friend, Audrey. We were suffering from extreme jet lag and exhaustion from the elements in the Congo, but, oh boy, I've never woken up so quickly as when I smelled the BBQ brisket that Emily's dad had made (I'm a sucker for BBQ!). We also ate chicken breasts with more meat on them than on a whole scrawny chicken in the Congo. And we had salad. Lots of it. I was almost positive I got typhoid fever from eating a salad while I was in the Congo. At home, I knew the salad wasn't washed with dirty water, that the utensils going into my mouth weren't contaminated. I wasn't putting anything into my mouth that was going to make me extremely sick.

It's crazy all the simple luxuries that we take for granted here in the U.S. and other first-world countries. I felt both incredibly thankful for what I had and deeply saddened for so many, including my Pygmy family, who knew nothing better. After our long-awaited and emotional reunion, and back at my parents' home, I crashed in my childhood room, and basically slept for the next two days.

On our third day back, I drove up to Oklahoma City to prepare for the Water4 Gala being held that Saturday at the Cowboy Hall of Fame. Water4's biggest supporters, some of OKC's movers and shakers, the area's elite (like the mayor and pro athletes), and other well drillers from around the world were attending the 750-person fund-raising event. I was being given the opportunity to tell the audience firsthand of Water4's impact in the Congo. I wasn't going to miss the chance to personally thank them on behalf of my Pygmy family. In fact, I was sent with strict instructions from several of the Pygmy chiefs to express the immense gratitude of their village.

Emily drove up with my parents from Dallas and we all met at the venue. None of us could have expected that we'd have the mess blessed out of us in such a surprising way. I'd never been to an event even remotely close to this one in my entire life. There were black-tie tuxedos and evening gowns and fur coats and jewelry. Wearing a pair of charcoal slacks and a button-down shirt absent a tie, I was probably the most underdressed in attendance; even the waitstaff were all in tuxedos. There was both a silent and live auction, where all the proceeds went to funding more water wells around the world. There were dancers, singers, and other performers, and a decadent three-course meal.

I was scheduled to speak for ten minutes, but Water4 wanted to introduce me first with a video they'd made. The video came up on the big screen and we were back in the Congo with an amazing fly-over of the rainforest. I saw Upio, a Shalom driller, smiling, then it cut to Kikurata and Kakura working. These were our guys! Our Shalom Drillers! Water4 had sent over Derek, an incredibly gifted filmmaker, with Matt, Grace, and Emily to capture some of the stuff we'd been doing. I hadn't forgotten, but it was my first time seeing any of the images and I was blown away. I was watching my team drilling for my family, and then they showed some of my dearest loved ones celebrating, dancing, and guzzling the new, clean water together. I got pretty choked up when it came for my time at the podium.

Then we auctioned off a palm-print art piece from Kaptula, and another with Chief Alondo's and Alaina's handprints. We raised $17,000 for more Fight for the Forgotten wells with Water4.

At our table, we sat across from Mary Sue and Marvin Beard, the kind, elderly couple who had given Jeff the Water4 ad to pass on to me. Mary Sue and Marvin had no idea how things had gone with Water4 and me, and all the great work we'd done together in the Congo in the last year. Like Emily, my parents, and me, the Beards were taken aback by the chic event. Mary Sue told me that just the week before, her pastor had given a particularly moving talk, citing Matthew 12:33 (NLT), which says, "A tree is identified by its fruit. If a tree is good, its fruit will be good. If a tree is bad, its fruit will be bad."

"Justin, I was thinking of what we had to show for fruit in our lives," Mary Sue told me. "Were we too old to do things now? We used to be able to. We thought we might not have anything to offer anymore. Then I got the call from Jeff and you with the invitation to tonight's gala."

"Thank you so much for listening to your heart Mary Sue," I answered, followed by a hug.

It's always ten times harder for me coming back from the Congo and readjusting to our culture than it is to adapt to the Pygmy way of life. In our culture, it's too easy to become busy with actions that don't really matter and overwhelmed with too many choices that don't mean much in the grand scheme of things. It's also easier to withdraw, be depressed, and hide. The people in the world I just came from have so few food choices that they are lucky to have one option of bland food to eat. Basically, they eat the small amount they've found, worked for, or slaved for to survive. The world I just came back to has too much food, too many choices, so many recipes and options of how to prepare the food that we can actually end up wasting more than we consume.

I got crazy looks the first time I ate chicken after coming back. I didn't want to unlearn some of the things that the Congo and the Pygmies have taught me, like eating *every* edible part of the animal—from its organs and, in a lot of cases, the bone, in order to get down to the marrow and not waste a single bit. It's been quite an adjustment.

Now that I was back, it was time to fulfill the proposal I'd made. I'd known that I was going to marry Emily after only a couple of weeks of knowing her. I know that may sound crazy, but other than committing my life to Christ, it was the second-biggest time in my life where I'd felt an overwhelming peace and certainty about a decision.

If it were up to me, I would have married Emily before I left for the Congo—scratch that, years before going to the Congo, before going for one year was ever a thought in my mind. I was just so eager to be her husband. As much as we wanted to get married, we knew, just like with everything else, that there's a perfect time for everything. As hard as it was for us to wait, we knew it would be worth it. And it was, even more so than I imagined it would be.

I've heard of surprise parties for birthdays and engagements. Who doesn't love a good surprise? Yes, I'm definitely a fan of surprises, especially being the one doing the surprising. It's known among my friends and family that it's hard to really get anything, especially a surprise, past me. At least, that was the case before my EmmyBear.

On November 1, I stood in Jeff's bathroom, wearing the shirt Emily had bought me for our small bridal shower that evening, trimming my beard. My beard had grown quite massive over the year, so much so that while Emily was visiting me in the Congo, people called me her grandfather (no joke!). Emily had been subtly, or not so much, hinting at me to trim it for the wedding, so I'd decided to surprise her with that for the bridal shower. As I cut away, I remembered thinking, *I can't wait to see the look on her face!*

Jeff, his wife, Amy, and my best friend, Josh, were driving me to another friend's house, where the shower was being held. Just down the street from the place, Jeff pulled the car over. Josh grabbed a laptop, which he handed to me.

"Emily wants you to watch this before we get to the house," they said.

I pressed play, and there was my beautiful bride, melting my heart in a video, telling me how much she loves me and how proud she is of me, using pictures and videos from our time in the Congo together.

And then she asked me a question that I did not see coming. She asked if I would marry her—that night! I'm not too proud to say that I cried an ugly cry. I couldn't wait to get to the house and marry the woman beyond my dreams.

Pulling up to our wedding venue, I was overwhelmed by the beauty of it all. All the planning, all of the details, everything Emily had dreamed up was all before me.

The Woods' house was down a long driveway at the bottom of a hill. The ceremony was set up to the left on the grass lawn just beyond a cluster of trees. As you approached, there were wooden benches with monogrammed *Mr. & Mrs.* pillows and handmade wooden signs propped up against trees. The "rustic eclectic" altar included candles, a picture frame, and a bouquet of flowers atop a cornflower-blue dresser and a few smaller tables. In the center background, a forking tree glowed with strings of warm orange lights that were quite stunning after dark. Off to the side, there was a white-and-blue bench with a bowl of steaming water and a towel at its feet. That would come in a little bit later.

The blue dresser had been Emily's great-grandfather's. A tin candleholder on the dresser was a gift to Emily from my mom. Emily had made the majority of the decorations and signs and it all looked and felt so sweet and sentimental. A lot of the people there said the wedding/reception/decor felt and looked just like us, which warmed both of our hearts.

Emily walked down from the house on a path lit by candles in mason jars. I couldn't help it, but I cried when I saw her. We exchanged vows and Emily took the ring she'd given me, the one I wore around my neck the entire year in the Congo, off my necklace and slipped it on my finger. We used the bench and water bath to wash each other's feet the way Jesus had done for his disciples the night before he was taken and crucified. That was Jesus's way of saying, "I'm here to serve you."

In our relationship, it was mine and Emily's way of saying we'd serve each other. We were putting each other first. We wanted to take a minute to humble ourselves, to lay our wants and desires down and instead focus on the desires and needs of the other.

Loved ones came to the ceremony from all around the country: New York, Virginia, Tennessee, Georgia, Mississippi, Oklahoma, Colorado, California, and more. Even Tom from Uganda made it out. Everyone was in on it. There'd been fake wedding invitations with the fake date sent out—I saw them at Emily's and my parents' houses. I couldn't believe the lengths Emily took to make sure this day was a surprise.

The wedding was everything I could have hoped for and more. It was perfect. It was the most perfect day of my life. What made it so perfect wasn't the beautiful lights, flowers, or music, though it was all so wonderful. What made that night perfect was that I had the moment to marry the love of my life fulfilled. The wait was over, and I'm so thankful that we did wait, and it was so worth it. God is faithful and I only need to look at my wife to know that is true.

I THINK THIS is where my story comes to an end for now. I learned some things about myself during my time in the Congo. I can put my body through almost anything, and the only motivation I needed to stay there and get through all the bad stuff—the corruption, the danger, the malaria, typhoid fever, shigella (a brutal intestinal bacteria)—was the motivation of love. I found out that I am a tender warrior. I want to fight, but I want to love at the same time.

I know love is what saved me. It wasn't some deep theological debate that sparked a lightbulb moment. It wasn't some well-thought-out doctrine to live by, it wasn't a dry and dull religion to dedicate myself to, I wasn't beat over the head with a Bible, and I wasn't guilted into it. It was a raw, real, no-strings-attached love that loved the Hell out of me. I was loved into it. God is love, and I truly and deeply felt loved by the God of the cosmos and everything in existence. That's what Jesus graciously did for me with God's grace. He forever loved me into God's Kingdom. That's what Jesus does.

Since I've found my personal faith in Christ, I've been asked what it means to "give your life to Christ." I think another way of asking that could be "How do you receive Christ into your life?" or "How does someone become a Christian (a believer, follower, or disciple of Jesus)?" It's not an easy question with one generic answer. It's a very personal connection made between the person and God, and when it happens, you know it.

I could tell you what becoming a Christian is not. It isn't following a religious checklist. Giving our life to Christ is not devoting our lives to a daily, weekly, or annual checklist of rules to do or not to do. I believe being a Christian is receiving God's grace and love in our life through a relationship with Jesus. When we give our hearts, minds, and souls over to be changed, we can discover God's best plan for our life, the life we are meant to live.

Being a Christian doesn't mean personal perfection. Receiving Jesus into our life isn't a magic potion that makes us perfect. In fact, I think it means you know you aren't perfect, but you now know who was and is. For me, that adds incredible meaning to my life and takes the pressure to be perfect off at the same time. The personal proof of God changing our lives, to me, is by seeing all the evidence in the new way we live, and in the big way we love.

Giving one's life to Christ doesn't mean a perfect life. Entering into a relationship with God doesn't mean our life will be easy-peasy and full of sunshine, rainbows, and butterflies. We will have times of suffering; in fact, Jesus promised it. Mostly, he lived it. His passion was so great that he brutally suffered so that we could also know God's love.

It doesn't mean the battle is over. Choosing to enlist ourselves as Christian doesn't mean we won't struggle, face trials, have immense heartbreak, or fall flat on our faces. Life is a battle and sometimes love is a fight. However, we aren't meant to lose! When we fall, we can look to Jesus and the heavens for our source of strength to get back up. I see my enlistment as choosing to fight the good fight in a dark world.

Opening one's life to God isn't boring. Just because someone now desires to know the God of the universe doesn't mean the fun is gone, that everything has to be serious, or that the laughs and good times are over. That seems so counterintuitive to me. I think it's quite the opposite. It means the fun adventure we were created for has just begun!

At the same time, becoming a Christian doesn't mean giving in or giving up to a hypocritical or man-made religion. Beginning a personal relationship with Jesus doesn't set us free from our sins only to enslave us to religion and endlessly long sheets of rules to follow. When the focus is a relationship with Jesus, we can now see, and walk free from any religious counterfeits trying to be passed as authentic. When we look to Christ, we can be loose of *all* chains.

Love is needed in every nook and cranny on planet earth, and we can be the ones to share it with our fellow man, our brothers and sisters. However, receiving the life God intended you to live doesn't mean you have to go to the same extremes and distances I did, but for a few of the people reading this, I think you will, because you'll want to or feel led to. Maybe you'll be like me and not be able to say no and escape it. The main thing I hope people walk away with from this book is that we can take part and live out what Jesus said were the two greatest commandments, and the very reason and foundation of all the biblical rules and laws: To love God and love people. We can do that anywhere!

Many have asked why I go halfway around the world to help

others when there's so much that could be done here in America. I've gotten this question a lot, and I know I will get it again. When I'm in the States, I try to get involved locally on a weekly basis. Nationally, I try to do something monthly. Internationally and annually, I have to jump in and get my hands dirty at least once. For the rest of my life, I'm committed to visiting and putting love and compassion into action for my Pygmy family. Other people don't have to adopt this local, national, and international approach; it's just how I like to try to live.

If you're able to, why not help here, there, and everywhere? Wherever you are able. Why not focus on what you can, where you can? Love where you are, wherever you are. If you see someone in need of a reasonable and practical form of love and kindness, or aid that you are able to give them, why not do it? Love whoever, whenever, however you can for those who need it. I bet you'll love doing it!

I mentioned how Isaiah 58:6–7 has guided me through this experience a couple of times already. Now I'd like to share a few other parts of Isaiah 58 with you:

> No, this is the kind of fasting I want: Free those who are
> wrongly imprisoned; lighten the burden of those who
> work for you. Let the oppressed go free, and remove the
> chains that bind people. Share your food with the hungry,
> and give shelter to the homeless. Give clothes to those
> who need them, and do not hide from relatives who need
> your help. Then your salvation will come like the dawn,
> and your wounds will quickly heal. Your godliness will
> lead you forward, and the glory of the Lord will protect
> you from behind. Then your light will shine out from the
> darkness, and the darkness around you will be as bright
> as noon. The Lord will guide you continually, giving you

water when you are dry and restoring your strength. You
will be like a well-watered garden, like an ever-flowing
spring. Some of you will rebuild the deserted ruins of your
cities. Then you will be known as a rebuilder of walls and
a restorer of homes.

God has delivered on all of this and more. Not only did He
heal my wounds quickly, God provided an abundance of land and
a safe refuge for the Pygmies. When I was giving clean water to my
family, God was quenching the thirst of my soul and restoring all
of my strength. Now well-watered gardens are being planted, and
strategies to build healthier communities are being put into action.
It's been quite the long journey, but to be honest, I see it only as
scratching the surface, and what I see now, I believe, is only the tip
of the iceberg.

Emily and I have had many discussions about living in the
Congo full time, and that is definitely still a serious option for us,
but maybe just not in the immediate future. We want to make the
greatest impact, with as much love as possible, and that is what we
are contending to do. We have a great, dedicated, full-time team
in the Congo that we want to be able to fan the flames for in the
meantime, and see them fly with their own wings—they are ready,
and are already doing it. It makes me so happy to see! For the next
few years, we will stick to numerous monthlong trips each year to
keep pushing things along.

Also, there is an opportunity to walk through a door I thought
was forever closed to me. The dwindling ember of a dream that I
thought had gone completely cold has come blazing back again.
Fighting was a sport I had my identity completely tangled in, it
was my source of purpose, and it led to the biggest downfall in my
life. I was fearful of becoming that person again, and thought I'd
successfully killed that desire in me. I thought I'd never step back

into professional sports, but with a lot of personal prayer and re-flection, and discussion, guidance, and repeated confirmation from those who love me, I see a green light to fight again, but with a whole new purpose.

I believe God uses people's gifts, talents, and different platforms to bring Him glory, and uses those as "tools for good." For the next few years, this could be one of those God-given tools to use for good. I will get to keep fulfilling my first promise I've ever made to the Pygmies: to give them a voice. I will get the opportunity to actually fight for the Forgotten, and fight for my family. I could never have more motivation. Maybe by the time this book is in your hands, I'll be in an MMA cage or in a rainforest in the Congo. Wherever I am, I know that it's going to be one hell of a fight.

Acknowledgments

The authors would like to thank Becky Nesbitt and Howard Books for taking a leap of faith with this project. We'd especially like to thank our wonderful editor, Amanda Demastus, who was there for us every step of the way. Our gratitude also goes out to our generous photographers, Colin J. Reed and Agung Fauzi, who risked their lives in the DRC and captured beautiful and stirring images for us to share. We'd also like to thank Jason Probst, our lightning-fast transcriber, and Bruce Gore, who created a sweet book cover! A special thank-you goes out to our publicity team, led by Bonnie Macisaac and Jennifer Smith.

We'd be amiss not to thank our Foundry Literary + Media agents, Chris Park and Yfat Reiss Gendell, who shepherded the project along, as well as the media outlets who caught the Fight for the Forgotten vision and got the ball rolling. Finally, we'd like to thank everyone who's volunteered their time, donations, and well wishes to Fight for the Forgotten. Together, we loved the Pygmies with all our might. God is good!

Justin, the signs brought us together and I'm so glad they did. Thank you! To Emmett and my husband, Shane. I love you.

—Loretta